THE
EPISTLE OF BARNABAS
RE-EXAMINED AND
RE-EXPLAINED

FR. PHILLIP HAEUSER

edited and translated by
Dr. William G. von Peters

Catholic Resources
Chattanooga, TN

https://www.lulu.com/spotlight/rheims

Ordering Information:
Quantity sales. Special discounts are available on quantity purchases by corporations, associations, and others. For details, contact the "Special Sales Department" at the address above.

The Epistle of Barnabas Re–Examined And Re–Explained, Dr. Phillip Haeuser, Ed., Dr. William von Peters
ISBN 978-1-962709-00-2

9 781962 709002

Contents

Imprimatur.

Paderbornae, d. 4. Iunii 1912.

Vicarius Generalis

Schnitz.

F

FOREWORD

With the exception of extensions in the "Conclusions", this study and explanation of the Letter of Barnabas was submitted as a dissertation to the Faculty of Theology at the Albert–Ludwigs–Universität zu Freiburg i. Br. To the H.H. professors of this faculty I would like to express my most sincere and sincere thanks for the good reception of this document. My special thanks go to University Professor Dr. G. Pfeilschifter, since he has helped me with advice on so many occasions in the most gracious manner. His Magnificence the Rector of the Royal University of Strasbourg, Professor Dr. A. Ehrhard, I owe my deepest thanks not only for including this work in the "Research on the History of Christian Literature and Dogma", but above all for the numerous hints and suggestions Lessons which he had the great goodness to give me for the final execution of the work,

Strassberg near Augsburg, October 1911.

The Author.

PRELIMINARY REMARK

Among the writings written in letter form from the most ancient time of the Church, the Epistle of Barnabas is not exactly one of those that can enjoy a special popularity. Dryness of style, the vagueness of the disposition, complete lack of personal remarks from the life of the author and the addressees are to blame for this. For example, what difference between the Epistles of St. Ignatius of Antioch and the Epistle of Barnabas! There everything breathes love and life, and the reader is carried away to love and live with the Saint, and may envy him his desire for martyrdom. Here the reader's mind laboriously searches for figures with whom it could feel an identification; it must first laboriously figure out the circumstances in order to get used to them. Nevertheless, the Epistle deserves our attention again and again as a witness of a precious time. And he found them as such in the richest measure.

Anyone looking over a list of the text editions of the Epistle and the various works on it might perhaps say that it has already been sufficiently appreciated and that nothing new can be offered about it. But anyone who closely follows this literature on Barnabas in its individual versions will recognize: so many adaptations of the Epistle, so many different opinions about him. If the author of this treatise dares to go public with a new work on Barnabas, it is not just to add a new opinion to the various opinions already put forward, he hopes that he will succeed, at least to achieve a uniformity of views in several places and, furthermore, to withdraw the necessary basis for future interpolation attempts by means of a detailed proof of uniform ideas. Even if the interpolation attempts by C. Heydecke,[1] J. Weiss,[2] D. Volter[3] were rightly rejected in many cases from the outset without further assessment, it must be admitted that partly because it is due to a detailed proof of the unity of thought in the writing was lacking, such attempts were possible and justified.

---

[1] Dissertatio qua Barnabae epistula interpolata demonstretur. Braunschweig 5874. Cf. Jenaer Literaturztg. 1875. pp. 491–493; journal f, scientific theol. 1875, p. 600; theol. literature 1876, cols. 210–213 ; theol. quarterly 1876, pp. I10–I14. In general, the interpolation hypothesis is rejected, but the work is recognized as ingenious.

[2] "The Barnabas Epistle, critically examined." Berlin 1888. Cf. Theol. Literaturztg. 1889, Sp. 393–399. Alb. Ehrhard, "Die altchristl. 1st Dept. (Freibg. 1900): "It may be part of the conditions of human progress that paths are also taken that lead into darkness; but these paths should be walked at least once" (p. 85).

[3] " Die apostolischen Vater" I. Leiden 1904. This work is an extension and revision of "Der Barnabasbrief, re–examined" in Jahrb. f. protest. theol. XIV, pp. 106–144.

The whole epistle is examined according to its purpose and content, taking into account the opposing views. In order not to interfere with a coherent, clear presentation of the train of thought, the conflicting opinions of other explainers of the letter are usually indicated and confirmed separately in notes. Explanatory remarks and references, which can already be found in the previous editions, are usually not repeated.

The epistle has been handed down in full in the codex Sinaiticus (= S) from the 4th or 5th century discovered by Tischendorf in 1859 and now in Petersburg and in the codex discovered by Ph. Bryennius in 1875 and now in the Patriarchal Library in Jerusalem Hierosolymitanus (=H) from the year 1056 (also called Constantinopolitanus). Before 1859 the editors of the Greek text had to rely on eight mostly younger manuscripts that flowed from an archetype (=V), in which the first chapters of the letter up to 5:7 are missing. An old Latin translation (=L) can also be used for the text, in which the final chapters 18–21 are not found. The manuscript for this came from the Corbie Monastery in northern France and is now in Petersburg. According to the investigations of J. M. Heer[4] it can be placed in the time before Cyprian and after Tertullian. Until finding S came for Barn. 15:7 only L eligible apart from two barns. 1:5 and 2:2, 3 quotes taken from Clement of Alexandria.[5]

Of the more recent Greek and Latin text editions, the works of Ad. Hilgenfeld,'[6] Gebhardt and Ad. Harnack,[7] Fr. X. Funk[8] and the aforementioned writing by Heer are mentioned.

---

[4] "The versio Latina of the Epistle to Barnabas and its relationship to the Old Latin Bible." Freiburg 1908. An afterword by Heers in Ram. Viertelschr. 1909, pp. 215–245. See also Berliner Philog. Wochenschrift, 1910, No. 17.

[5] Strom. II 6. 31. O. Stahlin, Clement Alex. II. (The Greek Christian writers. Vol. 15. Lpz. 1906).

[6] Barnabae epistula. Lpz. 1877. Addenda to this in Zeitschr. f. wiss. Theol. 1878. p. 150 and 295.

[7] Barnabae epistula, published in Patrum Apostolicorum opera I. 2. Lpz. 1878. Gebhardt took care of the text and the prolegomena relating to the text, and Harnack did the rest.

[8] "Patres Apostolici" 12. Tubingen 1901. Funk also took care of "Die apostolischen Vater" in "Collection of selected church and dogma–historical source writings, edited. von Kruger" (2nd row, 1st issue). The first edition, as well as the editions by Hilgenfeld and Gebhardt and Harnack are quoted only with the author's name, not the script.

THE CONTENTS OF THE
EPISTLE OF BARNABAS

The Introduction (Chap. 1:1–2:3)

The introduction consists of two parts: 1:1–5 and 1:5–2, 3. The first part briefly touches on the personal relationship between the writer and reader, the second gives the theme of the writing. First the second part will be examined; only when this is clear can the first be understood exactly.

Chap. 1:5–2:3. — Barnabas 1:5 indicates the purpose of the epistle with the words: "I hastened to write to you briefly, so that with your faith you would have complete Gnosis with your faith."[9] The gnosis of the already believing addressees still needs to be perfected.[10] The meaning of Gnosis can be concluded from 1:6–2:3. 1:6: "Three now are the teachings of the Lord: the hope of life is the beginning and the end of our faith; and righteousness is the beginning and the end of judgment; Love, which is manifested in joyful and cheerful deeds, is a testimony to righteousness."[11] The first of the three tenets states the reason and goal of faith, the

---

[9] Since γνῶσις is understood by Barn. in the sense of moral knowledge, which is at the same time connected with a corresponding attitude and activity, the term remains untranslated.

[10] According to L and Clem. Alex, Strom. II, 6. 31 (Stählin II. pag. 129) the letter wants to perfect faith and knowledge (scientia).

[11] The transmission in L and S is deficient. Weiss p. 52 does not want to presume to judge the origin of this sentence, since it can hardly be deciphered at all. Völter p. 339 declares those words to be incomprehensible at the point where they are located. In "Handbook to the New Testament Apocrypha" (edited by E. Hennecke, Tüb. 1904), p. 210 H. Veil 1:6 describes "as an old marginal comment, not belonging to the text, by a thoughtful reader who, perhaps in memory of the sentence of Ignatius Eph. 14: that faith and love are the beginning and the end of life, from the content of 1:4 the edifying application drew." Since 16 in the entire following letter finds no further explanation or connection, the sentence is "an erratic one Block, which a strange approximation pushed into this context" (ibid.).

second and third the way to this goal. The first sentence follows on from what the readers already have after 1:5, on the faith.

When the hope of life is described as its beginning and end, this means: eternal life is the basis and goal of faith. According to the second teaching, the way to this goal is justice, according to the third, love as a testimony of justice. The relation of the second teaching to the first is not expressed clearly enough. One would like to expect the words: Justice is the beginning and end of life, i.e., Righteousness (holiness) is the reason and cause and purpose of the eternal life hoped for through faith. Apparently, the author's thought of life was so closely connected with that of judgment that he readily interchanged the words life and judgment.[12] For him, life is judgment, the decision of the Divine Judge over believers.

1:7 indicates the content of the Gnosis with reference to the previously mentioned teachings of the Lord. "In fact, as the content of the Gnosis, the ruler has made the past and the present known to us through the prophets (ἐγνώρισεν), also giving us a foretaste of the future." The verbum ἀγνώριοεν is chosen with respect to γνῶοις, which is now being determined in more detail, as the transferring particle γάρ[13] shows. Gnosis includes prophetic revelations, past, present and future. The expressions παρεληλυθότα, ἐνεστῶτα, μελλόντων are too general to be readily understandable.

The words are only clear when 1:6 is taken into account. The words are only clear considering 1:6. There is probably nothing else possible than to assume that they are intended to repeat the teachings of the Lord mentioned there in a more general form—perhaps already known to the readers themselves from Barnabas' oral lecture. The first teaching of the Lord spoke of the future, i.e.,eternal life, of which the believer already gets a foretaste in this life. The past and the present must be related to the propositions that justice is rewarded with life, and that laboring love bears witness to love for justice. In the past and present, in the times of the prophets and Christianity, justice and love have in the same way such high power and exist so justly that Barnabas dares to use the expressions τά παρεληλυθότα and τά ἐνεστῶτα instead of these terms. 1:7a, however, not only determines Gnosis more closely by relating to it the three teachings of the Lord.

The same are also considered from a new point of view. What as the teaching of the Lord (κύριος), that is, Christ is known, 1:7 is referred to as the teaching of the God who revealed himself in the Old Covenant (ὁεβπότης). 1:7b[14] tells what

---

[12] κρίσις can like 11:7; 19:10; 21:6 have only the meaning "judgment".

[13] Gebhardt and Harnack p. 6. "Frustra in γάρ illo laborabis; verisimile est, γάρ hic et aliis huius libri locis esse = δὲ

[14] In Barn. 4:3 is contrasted with the δεσπότης. Τὸ δεσπότης in contrast to Christ cf. Doctr. Apost. 10:2, 3: εὐχαριστοῦμέν σοι, πάτερ ἅγιε, . . . υπέρ τῆς γνώσεως . . . ἧς ἐγνώ– ρισας ημῖν διά

effect the knowledge of "past and present" has on the behavior of believers. "If we see the individual as effective in this, as he has said, we must, on the basis of more abundant knowledge, also ascend all the higher to his altars."

The "effective"[15] is righteousness and love, since they confer eternal life. 1, 8 contains the writer's declaration that he still has to learn for himself, and reminds of the "foretaste of the future" in the reference to the joys in this world. 2:1 follows the invitation to take care of oneself and to search for the statutes (δικαιώματα) of the Lord, δικαιώματα is what secures the μαρτυρία δικαιοοονης (1:6) to the one who is looking for it. So it is to be understood by these the commandments, which demand justice and love. The invitation is justified by the wickedness of the times and the power of the one who causes it.

How to counteract these dangers is taught in 2:2: "Allies of our faith are now fear and perseverance, our comrades in battle are fortitude and renunciation." Whoever is able to resist the mentioned power in this way is promised 2:3 "Wisdom, understanding, knowledge, gnosis". This appropriately refers back to the announcement of the topic in 1:51[16] and concludes the introduction.[17]

Chap. 1:1–5:1:1 the "sons and daughters" are welcomed "in the name of the Lord who loved us". The apposition given to the Lord is striking. With the intention of educating for love (1:6), the writer immediately recalls the love of the divine model at the greeting.[18] 1:2 prepares the requirement in 2:1 by choosing the statutes (δικαιώματα) of God. These are called great, probably with regard to the previously mentioned love of Christ, who, as a divine example, is the most beautiful and best teaching and requirement of God. But they may be mentioned abundantly with reference to the numerous admonitions of the various prophets (cf. 1:7). The "great and bountiful statutes of God" are contrasted by μέν. The same can

---

Ἰησοῦ τοῦ παιδός σου ... σν, δέσποτα παντοκράτορ, ἴκτισας ..., ημῖν δέ ἐχαρίσω ... ζωήν αιώνιον διά τοῦ παιδός σου. ι. Clem. 7:4, 5 : ἀτενίσωμεν εις το αἷμα τοῦ Χριστοῦ και γνωμεν, ὡς ἐστιν τίμιον τω !)εω και πατρί αυτοῦ ... καί καταμα&ωμεν, οτι ... μετάνοιας τόπον εδωκεν ο δεσπότης ... I. Clem, 20:11; 24:1; 36:1; 2:4; 59:4 — L translates κύριος and δεσπότης with dominus.

[15] τά ενεργούμενα. though it is unknown to the ancient profane writers and LXX as a medium, it is often found at St. Peter's Basilica in Rome. Paul (Ro. 7:5; 2 Cor. 1:6; 4:12; Gal. 5:6; I.Th. 2:13; II.Th; 2:7; Eph. 3:20; Col. 1:29), also James 5:16; I.Clem. 60:1. In all these places the medium of impersonal concepts is used. For people, as well as Barn, 2:1, the active is used.

[16] L translates γνῶσις as scientia in 1:5, while in 2:3 he translates sapientia et intellectus.

[17] Only H. Veil in Neutestamentliche Apocrypha (edited by E. Hennecke, Tüb. 1904) expressly combines 1:5–2:3 into a whole.

[18] Harnack p. 2: "Magni momenti est, auctorem dpntinu.m nullo alio nomine hic nominasse nisi ἀγαπήσας ημάς." This designation shows an appeal to Pauline phrases.

only be found in 2:1. For while the greatness and richness of the statutes are emphasized in 1:2[19], it is required that man should also conform to them.

The thought that put the pen in the writer's hand was: the demands of God are so great and so plentiful, but they are still too little taken into account. However, Barnabas, being considerate, does not immediately accept the invitation to search for the statutes of the Lord. Among other things, he points out the spiritual advantages of the readers for the time being.[20] Their spiritual gifts not only already make those who possess them happy, they have already established themselves favorably before the world. Although they are divine gifts of grace, they have almost become natural to the readers.[21]

In a considerate manner, the writer 1:4 also gives the explanation to his own that he himself has the same duty as they do. "I am convinced[22] and aware[23] of this and conscious of the fact that, since I have preached among you, I possess abundant knowledge, because the Lord came to my side on the way to righteousness, so I also (still) see myself completely compelled to love you more than my life, because great faith and great love dwells in you in the hope of his life." The author compares himself to someone who, like him, has already acquired certain spiritual treasures, a "knowledge"[24], but still needs to be perfected. Since he now praises the spiritual gifts of the addressees in 1:4 as well as in the preceding and subsequent verses, and in 1:5 declares that their gnosis[25] needs to be perfected, he obviously wants to compare himself with them. Barnabas wants to say in 1:4: your task is also my task.[26]

---

[19] J. G. Müller, "Explanation of the Epistle of Barnabas. An appendix to de Wettes exeget. Handb. zum NT" (Leipzig 1869) p. 54: "The μίν does not correspond to a δέ. But in substance follows the contrast 1:5. In addition to what pleases the author about the readers, there should also be something from him." δικαίωμα is both 1:2 and 2:1 a praiseworthy quality of the readers (p. 54 and 72). The same explanation is given in the first place by C. J. Hefele, "The Epistle of the Apostle Barnabas Reexamined, Translated, and Explanated" (Tüb. 1840).

[20] 1:2: ὑπερευφραίνομαι ἐπὶ τοῖς μακαρίοις καὶ ἐνδόξοις ὑμῶν πνεύμασιν

[21] 1:2: οὕτως ἔμφυτον τῆς δωρεᾶς πνευματικῆς χάριν εἰλήφατε. 1:3, ἀληθῶς βλέπω ἐν ὑμῖν ἐκκεχυμένον . . . πνεῦμα ἐφ' ὑμᾶς. οὕτω με ἐξέπληξεν ἐπὶ ὑμῶν ἡ ἐμοὶ ἐπιποθήτη ὄψις ὑμῶν.
ουτω ἔμφυτον τῆς δωρεᾶς πνευματικῆς χάριν εἰλήφατε. ι, j: ἀλη&ώς βλέπω ἐν ὑμῖν ἐκκεχυμένον . . . πνεῦμα ἐφ' υμ–άς. ουτω με ἐξέπληξεν ἐπὶ ὑμῶν ἡ ἐμοι ἐπιπο^ήτη οψις ὑμῶν.

[22] πεπεισμένος, refers to the belief of the reader's mental state.

[23] ουνειδώς, refers to the conviction of one's own mental state.

[24] ἐν ὑμῖν λαλήσας πολλὰ ἐπίσταμαι.

[25] ἐπιστήμη (ἐπίστασθαι) and γνῶσις are obviously synonymous to the author. At the end of the introduction (2:3) both words are put together on purpose.

[26] Hilgenfeld p. 72 and Funk p. 39 remark on κάγώ in 1:4: sicut alii. Müller p. 61: "Your love has also forced mine on me. Harnack p. 4: Auxilium dei et caritas vestra etiam me cogunt.

II. The Old Testament: The Commandments of Sacrifice and Fasting (Ch. 2:4–4:8)

The epistle consists of three main parts: Chap. 2: 4–4:8; 4:9–12, 11:13–16. In the first, Barnabas starts with the call to moral life, perseverance and patience from the OT regulations on sacrifice and fasting. In the second main part, the power of evil in this world and at the same time the final, eternal victory of good is taught mainly in connection with the suffering of Jesus, which is reported about from OT revelations.

In the last paragraph, the author refers to the Old Testament. To the celebration of the Sabbath and the Temple of the ancient Jews, in order to warn against evil and to admonish to persevere in the good. Since one reason for the division of this disposition is not quite recognizable, it may perhaps be assumed that these three sections were partly three different sermons or catecheses, which Barnabas delivered at the time when he was personally among the addressees, and which he now wants to present in this epistle — probably more or less modified and revised — in order to render a service to the addressee also by the written word and to support his former activity.

2:4–10 will discuss the importance of Old Testament Sacrifices, 3:1–4:2 taught those of the lenten commandment. The end of the section warns of discouragement and despondency.

2:4–10. — From Is. 1:11–13 and Jer. 7:22, 23 it is proved that the true meaning of the sacrifices is not to be found in the outward, literal act and performance. The purpose of the sacrificial regulations is to inspire goodwill. "None of you plot evil in your heart against your neighbor, and love not a false oath."[27] a savor of goodwill is a heart to the Lord that praises its Creator."[28] Humility, love and honesty, sacrifices that are not demanded with external coercion[29] and are not offered by the external man,[30] correspond to the "intention of our benevolent Father" and lead to life.

3:1–4:2. — The commandment of Fasting also aims at moral life. Barnabas is referring to Is. 58:6 –10. The true fast consists in avoiding all unrighteousness

---

There is no mention anywhere of the readers' love for Barnabas. Her love, her faith and her hope are only praised in 1:4 because she is the necessary activity of God but only mentioned to explain the "abundant knowledge".

[27] Zach. 8:17.

[28] Ps. 50:19 + ?

[29] ἀρχὴ καὶ τέλος πίστεως (2:6).

[30] προςγορά μη ἀνθρωποποίης (2:6) = πρ. ἀπερίτμητος. on the other hand Müller: ab hominibus institutum sacrificium. L: humana ablatio.

and in the works of mercy. The writer summarizes the demands made by the Prophet in the term "integrity"[31]. 4:1 & 2: "Let us therefore flee completely from all the works of lawlessness, so that the works of lawlessness may not become master over us, and let us hate the error of the present time,[32] in order to experience love in the future! Let us not grant our soul the freedom that it has the opportunity to rush along a path with sinners and wrongdoers, so as not to become like them! With a special intention, 2:9 is spoken of "our kind Father" and 3.6 of the "long–suffering" God. The writer, referring to the divine example, wants to preach love and long–suffering with even greater emphasis, as already 1:1.

4:3–8. — "The annoyance has reached the highest degree." The trouble is the bad times (2:1), is the error of the present time (4:1). But Barnabas would like to ensure that this development does not make the evil power hesitant and does not prevent it from courageously and trustingly opposing it and following the moral warnings without hesitation. That is why he explains that it is not without God's prior knowledge that the conditions· have become so unfavorable at the moment; according to Enoch, they had already been predicted.[33] Out of this concern, he also assures that God has shortened these times so that his beloved Son will soon come and enter into his inheritance.[34] This assurance is further confirmed in 4:4 and 5

---

[31] ἀκεραιοσύνη (3:6). See 10:4.

[32] πλάνην τοῦ νῦν καιροῦ = ἡμερῶν πονηρῶ (2:1). πλάνη is, as the context shows, sin = τῆς πλάνης ἀνομία (14:5; cf. Rom. 1.27). On the other hand, K. H. v. Weizsäcker, "On the criticism of the Epistle of Barnabas from the Cod. Sinaiticus" (Tüb. 1863), p. 20: "According to the wording, the talk is of πλάνη τῆς ἀνομίας, according to the substance it is the seduction to the law."

[33] τὸ τέλειον σκάνδαλον ἤγγικεν, περὶ οὗ γέγραπται, ὡς Ἐνὼχ λέγει (4:3)·It shines on Enoch Chap. 85–90, where in a prophetic outline of world history the flock of God is finally given up to 70 heathen shepherds. The offenses given by these to the entrusted sheep are recorded by the command of God. Worst of all is the government of the last twelve shepherds in the fourth age. G. Beer in Kautzsch "The Apocrypha and Pseudepigr. of the Old Testament" 1906, II, pp. 294—298. Veil in Manual e.g. i.e., OT Apocr. P. 212. — In the τέλειον σκάνδαλον, Veil sees the possibility, unexpectedly offered under Emperor Hadrian, of the reestablishment of the Jewish temple and temple service, which any Christian teacher of the East, who saw in it a danger to the salvation of Christians brought about by Satan himself. There was reason to take up pen to avoid the danger of being seduced to preserve a Jewish religious conception and practice based on the letter of the OT or halfway to a Judaistic Christianity (NT. Apkr. p. 149).

[34] 4:3b: Εἰς τοῦτο γὰρ ὁ δεσπότης συντέτμηκεν τοὺς καιρούς . . . γάρ establishes the importance and necessity of the 4:1 and 2 given reminders. Hilgenfeld ld p. 78: perfectum scandalum iam appropinquasse Barnabas hoc argumento probat, quod deus tempora statuta propter filium suum imminuerit. After that, then, the "perfect scandal" would be proved by abbreviating the times. But this scandal is already something given (cf. 2:1), its existence does not

by reference to the prophecies of Dan. 7:24 and 7:7–8. In spite of the greatness and wide spread of evil, Barnabas wants to say that the hitherto restrained rule of the Son of God will come into its own, because, respectively, the power of the Son of God will be restored. just as, according to Daniel, "one little king" is to become master of "three kings at the same time" and "one little subsidiary horn" of the "fourth beast" will cope with "three large horns at the same time".[35] However, the statement that, despite the power of evil, the rule of the world and the final victory belong to God can be misused by those who trust. Barnabas 4:6–8 wants to warn His people about this. In part, as it seems, they gladly listened to the teaching of their former preacher that God remains faithful to the believers, does not break the covenant with them and does not leave them; they speak willingly, despite the fact that the power of evil is revealed so much, according to him the word "Your covenant (with God) remains with you".[36] But by giving him in this regard, faithfully repeating

---

need any proof, the power of evil is not doubted. What is supposed to be justified by γάρ is that one must not allow oneself to be deceived and influenced by this power of evil. — Weizsäcker p. 27, Weiss p. 56, Harnack p. 14 explain 4:3b as words from the book of Enoch. Weiss: "This τέλειον σκάνδαλον ἤγγικεν, περὶ οὗ γέγραπται must have been a well–known term, which may also have been borrowed from the Book of Enoch. Only the sentence Εἰς τοῦτο, constructed in Hebrew parallelism, is expressly quoted as a word from Enoch ... ἥξη." But such a word is not handed down in the book of Enoch that has survived, and moreover Barnabas in no way indicates that he wanted to quote Enoch with 4:3b. The meaning of 4:3a is: Enoch tells us that records have been made of the great scandal.

[35] See p. 21 ff below for more details.

[36] I follow the reading H: ὅτι ἡ διαθήκη ἐκείνων καὶ ἡμῶν. Likewise Funk, only that he reads ἡμῶν ἡμῖν, "which is not subject to any decency, since such mistakes are very common in the manuscripts" (Theol. Viertelschr. 1878 p. 153 f., 1889 p. 127); S: ὅτι ἡ διαθήκη ἡμῶν μεν, L: quia testamentum illorum et nostrum est. nostrum est autem. L follow: Müller p. 112; C. J. Riggenbach, "The so–called letter of Barnabas" (Basel 1873) p. 8; Hilgenfeld p. 8; Harnack p. 16; Funk p. 46; Völter p. 342 f.; NT Apocr. p. 152; Heer p. 30. Ad. Link in Theol. Literaturzeitung 1889 Column 596. Weizsäcker p. 10 f. sticks to S with the unconvincing remark "The author has not explained the contrast to μέν because the same immediately in his own reply introduced with ἀλλά against the thoughts of the speaker because he really could not put the principles of life, which alone can form that contrast, into the mouths of the speakers themselves. S may well be disregarded entirely, since its reading indeed makes no sense. It is also striking that the line in S in question is the shortest in its column; it has only nine letters, while the others all range between 11 and 15, only one line has ten letters (cf. Tischendorf, Nov. Test. Sin. 1863, p. 136). Only the words ὅτι ἡ διαθήκη ἡμῶν μεν ὑμῶν ὑμῖν μένει fit into the train of thought, which Weiss p. 58 is also inclined to accept. For, as 4:1–2 clearly shows, the aim is to deter the reader from the paths of sin; Now that "the finished stumbling block", this main cause for sin, has been discussed, the author wants to go into something new, which, in addition to what has been mentioned, can also be an impetus for sin (ετι και τουτο ε ἔτι δὲ καὶ τοῦτο ἐρωτῶ ὑμᾶς ρωτώ ίμας 4:6). This second reason is now given in the one–

and trusting only in God's faithfulness and power, they pile up sin upon sin. For the instruction of such trusting persons, Barnabas refers to the story in which God has already shown to the Jewish people that the covenant can also be lost again. As soon as Moses received the covenant, Israel had already completely lost it.[37]

The writer's intention to give the reader "understanding" (οἴνεσις 2:3) is repeatedly recalled in the present passage. Of Moses, who is placed in contrast to his sinful people, it says 4:8 "he had understanding".[38] After instruction about the sacrificial laws, 2:9 the admonition is given not to be "ignorant".[39] After the reference to the prophecies of Daniel 4:6 are followed by the request: "You must therefore be understanding".[40]

In sections 2:4–4:8, after the explanation given, Barnabas intends to admonish virtue and perseverance. The question remains, however, whether he does not want to fight the Atian sacrifice and fasting customs at the same time, perhaps even denying their relative validity, whether he only wants to strengthen believers morally or warn half–Christians, some of whom still lean towards Judaism, against halfheartedness want. A more or less sharp opposition to Judaism is almost universally ascribed to the epistle, especially to the present section.[41] Certain statements seem to speak in favor of this.

---

sided judgment of the preached words: "Your covenant remains with you." Even afterwards, belief in the covenant becomes a reason for indifference in moral life; however, some of the readers also justify themselves with the fact that not only they, but also the Jews, have the covenant with God. But what does this reference to the Jewish people mean here? Understandably, only the author himself was able to point to the people of Israel in order to demonstrate this error with an example from history.

[37] Heydecke, p. 16, and Weiss, p. 58 f., declare the story of Sinai 4:6–8 to be interpolated, since it is a repetition of 14:1–3. But the narrative has a different purpose each time.

[38] καὶ συνήκεν Μοϋσῆς. See 10:1 (S. V.).

[39] αἰσθάνεσθαι οὖν ὀφείλομεν, μὴ ὄντες ἀσύνετοι, τὴν γνώμην...

[40] συνιέναι οὖν ὀφείλετε.

[41] Hefele e.g. B. claims claims that the letter explains the ceremonies, which appeared to the Jewish Christian as a command of God that was binding up to the most recent times and was only abolished by Christ, as a custom that God had already rejected long before Christ (p. 172; cf. p. 50; 51 A. 9; 136; 243). According to Müller, the topic of Chap. 2 and 3: the Jewish sacrifices and fasts are not valid. Similar to O. Braunsberger ... The Apostle Barnabas. His life and the letter enclosed with him, scientifically appreciated" (Mainz 1876) p. 220f. Hilgenfeld p. XXXI: the Christian faith does not need the sacrifices of the Jewish law; the same, "The Apostolic Fathers" (Halle 1853) p. 14: already the OT Prophecy invalidated the Jewish ceremonial law. The basic idea of Chap. 2–4 is according to Harnack LX, A. 9, the Old Covenant already belongs to the Christians, its ceremonies are not to be observed. Funk claims that Barnabas wanted to warn against Jewish errors (p. XXVI). Völter p. 368 f.: the

1. First of all, 2:6 can give some reason for this: The Lord has abolished the sacrifices "so that the new law of our Lord Jesus Christ, free from the yoke of compulsion, may have no sacrifice that man offers externally."[42] A removal, cancellation of the OT sacrifices by God himself is pronounced. But it does not follow from these words that Barnabas wants to teach that the sacrifices in the Old Covenant are invalid. The meaning of ταυτα οὖν κατήργησεν is not: At that time God, when he rendered the words of Isaias 2:5 "What shall the multitude of your sacrifices do for me? . . ." said, with this explanation the sacrifices lifted, οὖν connects to the divine thought quoted in 2:5 and points to a divine action corresponding to this thought, which follows from it but was only carried out in the time of the New Covenant. According to Barnabas, this thought is just as irrelevant as that of Isaias himself: God did not want any external sacrifices at all and never ordered them. Rather, it is: External sacrifices alone are not enough for God, and he hates them if the appropriate attitude is lacking. 2:6 is now to be interpreted in the following way:

Since the OT sacrifices only had relative importance and the main intention of the Lord was aimed at the inner, spiritual revival of man, he now has (ουν) now, after the appearance of Christ, since his New Law came into effect, the various OT sacrifices have been abolished, so that in the force of this New Law the sacrifice of the heart may be made in free activity of the will on the basis of the right moral frame of mind. The spiritual sacrificial life should no longer need to be stimulated through external sacrifices based on strict ceremonial laws that enforce sacrifices.

The purpose of sentence 2:6 is not to be found in dogmatic instruction, not in an explanation of the validity or invalidity of the ancient sacrificial laws, but in the call to sacrifice, so that the comparison of the Old Testament with the New Law only happens with the intention of no longer making an external law, but rather man's free will, his sense of duty, the reason for spiritual sacrifices.

---

writer teaches the sharp distinction between law and prophets and proves that Christianity is the true religion compared to Judaism. O. Bardenhewer, "Patrologie" (3rd edition!, Freibg. 1910) p. 20 f.: 2–17 "wants to put the Old Covenant in the right light according to its value and meaning. However, the author does not content himself with teaching the New Testament that the Old Covenant has been annulled, that the Mosaic law has been abolished; Rather, he claims that the Old Covenant never had any validity at all, that Judaism with its statutes and ceremonies was not based on divine decree. . . A. Marmorstein, "L'epitre de Barnabd et la poldmique juive" (Revue des dtudes juives 1910) p. 214: "Les lois et coutumes des Juifs ne sont pas voulues et commanddes par Dieu."

[42] τοῦτο ἐρωτῶ ὑμᾶς ὡς εἷς ἐξ ὑμῶν ὤν, ἰδίως δὲ καὶ πάντας ἀγαπῶν ὑπὲρ τὴν ψυχήν μου, προσέχειν.

2. In the reference to the will of the Lord that we "should not seek like them in error" (2:9),[43] is often seen as a warning against dogmatic errors. The "erring ones" are considered to be those who still believe they are bound by the old Jewish sacrificial laws. However, the error in question is primarily attributed to the Jews. But if these are also accused in the foregoing of placing so much value on sacrifices, it does not follow from this that the error lies in the offering of the sacrifices and in the belief in their necessity. What the readers should not make common cause with the Jews on is rather the lack of a spirit of sacrifice, as the already explained meaning of 2:5 and 6 and the quote from Psalm 50 following 2:10 reveal.

A contrite heart was required of the Jews when performing the ceremonies. Israel sinned against this demand, and the Christian reader should have no part in this sin. The writer does not want to emphasize that the way which leads to God, according to God's own explanation,[44] no longer has sacrifices of the kind known in the Old Covenant, but that it consists in good disposition, in a moral life.[45]

3. The assertion that there are dogmatic discussions in the chapters in question also seems to find support in the remark 3:6 that the long–suffering person had predicted that the people would believe in integrity.[46] It is written afterwards and with reference to the prophecy of Isaiah mentioned above. If the tone has to be set to πιστεύσει, then the explainers are right, who see a teaching about faith here and understand by πιστεύσει εν ἀκεραιοσύνῃ "pure faith with higher insight", "who wants nothing to do with the law".[47] But Barnabas does not want to

---

[43] ἡμῖν λέγει, θέλων ἡμᾶς μὴ ὁμοίως πλανωμένους ἐκείνοις ζητειν, πῶς προσάγωμεν αὐτῷ.

[44] The indirect question in 2:9 (πῶς προσάγωμεν αὐτῷ) may well depend on λέγει, since the ζητειν immediately preceding the question can be omitted as an expression of the uncertain and little goal–conscious striving of an object, or it may refer to λέγει and ζητειν are obtained at the same time. On the other hand, Müller summarizes p. 81 λέγει absolutely.

[45] Only Weiss p. 54 emphasizes that there is no trace of polemics in 2:9. P. 88 on the spot: "The author looks back with gratitude on this liberation from the uncertain, groping state brought about by the goodness of God; the possibility of a seduction to that lack of freedom lies so far, the ἐκείνοι are so little close to the reader's field of vision that one would not even think of finding a warning against Judaistic seducers here if this tone had not been struck by the critics would be, who are still consistently ruled by the spell of the Tübingen view of history."

[46] ὁ μακρόθυμος προβλέψας, ὡς ἐν ἀκεραιοσύνῃ πιστεύσει ὁ λαός, . . . προεφανέρωσεν ἡμῖν περὶ πάντων, ἵνα μὴ
. . .

[47] Müller, p. 92. Harnack, p. 12: ... ἐν ἀκεραιοσύνῃ i. e.· legis Iudaicae opera non admiscendo." Funk p. 44 f.: „Auctor de fide in cognitione perfecta loquitur et sensum allegoriae altiorem appellat simplicem." Weiss, p. 55 zu iv ἀκεραιοοοην: "without admixture of Jewish customs.·

place special emphasis on πιστευειν and does not prefer one particular faith to another through the addition εν ἀκεραιοσύνῃ. Believing in and of itself is of secondary importance to him here. At this point, it is a broad, unspecified and narrowly limited term that refers to the OT and NT God's people is applied at the same time and forms something common to both of them, the turning to God in general, while the ἀκεραιοσυνη as the moral life will differentiate and distinguish one people from the other. What "the long–suffering foresaw" in Is. 58:6–10 in relation to the NT People are righteousness and mercy. Whether this people of the future will also adhere to fasting commandments or not, there is no question. When the author writes προβλέψας . . . προεφανερωσεν ἡμῖν περί πάντων, so he has made it clear enough what he intends, πάντα can only be referred to the good works enumerated at Isaias, peculiar to the true People of God, and not to fasting alone, not even to the various expressions of this fasting mentioned in 3:1 and 2; for everything that the Lord has "revealed before us" does not refer to the 3:1, 2 mentioned Isaiah's passage, which Barnabas introduces with the words "he speaks. . . to them", but only to the quotation 3:3–5, since only this "to us" is spoken.[48]

4. Especially favorable for the ordinary view of the meaning of the sections of the epistle in question seem to be the words with which the author 3:6 indicates the purpose of divine revelation in Isaiah προβλέψας, ὡς ἐν ἀκεραιοσύνη πιστεύσει ὁ λαός, ὃν ἡτοίμασεν ἐν[49] τῷ ἠγαπημένῳ αὐτοῦ). Many[50] find here a warning against proselytism and against accepting the Jewish ceremonial law. Decisive for the correct interpretation of the passage is the meaning of νόμῳ. Does the word here have to be understood from the ceremonial law? Probably nothing should force this, νόμῳ μος is mentioned in the letter only 2:6: "the new law of our Lord Jesus Christ". If, as may be assumed, "the law of those" in 3:6 is in contrast to this law of the Lord, then, as the above–given explanation of 2:5 and 6 concludes, this does not mean the law that prescribes sacrifice and fasting, but that direction and conception of the law that, despite sacrifice and fasting, does not also know sacrificial disposition, love and mercy. "The law of those" is therefore synonymous with the ἀνομίας (L: iniquitas) called in 4:1b. Also, b ἐκείνων νόμος stands in intentional contrast to the previous πάντων, so that because of this juxtaposition, everything that contradicts all the moral admonitions of the Prophet Isaiah is to be understood by it.[51]

---

[48] πρὸς ἡμᾶς δὲ λέγει (3:3).

[49] H und L: προσήλυτοι. S: ἐπίλυτοι.

[50] Z. B. Hefele p. 54, 136. Müller p. 93 — 95. Hilgenfeld p. XXXI; Ap. Väter p. 15. Harnack p. 13. Funk p. XXVII. Völter p. 364 und 368.

[51] Weiss p. 88 explains to 36: the passage "gives the impression that a real seduction against Judaism is completely out of the realm of possibility. The ἐκζητεῖν puts the matter at a great distance and the expression προσρησσώμεθα is so indefinite and general that the author can hardly have had any concrete view of Jewish aspirations at his command." — Weizsäcker p.

All the above–mentioned concerns and objections can still be met by the following considerations:

a) The peculiar distribution of the prophet's words is significant. One is addressed to the reader by the author, the others to the Jews. Some are introduced with the words λέγει δὲ οὕτως,[52]– Λέγει οὖν πάλιν περὶ τούτων πρὸς αὐτούς (3:1). So he quotes the others: ἡμῖν οὖν οὕτως λέγει (2:10), πρὸς ἡμᾶς δὲ λέγει (3:3). Why does Barnabas not apply all the scriptures to his readers in the same way? Why does he address only the Jews with those sentences that speak of the uselessness of sacrifices and fasting? Probably only because these prophetic words were irrelevant in their next meaning for the addressees of the missive, since they did not observe those ceremonies and should not be warned about their observation either. For them, only that which was expressed indirectly in these passages of the Bible, the admonition to a sense of sacrifice, to love and mercy, had meaning, which is why the author was only able to have those words which convey these deeper, moral thoughts directly reach the address of His own people.

b) Some expositors openly admit that, assuming the dogmatic character of chapters 2 and 3, they are somewhat embarrassed by the subsequent moral instructions in 4:1 and 2. Müller writes in an introduction to chapter 4: "Looking at the present and the near future, our author suddenly admonishes readers to avoid sins. Since he previously spoke of the nullity of sacrifices and fasting, the transition to this exhortation does not seem motivated enough." Heydecke is so unable to understand the relationship of the fourth chapter with its moral admonitions to the two previous chapters that he takes that from the traditional contexts in order to place it only after the end of the didactic part of the epistle (= chapters 2–3; 13–16) (loc. cit. pp. 10–12).

Since he sees a warning against proselytism in 3:6, Hilgenfeld finds the train of thought interrupted when this is immediately followed by a warning against sin in 4:1 f. and in 4:6b a new invitation is issued, similar to 3:6, to not to make a common cause with the Jews. With 3:6 he therefore first associates 4:6b, 4:9a (incl.) and only then adds 4:1–4, 6a[53]. It thus forces the assertion that chapters

---

13 f.: ","there is no doubt thatit is to be understood according to the fixed meaning of επιλνειν, επιλνοις, according to which this is the art expression for written explanation. Therefore, we probably have to read: ὡς ἀπιλύτῳ εκείνων νόμῳ . . . The meaning is, therefore, that we do not come across the law, fall in love with it or become confused by it, accept it as it is, as if it were a declared (by itself), while it is only through the Lord's own revelations . . . receives for us his true explanation in a higher sense, which protects us from being attached to him."

[52] 2:7. Because of πάλιν, προς αντοίς must also be added to λίγων διέ μίν in 2:4.

[53] P. XIX ff, Harnack p. 13 remarks on this view of Hilgenfeld: Libenter viro doctissimo concedo, sententiarum ordinem ab eo propositum perspicuum atque bonuni esse. At cum

2 and 3 contained doctrines to abandon and disregard the old, multiple and well–preserved testimonies.

Special attention was often paid to the two Daniel passages in 4:4 and 5 for the chronological fixation of the Epistle of Barnabas. But the figures in the two passages of the prophets have no other purpose in the eyes of Barnabas than to indicate the power of sin on earth until the appearance of the divine judge, as has resulted from the context. That the author has mentioned the numbers Βασιλεῖαι δέκα — τρεῖς ὑφ' ἓν τῶν βασιλέων; δέκα κέρατα — ἓν τρία τῶν μεγάλων κεράτων) in a mystical sense, may suggest his number mysticism applied elsewhere (9:8).

That the author has mentioned the numbers (βασιλεααι δέκα — τρεις ιφ" ἑν των βαοιλέων; δέκα κέρατα — νφ εν τρία των μ εγάλων κεράτων) in a mystical sense, his number mysticism applied elsewhere (9:8) may suggest.

Barnabas did not think of ten or three certain historical figures, regents, as was most often assumed.[54] For this reason, in Paragraphs 4:4 and 5 he does not offer any indication for determining the writing time of the missive. Harnack and P. Ladeuze also deny that the above–mentioned Daniel passages allow the writing time of the epistle to be determined. However, they come to this view mainly because they consider the various attempts already made to find the dates offered by Daniel in the Roman imperial history to be failures.

Harnack writes: "In view of the impossibility of finding an explanation of the corrected prophecies from the time between Vespasian and Hadrian, this may be borne in mind . . . to be raised more seriously again: did the author really correct the divination himself? did he just record the prophecy of Daniel — modified for a

---

constet, scriptorem epistulae saepius verum ordinem turbasse, quominus Hilgenfeldium sequar impedior. Funk expresses his opposition to Hilgenfeld's conversion to Theol. Quarterly. 1878, p. 157. But Hilgenfeld stops in Zeitschr. for scientific Theol. 1879, p. 267 against Funk, upholds his view. The fact that the above–mentioned change in the sentences of the fourth chapter by no means simplifies the train of thought is shown by the fact that Hilgenfeld, in order to be able to combine the warning against Judaism, which concludes with 4:8, with the moral admonitions that then follow, now feels compelled to suddenly set a new goal for the author at 4:9, to let him fight first against the Jews and then immediately afterwards against the Gentiles: Hoc igitur epistulae introitu duplex, admonitio indicatur, primo ne Christiani causam suam cum Iudaeis communicent, tum ne gentilium opera iniqua exerceant (p. XXXI).

[54] For more details, see Harnack, Hist. of the Old Christian Lit. II. i, p. 420 ff.; Funk, Church History Treatise And Examination II, p. 77 ff.; Ehrhard, *The Old Testament Lit. and Their Research.* from 1884–1900, pp. 81 f. Most recently, Barn. 4:4 and 5 used historically by M. d'Herbigny S.I. in the *Recherches de Science religieuse 1910*, I, 417–443, 540–566 (*"La date de l'Epitre de Barnabe"*).

certain situation (in Egypt) decades before, which was not understandable to him himself — because he hoped that it would come true in the near future, perhaps also because he was counting on a witty reader who would be able to interpret it? Does the prophecy perhaps originate from the time of Christ and does it refer to Roman–Egyptian conditions? Until this question is answered, it is necessary to leave aside the passage when fixing the date of our epistle" (II, 423).

Ladeuze[55] explains: "C'est a tort qu'on pretend que Barnabe, en cet endroit, consider la prophetie de Daniel comme realisee de ses jours, et qu'il voit cet accomplishment dans la succession des empereurs de Rome . . . Avons–nous, dans ce v. 4, une nouvelle preuve de l'assertion qui commence le v. 3: ‚le grand scandale approche ? L'auteur semble plutöt, apres avoir brivement prouve cette assertion, indiquer ä ses lecteurs un signe auquel il faudra reconnaitre la fin du monde, quand eile s'annoncera, et en laisser l'interpretation ä leur sagacite (συιέναι οὖν ὀφείλετε)."[56]

A. Ehrhard claims that the "interpretative skills" made for the chronological evaluation of the Daniel passages are suitable for discrediting both the interpreters and the author of the epistle himself. "If one reads the passage without the preconceived opinion of gaining in it a chronological clue to the time of its writing, one does not get the impression that the author had a certain Roman emperor in mind, but he leads the prophecy to the heedfulness of his addressees" (p. 82).

Most recently, Veil has again been featured in [Edgar] Henneke's Handbuch zu den Neutestamentliche Apokryphen (1904), pp. 215 et seq. He used the above–mentioned prophecies of Daniel for the dating of the epistle and, especially because of the changes made by Barnabas in the passages of the prophets, rightly believed that the author wanted to refer to certain contemporary historical events. p. 217.

He makes the assertion: "A close examination of the wording has shown that there is nothing in it that contradicts the interpretation of Hadrian, but rather that his numerous and significant deviations from the Danielian text can hardly be explained otherwise than by the intention to point out Hadrian as clearly as possible;" his interpretation of the passage gives "for the first time a satisfactory solution

---

[55] L'Epitre de Barnabe. Extrait de la Revue d'histoire ecclesiastique I, 1 — 2. Louvain 1900, p. 9 f.

[56] Ed. "It is a mistake that it is claimed that Barnabus, in this place, considers the prophecy of Daniel as fulfilled in his days, and that he sees this achievement in the succession of the emperors of Rome. . . Do we have, in this v. 4, a new proof of the assertion that begins v. 3: ‚the great scandal is approaching? The author seems rather, after having briefly proved this assertion, to indicate to his readers a sign to which it will be necessary to recognize the end of the world, when it will announce itself, and to leave the interpretation to their sagacity (συιέναι οὖν ὀφείλετε)."

to the riddle, which his author with the imposition: it is then necessary for you to show understanding, to his readers, and which Harnack II, p. 422 et seq. has recently called unsolvable, even suspected as pointless"; he offers "a solution of full evidence and without rest". But despite the certainty and confidence that speaks from these words, I think I can use the changes made by Barnabas for my opinion. A comparison of these changes with the original text of the LXX will provide the proof:

Original Text (LXX):	Text by Barnabas:
Dan. 7:24. καὶ τὰ δέκα κέρατα τῆς βασιλείας δέκα βασιλεῖς στήσονται καὶ ὁ ἄλλος βασιλεὺς μετὰ τούτους στήσεται καὶ αὐτὸς διοίσει κακοῖς ὑπὲρ τοὺς πρώτους καὶ τρεῖς βασιλεῖς ταπεινώσει	βασιλείς (H; βασιλεῖαι S. and L) δέκα ἐπὶ τῆς γης βασιλεύοονοιν, καὶ ἐξαναϋτήϋεται οπισϑεν (αυτών S) μικρός βαοιλεύς, ὃς ταπεινώσει τρεις ὑφ έν τῶν βασιλέων.
Dan. 7:7 f. μετὰ δὲ ταῦτα ἐθεώρουν . . . θηρίον τέταρτον φοβερόν. . . . διαφόρως χρώμενον παρὰ πάντα τὰ πρὸ αὐτοῦ θηρία εἶχε δὲ κέρατα δέκα . . . καὶ ἰδοὺ ἄλλο ἓν κέρας ἀνεφύη ἀνὰ μέσον αὐτῶν μικρὸν ἐν τοῖς κέρασιν αὐτοῦ, καὶ τρία τῶν κεράτων τῶν πρώτων ἐξηράνθησαν δι' αὐτοῦ	καὶ εἶδον τό τέταρτον θηρίον τό (> S) πονηρόν και καχυρόν χαῖ χαλεπώτερον παρά πάντα τά θηρία τῆς θαλάσσης (H L; γης S) καὶ ὡς ἐξ αυτού ἀνέτειλεν δέκα κέρατα και εξ αυτών μικρόν κέρας παραφυάδιον, καὶ ὡς ἐταπείνωσεν ὑφ έν τρία τών μεγάλων κεράτων.

Of the changes that indicate the author's intention to show that the small and unnoticed can defeat the great and powerful, the following four additions made by Barnabas can be considered: μικρός (βασιλεύς) and υφ' εν in the first Prophet passage of the prophet and from the second παραφυάδον and ύφ' εν, as well as the predicate μεγάλων (κεράτων). The omission of the words: και. αυτός διοίσει κακοῖς ... in Dan. 7:24 proves that the one whom the author wishes to call victor over the great powers must be a good ruler and not represent a bad power, as the original text states and as the interpreters of the missive usually assume. Harnack, on the other hand, suspects that the changes that the two passages of the prophets in the epistle of Barnabas have in comparison with the LXX text were not made by the author of the epistle himself, but that Barnabas has received the two passages in an already changed form. "They seem to come from an apocalyptic collection of passages" (II, 419). In any case, Barnabas made no attempt to interpret the main changes, or even gave a hint (p. 420).

CHAPTER 2

THE OLD TESTAMENT: THE COMMANDMENTS OF SACRIFICE AND FASTING (CH. 2:4–4:8)

a) Transition (Chap. 4:9–5:13)

4:9 — 14 is usually still connected with the preceding sentences of the fourth chapter as belonging together.

Already in 4:9a the conclusion of the previous train of thought and the transition to new thoughts are clearly indicated. "But although I wanted to write many things — not in the tone of a teacher, but in the manner of a loving friend — I have hastened to write (yet only) what we cannot ignore (in the manner mentioned), thus as your least servant."[57] The meaning of these words is: Although I wanted to discuss a lot of the things that have already been discussed, I have to hurry, and in my haste I only write what is absolutely necessary. The words that he did not want to be a teacher but a friend are not intended to make his intention to write a lot appear intrusive or bold. The declaration of subservience at the end of the sentence points back to this: since I want to interact with you in the manner

---

[57] πολλὰ δὲ θέλων γράφειν — , οὐχ ὡς διδάσκαλος, ἀλλ' ὡς πρέπει ἀγαπῶντι ἀφ' ὧν ἔχομεν μὴ ἐλλείπειν, γράφειν ἐσπούδασα, περίψημα ὑμῶν. Veil translated: . I have endeavored to remind this in my letter, dal! we must not let go of what we possess." But σπουδάζειν, like 1:5, can only mean "hurry up". Then a warning 'Don't let go of what we have!' doesn't fit into the train of thought. There is no talk of a possession that should not be given up. The simplest is the expression ἀφ' ὧν . . . To contrast ἐλλείπειν with πολλά. The connection of ideas in Riggenbach's translation is unnatural: "Since I wanted to write a lot, not as a teacher, but as befits a lover, not to lag behind what we have, I made an effort to write."

proper to a willing friend and benefactor, I now mark myself "therefore"[58] as your submissive servant.

The personal remark in 4:9, unfounded by the preceding train of thought, shows that Barnabas interrupts his discussions here in order to move on to a new matter. The matter is becoming more important, and that is why it is necessary, for better conviction and more effective instruction, to let the power of one's own personality come into its own beforehand. In those words, the transition is not only indicated to a new section, but also one with a heavy content. Because the author could have said a lot more from the way he has already presented it to his readers; but he doesn't have time for that, he's too pressed to move on to something else quickly, precisely because he can't under any circumstances omit or shorten the new teaching point.

In the event that 49 remains connected with the preceding sentences of the chapter as belonging together, the repetition of the same ideas, the moral instruction, is on the one hand in 4:1 and 2, and then again in 4:10–13, and that in part inexplicable in the same and related expressions.[59] Surely it is not to be expected that a writer, in quick succession, twice addresses the same or nearly the same admonitions to his readers in the same passage, that Barnabas twice lays the cap–stone to the teachings of chapters 2 and 3. But the writer can, in order to emphasize the purpose of his writing with sufficient urgency, at the introduction of a new section, emphasize the very ideas with which he is primarily concerned throughout the entire work.

If Chapter 4 were an internally self–contained whole, then another thought would also recur twice in quick succession in the same section. 4:7–8 & 4:14 contain the same teaching that the external covenant relationship or calling alone is not sufficient and does not yet imply election to eternal life. However, the phrase ετι δέ κακείνο . . . . . . νοείτε (4:14), shows that the author was very far from repeating this same admonition, albeit each time in a different form, in one and the same section which clearly states that the following words contain something quite new for the present section.

---

[58] διό. — διό comes after H and S before περίφημα, while after L it comes before the following verb προσέχωμεν. L follow all editors and commentators. But the testimony of the best manuscripts is to be recognized here. Because διό gives a good sense before περίφημα, and moreover it can also be explained how the displacement by L could happen. Because of other personal circumstances, the whole sentence πολλὰ δὲ . . . περίψημα ὑμῶν was useless and he therefore omitted it, he had to look for a compound for the words προσέχωμεν . . . search and now borrowed διό from that sentence.

[59] φύγωμεν . . . μισήσωμεν (4:1 and 10), μη δώμεν ανεσιν (4:2) — " ἵνα μήποτε ἐπαναπαυόμενοι . . . ἐπικαθυπνώσωμεν . . . (4:13).

4:9–14. — As in the introductory sections 1:5, 2:3, 4:9–14 also calls on the addressees to love and justice in the interest of their salvation and to perseverance and patience in love because of the power of Satan.

As in 1:6, Barnabas also in 4:9 first reminds of faith and its position in relation to salvation. Only under certain conditions would "all the time of our belief" be of use.[60] Then he calls for the common good to be in view, to become spiritual men and temples of God, to observe the commandments of the Lord. He warns against all vanity, the works of the vicious path and against selfish seclusion. He preaches justice, makes his followers aware that they should not believe they are already justified. "If a man is good, righteousness will go before him." He recalls the troubled times and the power of Satan, writing of "the lawless days" and "the troubles to come" which are meant to give rise to resistance, "so that the black man may not sneak in".

Satan is called the "bad prince". Faced with this power there is no rest and no sleep; so perseverance is necessary. Also the reference to the fate of the Israelite people, which could enjoy so many divine graces, but were finally abandoned by God, can only serve the purpose of warning against flagging in moral zeal and the feeling of security and to encourage tenacious endurance.[61] The purpose of sowing

---

[60] ὁ πᾶς χρόνος τῆς πίστεως (S; on the other hand H: τῆς ζωῆς΄). Since the author speaks only of eternal life in 1:6 and, before he names the way to it, points out that the prospect of eternal life has caused faith, because of the similarity that also prevails elsewhere between 1:6 and 4:9 f. consists in preferring the reading S, according to which eternal salvation is related to faith. In chap. 1 as in chap. 4 the thought is expressed: The belief of the readers is generally not objectionable, it is the good on which to build. L combines both ways of reading: nihil enim proderit nobis omne tempus vitae nostrae et fidei.

[61] 4:14: ἔτι δὲ κἀκεῖνο, ἀδελφοί μου, νοεῖτε· ὅταν βλέπετε ματὰ τηλικαῦτα σημεῖα καὶ τέρατα γεγονότα ἐν τῷ Ἰσραήλ, καὶ οὕτως ἐγκαταλελεῖφθαι αὐτούς· προσέχωμεν, μήποτε, ὡς γέγραπται, πολλοὶ κλητοί, ὀλίγοι δὲ ἐκλεκτοὶ εὑρεθῶμεν." εὑρεθῶμεν. σημεῖα καὶ τέρατα are to be understood as the signs of the OT revelation, the extraordinary and wonderful intercourse of God with the people of the covenant of Israel. On the other hand, Braunsberger claims on p. 250 that with these words the author is referring to the destruction of the Jewish Temple, which is also mentioned in 16:4. — The question of the origin of the written word πολλοὶ κλητοί, ὀλίγοι δὲ ἐκλεκτοὶ has found different answers. The same remind of Mt. 22:14. For a quote from Mt.. by Riggenbach p. 36; Hilgenfeld p. XXXVII; Harnack p. 19f; others., History of the Early Christians, L. II. I p. 417; Sprinzl, "The Theology of the Apostolic Fathers" (Vienna 1880), p. 73. Zahn, History of the New Testament Canons I. 2 (Leipzig 1889) p. 848 Anni, 1: "It seems to me completely useless to deny those who cling to the possibility that the saying was already found by Jesus as a proverb or Bible saying, and that Barnabas drew it from the same source independently of Matthew 22:14, or that Barnabas confused the saying known to him from Matthew with the other in IV Esdras 8:5 multi quidem creati sunt, pauci autem salvabuntur and therefore quoted it as a biblical

love may already be expressed in the personal remark in 4:9, insofar as the author in the words ὡς πρέπει αγαπῶντι also intends to present himself to his readers as an example.[62] In 4:9–14 the author nowhere directly expresses the intention of enriching the "knowledge", the gnosis of his followers through his teachings, but he warns 4:11 those who would like to live in self–satisfied seclusion against selfish knowledge with the quote from Isaiah 5:21: οναί οἱ οννετοι εαντοίς καί ενώπιον εαυτῶν επιστήμονες[63].

5:1–13. — 5:1 gives the theme for chapters 5–12: the suffering of Christ warns against sin and admonishes for sanctification. "For this the Lord took it upon himself to give His flesh to destruction, that we might be sanctified by remission of sins, that is, by sprinkling his blood." This truth is urgently preached with reference to OT prophecies about Jesus' suffering from 5:13 onwards. But first, up to 5:12, the double purpose that is pursued by mentioning Jesus' suffering is emphasized. One is to turn away from sin and turn to good (5:1–4); the other is to present the power of evil and its authority as only apparent and temporary (5:5–12).

In 5:1, not only the final sentence refers to moral revival, but also the connection with the immediately preceding teachings by γάρ. To prove his claim, Barnabas quotes in 5:2 Isaias 53:5–7: "He was wounded because of our lawlessness and has been mistreated because of our sins. We were healed by his stripes . . . In 5:3 he

---

verse I have and the like." Lipsius in the Bible lexicon by D. Schenkel, vol. I (Leipzig 1869), p. 371: . . This expression in particular (γέγραπται) proves that the author used the relevant words in an OT script found." Weizsäcker S 34 rightly explains: "The words are therefore in any case the execution from a γραφή. But the more the application of this designation to a gospel writing contradicts the whole other behavior of the letter in this respect, the more certain we can assume that its source is different." Cf. Weiss p. 109 f.

[62] See 1:4 κἀγὼ ἀναγκάζομαι ἀγαπᾶν.

[63] Harnack p. 19: Totum capitulum in duas partes di vidi potest sibi respondere: vv 1–8, 9–14. In utriusque partis particula priore (vv 1–5, 9–13) auctor epistulae monuit, ut periculosam animarum securitatem lectores evitarent et opera iniquitatis fugerent; tum in altera parte (vv 6–8. 14). verbis ετι όέ καί τούτο ερωτώ (ἔτι δὲ κἀκεῖνο νοεῖτε) id egit, ut lectores a Iudaizantium cultu ac religione et a Iudaeorum imitatione a vocaret, historiae Iudaeorum cum triste initium (vv 6–8), tum tristem exitum (vv 14) eos respicere iubens. But if Barnabas had intended to emphasize in the second part precisely "its extremely fateful end" (cf. p. LV11I) in contrast to the "fatal beginning of Jewish history" mentioned in the first section of the chapter, then he would probably have in quite a different way Wisely, when it happened, must emphasize the two periods of this history. Whether the events mentioned formed the beginning and the end of Jewish history was irrelevant to the author; he does not cite them as a main idea of the chapter, but only adds them as occasional remarks suitable for better moral instruction.

explains that the promised prophetic revelations, the past, present, future[64] are now also present here, that gnosis, wisdom and understanding (2:3) would also be given to us here: "So we must be extremely grateful to the Lord, since he both made the past the content of gnosis for us, and gave us wisdom regarding the present; we are also not without understanding about the future."[65]

Since 5:3 is a conclusion from the above–mentioned Isaiah quotation, the revelation about the past and present — according to the explanation of 1:7 — is to be sought in the teaching that lawlessness and sin are hated by the Lord and man should purify himself from them. Even the instruction about the future can only encompass the truth that nothing sinful, but only that which is sanctified by Christ's wounds, will enter into bliss. That Barnabas wants to warn against sin is also suggested by 5:4: "A man will rightly perish who, although he has knowledge of the way to righteousness, keeps to the way of darkness."

In 5:5, the other purpose for which the suffering of the Lord is to be mentioned is indicated. "There, our Lord took it upon himself to suffer for our soul, although Lord of the whole world — to whom God spoke immediately after the foundation of the world, let us make man in our image and likeness[66] — so it is strange how he took it upon himself to suffer at the hands of men." The meaning of these words is: now that the remarkable thing has happened that the Son of God was subjected to foreign power and rule through his suffering, the question arises as to how his suffering took place. One wants an answer to the question of whether there is a final subjection of power of good to the evil one. The author wants to fulfill the desire for such knowledge. That is why he explains in 5:6–8 that the divine Lord only succumbed in order to finally triumph, that the purpose of his incarnation was to combat and overcome death, as well as the teaching of the

---

[64] τὰ παρεληλυθότα, τὰ ἐνεστῶτα, τῶν μελλόντων (1:7).

[65] καὶ τὰ παρεληλυθότα ἡμῖν ἐγνώρισεν καὶ ἐν τοῖς ἐνεστῶσιν ἡμᾶς ἐσόφισεν, καὶ εἰς τὰ μέλλοντα οὐκ ἐσμὲν ἀσύνετοι.

[66] ὁδοῦ δικαιοσύνης γνῶσιν.

resurrection,[67] that in this way he fulfilled the promise to the fathers,[68] and by work-ing the resurrection on himself, he wanted to show his power as a judge.[69]

His glorious humiliation in the flesh, his reputation on earth is referred to in various expressions. It is reminiscent of his founding of a new kingdom,[70] his activity as a teacher,[71] his wonderful and multifaceted effectiveness.[72] The power of the humbled Son of God is also taught in 5:8 by the words: "I will not speak of the fact that some proclaimed him and loved him infinitely."[73] The sermon and the love of the apostles are remembered, for the apostles and their preaching are immedi-ately referred to in 5:9 again. Barnabas wants to say: it was precisely the consequence of the humiliation under human nature that Christ gained disciples who pro-claimed him and his teaching, and that he reaped sacrificial love. But not only — as the further course of thought in 5:9 shows — the public appearance of the apostles gives evidence of the invincible power of Christ and his brilliant successes; they are already taught by the calling of the disciples, since the Lord has made righteous ones out of sinners in them.

"But when he chose his own apostles, who were to preach his gospel, alt-hough they were the greatest sinners, to show that he had not come to call the right-eous, but sinners, he revealed himself as the Son of God." Even a great development

---

[67] Völter declares section 5:5–7:1 to be interpolated. "It has nothing to do with what is said about the covenant in 4:1–8 and 5:1–4. This discussion has its clear conclusion in 5:5.4. Section 5:5–7:1 gives the impression of a subsequent appendix in which a single idea from the preceding exposition is made the subject of a detailed, apologetic treatment, namely the idea expressed in 5:1 that the Lord put his flesh in gave death. But while this thought is pre-sented quite harmlessly and impartially in 5:1, without the author being aware that he could be subject to all sorts of difficulties and objections, it is quite different in 5:5–7:1. The au-thor feels compelled to defend the thesis that the Son of God came in the flesh and suffered with all the means at his disposal. It is the intensification and development of Christological ideas, the conception of Christ as the essential Son of God, that has caused this difficulty, while the author of 5:14 still remotely thinks of it." (p. 345 f. cf. p. 416.)

[68] εἰ = ἐπεί very often in the New Testament.

[69] αὐτὸς δέ, ἵνα καταργήσῃ τὸν θάνατον καὶ τὴν ἐκ νεκρῶν ἀνάστασιν δείξῃ. . . ὑπέμεινεν (5:6).

[70] ἵνα τοῖς πατράσιν τὴν ἐπαγγελίαν ἀποδῷ (5:7) Weiss p. 5) posed the question" that "no consideration is given to the disturbing contrast between Christ's divine glory and his suf-fering at the hands of men". A further contradiction between the two final clauses is shown in the fact that Christ's incarnation is first shown to be necessary in a "more physical or met-aphysical way", while 5:7 "the person of Christ is considered in terms of its religious–histor-ical significance". 5:5 and the final sentence in 5:6 is interpolated.

[71] ἵνα. . . ἐπιδείξῃ ἐπὶ τῆς γῆς ὤν, ὅτι τὴν ἀνάστασιν αὐτὸς ποιήσας κρινεῖ (5, 7).

[72] τὸν λαὸν τὸν καινὸν ἑτοιμάζων (5:7)

[73] διδάσκων τὸν Ἰσραὴλ (5:8).

of sinful power can offer no obstacle to the incarnate God without it, but rather helps to reveal his divinity.[74] Thus it can now be understood that Christ even humbled himself to suffering in human nature precisely for the very purpose of bringing evil to its highest form. "So the Son of God appeared in the flesh for the purpose of filling up the measure of sin for those who had persecuted his prophets to death. So he took it upon himself (to suffer)."[75] With the words 5:13 "But he wanted to suffer, because it was necessary that he: suffering from the cross" is already being transferred to the execution of the topic. But they also emphasize once again the independence and power of Christ against the hostile power, by explaining in the second part that no unforeseen obstacle, not wanted by himself, was put in the way of the Son of God.[76]

---

[74] τηλικαῦτα τέρατα καὶ σημεῖα ποιῶν (5:8).

[75] οιχ (complete λέγω), ὅτι ἐκήρυσσον καί ὑπερηγάπησαν αυτόν. The tradition of these words is very different. H: ουγ ὅτι ἐκήρυσσε καί ὑπερηγάπησαν αυτόν. S: ἐκήρυσσεν καί ὑπερήγαπησαν αυτόν. V (only begins with 5, 7): ἐκήρυξε καί ὑπερηγάπησεν αυτόν (also army). L: non crediderunt nec dilexerunt illum. Gebhardt: ἐκήρυσσεν, καί ὑπερηγάπησεν αυτόν. Hilgenfeld: οὐχ οτι ἐκήρυσσον καί ὑπερηγάπησαν αυτόν (on the other hand in the first edition ἐκήρυσσεν, καί ουπερ ἡγάπησαν αυτόν), also earlier Funk, but which now prefers the reading ἐκήρυσσεν καί ὑπερηγάπησεν αυτόν (Theol. Viertelschr. 1889, pp. 129–133). I declare myself for H, only that I put both verbs in the plural, for the following reasons: The singular form εκήρυσσεν would become ουχ ότι. (S V) must be related to Christ, which would result in a repetition of the same idea, since Christ's teaching activity is already emphasized in διδάσκων τον Ισραήλ. The addition ουχ ότι, which H reads alone, is necessary because of the δε (5, 9) that follows in the next sentence. 5, 8b stands in contrast to 5, 9. The author wants to speak of the apostles insofar as it concerns the time of their calling, but he does not want to speak of the time of their later activity. "I will not go into great lengths about the apostles preaching and loving the Lord beyond measure. But I do want to mention that at that time, when the Lord chose his own apostles . . ., he revealed himself as the Son of God." οὐχ ότι expresses that it was not the writer's intention to particularly emphasize the activities of the apostles as proof of the authority of the divine Lord. Hilgenfeld, who also follows H, gives the following explanation of sentence 5, 8b in the Journal for Scientific Theology 1879, p loved, Jesus, as we will read shortly, had to choose his own apostles τους μέλλοντας κηρυσσειν τό εναγγέλιον αυτού." ὑπεραγαπάν recalls 1:4 and 4:6: αγαπάν υπέρ την ψυχήν. The aorist ὑπερηγάπησαν in contrast to the imperfect ἐκήρυσσον indicates a unique ActsThis is the conclusion of the teaching activity (first comes ἐκήρυσσον, then ὑπερηγά¬πησαν) the devotion of life out of love to the Lord. Accordingly, we have here a chronological point of reference for the composition of the epistle, insofar as the apostles had already died at that time.

[76] The view that in Chap. 5 ff. out of opposition to Judaism the meaning and validity of the New Covenant should be proved. Hefele overwrites chap. 5: "The new covenant established in the blood of Christ brings us salvation, the Jews to destruction." Funk p. XXVII: Dominum prophetis praenuntiantibus, Judaeis vero non intellegentibus, propterea passum esse,

A great development of sinful power cannot offer any obstacle to the Son of God who has become man, but rather helps to reveal his divinity.[77] So it can now be understood that Christ even lowered himself to suffering in human nature for the very purpose of bringing evil to its highest form. "So the Son of God appeared

---

ut nos per sanguinem ipsius sanctificaremur, peccata Judaeorum autem consummarentur." Likewise Hilgenfeld p. XXXI; the same "Apostle Fathers" p. 17. Harnack p. LVIII f. — Barnabas also wanted to counteract docetical errors. So Hefele p. 138 (cf. p. 182 f. and 249 f.). Müller p. 128 writes about chap. 5: "The emphasis is on the appearance in the flesh . . . This now points quite clearly to docetistic views, which are fought here and elsewhere in the letter." A writer who aimed to combat docetism could have written 5.6 and 7 with this intention, and the fact and meaning of the bodily resurrection and would have had to emphasize that Christ wanted to fill up the measure of the sins of his enemies in his bodily suffering. But by mentioning his teaching and his miracles (8) he would not have proved anything to a doctor. Furthermore, Barnabas would abandon the argument once taken in 9 and 10, where he shows that Christ is the Son of God and declares that Christ could not possibly have manifested himself in His divine splendor. This 5, 10 pronounced impossibility does not yet require any revelation in the flesh in the form of an actual incarnation. Hilgenfeld raises the following objection to Müller's statement: verum enimvero Barnabas non demonstravit, Christum in carne venisse, sed eum, qui in carne venit et ipsam mortem perpessus est, esse filium dei (p. 84; cf. Ap. V. p. 37 f.) . This objection is not precisely formulated. It should read: Barnabas showed that Christ, despite his incarnation and suffering, was the Son of God and as such had supreme power, having dominion over life and death. Weizsäcker rightly writes p. 15 f.: "In the exposition about the person of Christ in c. 5 the main thing is not the appearance of Christ in the flesh, but his suffering in death. Here, however, the phenomenon (v σαρκί) is also discussed, but not according to its reality, but according to its necessity." Ibid. p. 17: "The voluntariness of this suffering and the divine purpose of it was to be asserted: consequently to contest the opinion that his suffering was a human shame and a testament to the power of men over him."

[77] The harsh judgment on the apostles (ἀποστόλους . . . ὄντας ὑπέρ πάσαν ἁμαρτίαν ἀνομωτέρους) is viewed as evidence against the writing of the letter by the apostle Barnabas by Hefele, p. 160 f., J. Kayser, "About the so-called Letter of Barnabas" (Paderborn 1866) p. 77 f., Müller, p. 17, 144, Riggenbach p. 33 f., Harnack, History of the Altchr. L. II. 1. P. 411. Braunsberger, on the other hand, does not want this reason for the inauthenticity of the writing to be considered valid, Jassen (pp. 229–232). If the purpose pursued by the author in sentences 5:6–13 is taken into account, then that statement about the apostles will in no way cause particular offense. — Weizsäcker p. 37 comments on 5:9: Here "the author mentions the moment from which Jesus revealed himself as the Son of God during his earthly life. "He wants to give very precise information here." This claim is incorrect. As the context shows, the letter does not say in 5:9 that Jesus revealed himself as the Son of God from a certain point in time, but rather it offers a new moment that shows us that Christ was not just a man.

in the flesh for the purpose of filling the measure of sin for those whom his prophets had persecuted to the death. For this purpose he took it upon himself (to suffer)."[78] With the words 5:13 "But he wanted to suffer like this; because it was necessary that he, "suffering on the cross"[79] already leads to the development of the theme. But they also emphasize once again the independence and power of Christ in relation to the enemy power by explaining in the second part that no unforeseen obstacle that was not of his own will was put in the way of the Son of God.[80]

---

[78] 5:11 and 12

[79] ἔδει γάρ, ἵνα. . . Harnack p. 24 adds the infinitive παθεῖν to ἔδει. Sensus: Ut in ligno pateretur, pateretur necesse erat. But now the meaning of these words probably needs an explanation. Funk (p. 53) follows Harnack, as does Veil in the translation: "For this (i.e. suffering) he had to understand himself in order to suffer from the tree." The thought would certainly be understandable: Jesus suffered on the cross in order to suffer at all. But the claim is probably pointless: Jesus suffered in order to suffer on the cross. There is nothing left but to explain " ἵνα" here not as a final conjunction, but to make it dependent on δεί, since in the N.T. ἵνα follows synonymous expressions like this after χρείαν ἔχεις (Jo. 2:25; 16:30; 1 Jo. 2:27) or after expressions like συμφέρει (Mt. 18:6; 5:29–30; Jo. 11:50; 16:7). λυσιτελεῖ (Lk. 17:2), ἀρκετὸν ἐστιν (Mt. 10:25), ἄξιος (Jo. 1:27), ἱκανὸς (Mt. 8:8; Lk. 7:6), ἐλάχιστόν μοί ἐστιν (I. Cor. 4:3) See, for example, Grimm, Lexicon Graeco–Latinum in libros Novi Testament! 1888, p. 211. Blaß, Gramm, of the New Testament. Greek, 1902, p. 232 f.

[80] There is a widespread view that in Chap. 5 ff. The meaning and validity of the New Covenant should be proven out of opposition to Judaism. Hefele writes about chap. 5: "The new covenant established in the blood of Christ is for our salvation, for the Jews it is for destruction." Funk p. XXVII: Dominum prophetis praenuntiantibus, Judaeis vero non intellegentibus, propterea passum esse, ut nos per sanguinem ipsius sanctificaremur, peccata Judaeorum autem consummarentur." Likewise Hilgenfeld p. XXXI; the same "Apostolic Fathers" p. 17.. Harnack p. LVIII f. and others. — Barnabas also wanted to counteract docetic errors. So Hefele p. 138 (see p. 182 f. and 249 f.). Müller p. 128 writes about chap. 5: "The emphasis is on appearance in the flesh. . . This clearly points to docetic views that are combated here and elsewhere in the letter." A writer who aimed to combat docetism could also have written 5:6 and 7 with this intention and the fact and meaning of the physical resurrection and would also have had to emphasize that Christ wanted to fulfill the measure of the sins of his enemies in his physical suffering. But by mentioning his teaching and his miracles (8) he would not have proven anything to a Docetist. Furthermore, when confronted with a Docetist, Barnabas would again abandon the course of argument he had once taken in 9 and 10, where he shows that Christ is the Son of God and declares that Christ could not possibly have revealed himself in his divine splendor. This stated impossibility in 5:10 does not yet require revelation in the flesh in the form of an actual incarnation. Hilgenfeld raises the following objection to Müller's statement: verum enimvero Barnabas non demonstravit, Christum in carne venisse, sed eum, qui in carne venit et ipsam mortem per-

pessus est, esse filium dei (p. 84; cf. Ap. V. p. 37 f.) . This objection is not precisely formulated. It should read: Barnabas showed that, despite his incarnation and his suffering, Christ
was the Son of God and as such had supreme power, dominion over life and death.
Weizsäcker rightly writes p. 15 f.: "In the exposition about the person of Christ in chap. 5
the main thing is not the appearance of Christ in the flesh, but his suffering of death. Here,
however, the phenomenon (ἐν σαρκὶ) also comes up for discussion, but not according to its
reality, but according to its necessity." Ibid. p. 17: "It was necessary to assert the voluntariness of this suffering and the divine purpose of it: therefore to dispute the opinion that his
suffering was a human disgrace and a testimony to the power of men over him."

CHAPTER 3

THE SUFFERING OF JESUS PROCLAIMED IN THE O.T. CHAP. 4:9–12:11)

a) Transition (chap. 4:9–5:13)

4:9 — 14 is usually still connected with the preceding sentences of the fourth chapter as belonging together.

Already in 4:9a the conclusion of the previous train of thought and the transition to new thoughts are clearly indicated. "But although I wanted to write many things — not in the tone of a teacher, but in the manner of a loving friend — I have hastened to write (yet only) what we cannot ignore (in the manner mentioned), thus as your least servant."[81] The meaning of these words is: Although I wanted to discuss a lot of the things that have already been discussed, I have to hurry, and in my haste I only write what is absolutely necessary. The words that he did not want to be a teacher but a friend are not intended to make his intention to write a lot appear intrusive or bold. The declaration of subservience at the end of the sentence points back to this: since I want to interact with you in the manner

---

[81] πολλὰ δὲ θέλων γράφειν — , οὐχ ὡς διδάσκαλος, ἀλλ᾽ ὡς πρέπει ἀγαπῶντι ἀφ᾽ ὧν ἔχομεν μὴ ἐλλείπειν, γράφειν ἐσπούδασα, περίψημα ὑμῶν. Veil translated: . I have endeavored to remind this in my letter, dal! we must not let go of what we possess." But σπουδάζειν, like 1:5, can only mean "hurry up". Then a warning 'Don't let go of what we have!' doesn't fit into the train of thought. There is no talk of a possession that should not be given up. The simplest is the expression ἀφ᾽ ὧν . . . To contrast ἐλλείπειν with πολλά. The connection of ideas in Riggenbach's translation is unnatural: "Since I wanted to write a lot, not as a teacher, but as befits a lover, not to lag behind what we have, I made an effort to write."

proper to a willing friend and benefactor, I now mark myself "therefore"[82] as your submissive servant.

The personal remark in 4:9, unfounded by the preceding train of thought, shows that Barnabas interrupts his discussions here in order to move on to a new matter. The matter is becoming more important, and that is why it is necessary, for better conviction and more effective instruction, to let the power of one's own personality come into its own beforehand. In those words, the transition is not only indicated to a new section, but also one with a heavy content. Because the author could have said a lot more from the way he has already presented it to his readers; but he doesn't have time for that, he's too pressed to move on to something else quickly, precisely because he can't under any circumstances omit or shorten the new teaching point.

In the event that 4.9 remains connected with the preceding sentences of the chapter as belonging together, the repetition of the same ideas, the moral instruction, is on the one hand in 4:1 and 2, and then again in 4:10–13, and that in part inexplicable in the same and related expressions.[83] Surely it is not to be expected that a writer, in quick succession, twice addresses the same or nearly the same admonitions to his readers in the same passage, that Barnabas twice lays the cap–stone to the teachings of chapters 2 and 3. But the writer can, in order to emphasize the purpose of his writing with sufficient urgency, at the introduction of a new section, emphasize the very ideas with which he is primarily concerned throughout the entire work.

If Chapter 4 were an internally self–contained whole, then another thought would also recur twice in quick succession in the same section. 4:7–8 & 4:14 contain the same teaching that the external covenant relationship or calling alone is not sufficient and does not yet imply election to eternal life. However, the phrase ετι δέ κακείνο . . . . . . νοείτε (4:14), shows that the author was very far from repeating this same admonition, albeit each time in a different form, in one and the same section which clearly states that the following words contain something quite new for the present section.

---

[82] διό. — διό comes after H and S before περίφημα, while after L it comes before the following verb προσέχωμεν. L follow all editors and commentators. But the testimony of the best manuscripts is to be recognized here. Because διό gives a good sense before περίφημα, and moreover it can also be explained how the displacement by L could happen. Because of other personal circumstances, the whole sentence πολλά δὲ . . . περίψημα ὑμῶν was useless and he therefore omitted it, he had to look for a compound for the words προσέχωμεν . . . search and now borrowed διό from that sentence.

[83] φύγωμεν . . . μιοήσωμεν (4:1 and 10), μη όώμεν ανεσιν (4:2) — "ἵνα μήποτε ἐπαναπαυόμενοι . . . ἐπικαθυπνώσωμεν . . . (4:13).

4:9–14. — As in the introductory sections 1:5–2, 3:4, 9–14 also calls on the addressees to love and justice in the interest of their salvation and to perseverance and patience in love because of the power of Satan.

As in 1:6, Barnabas also in 4:9 first reminds of faith and its position in relation to salvation. Only under certain conditions would "all the time of our belief" be of use.[84] Then he calls for the common good to be in view, to become spiritual men and temples of God, to observe the commandments of the Lord. He warns against all vanity, the works of the vicious path and against selfish seclusion. He preaches justice, makes his followers aware that they should not believe they are already justified. "If a man is good, righteousness will go before him." He recalls the troubled times and the power of Satan, writing of "the lawless days" and "the troubles to come" which are meant to give rise to resistance, "so that the black man may not sneak in".

Satan is called the "bad prince". Faced with this power there is no rest and no sleep; so perseverance is necessary. Also the reference to the fate of the Israelite people, which could enjoy so many divine graces, but were finally abandoned by God, can only serve the purpose of warning against flagging in moral zeal and the feeling of security and to encourage tenacious endurance.[85] The purpose of sowing

---

[84] ὁ πᾶς χρόνος τῆς πίστεως (S; on the other hand H: τῆς ζωῆς'). Since the author speaks only of eternal life in 1:6 and, before he names the way to it, points out that the prospect of eternal life has caused faith, because of the similarity that also prevails elsewhere between 1:6 and 4:9 f. consists in preferring the reading S, according to which eternal salvation is related to faith. In chap. 1 as in chap. 4 the thought is expressed: The belief of the readers is generally not objectionable, it is the good on which to build. L combines both ways of reading: nihil enim proderit nobis omne tempus vitae nostrae et fidei.

[85] 4:14: ἔτι δὲ κἀκεῖνο, ἀδελφοί μου, νοεῖτε· ὅταν βλέπετε ματὰ τηλικαῦτα σημεῖα καὶ τέρατα γεγονότα ἐν τῷ Ἰσραήλ, καὶ οὕτως ἐγκαταλελεῖφθαι αὐτούς· προσέχωμεν, μήποτε, ὡς γέγραπται, πολλοὶ κλητοί, ὀλίγοι δὲ ἐκλεκτοὶ εὑρεθῶμεν." εὑρεθῶμεν. σημεῖα καὶ τέρατα are to be understood as the signs of the OT revelation, the extraordinary and wonderful intercourse of God with the people of the covenant of Israel. On the other hand, Braunsberger claims on p. 250 that with these words the author is referring to the destruction of the Jewish Temple, which is also mentioned in 16:4. — The question of the origin of the written word πολλοὶ κλητοί, ὀλίγοι δὲ ἐκλεκτοὶ has found different answers. The same remind of Mt. 22:14. For a quote from Mt.. by Riggenbach p. 36; Hilgenfeld p. XXXVII; Harnack p. 19f; others., History of the Early Christians, L. II. I p. 417; Sprinzl, "The Theology of the Apostolic Fathers" (Vienna 1880), p. 73. Zahn, History of the New Testament Canons I. 2 (Leipzig 1889) p. 848 Anni, 1: "It seems to me completely useless to deny those who cling to the possibility that the saying was already found by Jesus as a proverb or Bible saying, and that Barnabas drew it from the same source independently of Matthew 22:14, or that Barnabas confused the saying known to him from Matthew with the other in IV Esdras 8:5 multi quidem creati sunt, pauci autem salvabuntur and therefore quoted it as a biblical

love may already be expressed in the personal remark in 4:9, insofar as the author in the words ὡς πρέπει ἀγαπῶντι also intends to present himself to his readers as an example.[86] In 4:9–14 the author nowhere directly expresses the intention of enriching the "knowledge", the gnosis of his followers through his teachings, but he warns 4:11 those who would like to live in self–satisfied seclusion against selfish knowledge with the quote from Isaiah 5:21: οναί οί οννετοι εαντοίς καί ενώπιον εαυτών επιστήμονες[87].

5:1–13. — 5:1 gives the theme for chapters 5–12: the suffering of Christ warns against sin and admonishes for sanctification. "For this the Lord took it upon himself to give His flesh to destruction, that we might be sanctified by remission of sins, that is, by sprinkling his blood." This truth is urgently preached with reference to OT prophecies about Jesus' suffering from 5:13 onwards. But first, up to 5:12, the double purpose that is pursued by mentioning Jesus' suffering is emphasized. One is to turn away from sin and turn to good (5:1–4); the other is to present the power of evil and its authority as only apparent and temporary (5:5–12).

In 5:1, not only the final sentence refers to moral revival, but also the connection with the immediately preceding teachings by γάρ. To prove his claim, Barnabas quotes in 5:2 Isaias 53:5–7: "He was wounded because of our lawlessness and has been mistreated because of our sins. We were healed by his stripes . . . In 5:3 he

---

verse I have and the like." Lipsius in the Bible lexicon by D. Schenkel, vol. I (Leipzig 1869), p. 371: . . This expression in particular (γέγραπται) proves that the author used the relevant words in an OT script found." Weizsäcker S 34 rightly explains: "The words are therefore in any case the execution from a γραφή. But the more the application of this designation to a gospel writing contradicts the whole other behavior of the letter in this respect, the more certain we can assume that its source is different." Cf. Weiss p. 109 f.

[86] See 1:4 κἀγὼ ἀναγκάζομαι ἀγαπᾶν.

[87] Harnack p. 19: Totum capitulum in duas partes di vidi potest sibi respondentes: vv 1–8, 9–14. In utriusque partis particula priore (vv 1–5, 9–13) auctor epistulae monuit, ut periculosam animarum securitatem lectores evitarent et opera iniquitatis fugerent; tum in altera parte (vv 6–8. 14). verbis ετι όέ καί τούτο ερωτώ (ἔτι δὲ κἀκεῖνο νοεῖτε) id egit, ut lectores a Iudaizantium cultu ac religione et a Iudaeorum imitatione a vocaret, historiae Iudaeorum cum triste initium (vv 6–8), tum tristem exitum (vv 14) eos respicere iubens. But if Barnabas had intended to emphasize in the second part precisely "its extremely fateful end" (cf. p. LV11I) in contrast to the "fatal beginning of Jewish history" mentioned in the first section of the chapter, then he would probably have in quite a different way Wisely, when it happened, must emphasize the two periods of this history. Whether the events mentioned formed the beginning and the end of Jewish history was irrelevant to the author; he does not cite them as a main idea of the chapter, but only adds them as occasional remarks suitable for better moral instruction.

explains that the promised prophetic revelations, the past, present, future[88] are now also present here, that gnosis, wisdom and understanding (2:3) would also be given to us here: "So we must be extremely grateful to the Lord, since he both made the past the content of gnosis for us, and gave us wisdom regarding the present; we are also not without understanding about the future."[89]

Since 5:3 is a conclusion from the above–mentioned Isaiah quotation, the revelation about the past and present — according to the explanation of 1:7 — is to be sought in the teaching that lawlessness and sin are hated by the Lord and man should purify himself from them. Even the instruction about the future can only encompass the truth that nothing sinful, but only that which is sanctified by Christ's wounds, will enter into bliss. That Barnabas wants to warn against sin is also suggested by 5:4: "A man will rightly perish who, although he has knowledge of the way to righteousness, keeps to the way of darkness."

In 5:5, the other purpose for which the suffering of the Lord is to be mentioned is indicated. "There, our Lord took it upon himself to suffer for our soul, although Lord of the whole world — to whom God spoke immediately after the foundation of the world, let us make man in our image and likeness[90] — so it is strange how he took it upon himself to suffer at the hands of men." The meaning of these words is: now that the remarkable thing has happened that the Son of God was subjected to foreign power and rule through his suffering, the question arises as to how his suffering took place. One wants an answer to the question of whether there is a final subjection of power of good to the evil one. The author wants to fulfill the desire for such knowledge. That is why he explains in 5:6–8 that the divine Lord only succumbed in order to finally triumph, that the purpose of his incarnation was to combat and overcome death, as well as the teaching of the

---

[88] τὰ παρεληλυθότα, τὰ ἐνεστῶτα, τῶν μελλόντων (1:7).

[89] καὶ τὰ παρεληλυθότα ἡμῖν ἐγνώρισεν καὶ ἐν τοῖς ἐνεστῶσιν ἡμᾶς ἐσόφισεν, καὶ εἰς τὰ μέλλοντα οὐκ ἐσμὲν ἀσύνετοι.

[90] ὁδοῦ δικαιοσύνης γνῶσιν.

resurrection,[91] that in this way he fulfilled the promise to the fathers,[92] and by working the resurrection on himself, he wanted to show his power as a judge.[93]

His glorious humiliation in the flesh, his reputation on earth is referred to in various expressions. It is reminiscent of his founding of a new kingdom,[94] his activity as a teacher,[95] his wonderful and multifaceted effectiveness.[96] The power of the humbled Son of God is also taught in 5:8 by the words: "I will not speak of the fact that some proclaimed him and loved him infinitely."[97] The sermon and the love of the apostles are remembered, for the apostles and their preaching are immediately referred to in 5:9 again. Barnabas wants to say: it was precisely the consequence of the humiliation under human nature that Christ gained disciples who proclaimed him and his teaching, and that he reaped sacrificial love. But not only — as the further course of thought in 5:9 shows — the public appearance of the apostles gives evidence of the invincible power of Christ and his brilliant successes; they are already taught by the calling of the disciples, since the Lord has made righteous ones out of sinners in them.

"But when he chose his own apostles, who were to preach his gospel, although they were the greatest sinners, to show that he had not come to call the righteous, but sinners, he revealed himself as the Son of God." Even a great development

---

[91] Völter declares section 5:5–7:1 to be interpolated. "It has nothing to do with what is said about the covenant in 4:1–8 and 5:1–4. This discussion has its clear conclusion in 5:5.4. Section 5:5–7:1 gives the impression of a subsequent appendix in which a single idea from the preceding exposition is made the subject of a detailed, apologetic treatment, namely the idea expressed in 5:1 that the Lord put his flesh in gave death. But while this thought is presented quite harmlessly and impartially in 5:1, without the author being aware that he could be subject to all sorts of difficulties and objections, it is quite different in 5:5–7:1. The author feels compelled to defend the thesis that the Son of God came in the flesh and suffered with all the means at his disposal. It is the intensification and development of Christological ideas, the conception of Christ as the essential Son of God, that has caused this difficulty, while the author of 5:14 still remotely thinks of it." (p. 345 f. cf. p. 416.)

[92] εἰ = ἐπεί very often in the New Testament.

[93] αὐτὸς δέ, ἵνα καταργήσῃ τὸν θάνατον καὶ τὴν ἐκ νεκρῶν ἀνάστασιν δείξῃ. . . ὑπέμεινεν (5:6).

[94] ἵνα τοῖς πατράσιν τὴν ἐπαγγελίαν ἀποδῷ (5:7) Weiss p. 5) posed the question" that "no consideration is given to the disturbing contrast between Christ's divine glory and his suffering at the hands of men". A further contradiction between the two final clauses is shown in the fact that Christ's incarnation is first shown to be necessary in a "more physical or metaphysical way", while 5:7 "the person of Christ is considered in terms of its religious–historical significance". 5:5 and the final sentence in 5:6 is interpolated.

[95] ἵνα. . . ἐπιδείξῃ ἐπὶ τῆς γῆς ὤν, ὅτι τὴν ἀνάστασιν αὐτὸς ποιήσας κρινεῖ (5, 7).

[96] τὸν λαὸν τὸν καινὸν ἑτοιμάζων (5:7)

[97] διδάσκων τὸν Ἰσραὴλ (5:8).

of sinful power can offer no obstacle to the incarnate God without it, but rather helps to reveal his divinity.[98] Thus it can now be understood that Christ even humbled himself to suffering in human nature precisely for the very purpose of bringing evil to its highest form. "So the Son of God appeared in the flesh for the purpose of filling up the measure of sin for those who had persecuted his prophets to death. So he took it upon himself (to suffer)."[99] With the words 5:13 "But he wanted to suffer, because it was necessary that he: suffering from the cross" is already being transferred to the execution of the topic. But they also emphasize once again the independence and power of Christ against the hostile power, by explaining in the second part that no unforeseen obstacle, not wanted by himself, was put in the way of the Son of God.[100]

---

[98] τηλικαῦτα τέρατα καὶ σημεῖα ποιῶν (5:8).

[99] οιχ (complete λέγω), ὅτι ἐκήρυσσον καὶ ὑπερηγάπησαν αυτόν. The tradition of these words is very different. H: ουγ ὅτι ἐκήρυσσε καὶ ὑπερηγάπησαν αυτόν. S: ἐκήρυσσεν καὶ νπερήγαπησαν αυτόν. V (only begins with 5, 7): ἐκήρυξε καὶ ὑπερηγάπησεν αυτόν (also army). L: non credide-runt nec dilexerunt illum. Gebhardt: ἐκήρυσσεν, καὶ ὑπερηγάπησεν αυτόν. Hilgenfeld: οὐχ οτι ἐκήρυσσον καὶ ὑπερηγάπησαν αυτόν (on the other hand in the first edition ἐκήρυσσεν, καὶ ου-περ ἠγάπησαν αυτόν), also earlier Funk, but which now prefers the reading ἐκήρυσσεν καὶ ὑπερηγάπησεν αυτόν (Theol. Viertelschr. 1889, pp. 129–133). I declare myself for H, only that I put both verbs in the plural, for the following reasons: The singular form εκήρυσσεν would become ουχ ὅτι. (S V) must be related to Christ, which would result in a repetition of the same idea, since Christ's teaching activity is already emphasized in διδάσκων τον Ισραήλ. The addition ουχ ὅτι, which H reads alone, is necessary because of the δε (5, 9) that follows in the next sentence. 5, 8b stands in contrast to 5, 9. The author wants to speak of the apostles insofar as it concerns the time of their calling, but he does not want to speak of the time of their later activity. "I will not go into great lengths about the apostles preaching and loving the Lord beyond measure. But I do want to mention that at that time, when the Lord chose his own apostles . . ., he revealed himself as the Son of God." οὐχ ὅτι expresses that it was not the writer's intention to particularly emphasize the activities of the apostles as proof of the authority of the divine Lord. Hilgenfeld, who also follows H, gives the following explanation of sentence 5, 8b in the Journal for Scientific Theology 1879, p loved, Jesus, as we will read shortly, had to choose his own apostles τους μέλλοντας κηρνσσειν τό εναγγέλιον αντοῦ." ὑπεραγαπάν recalls 1:4 and 4:6: αγαπάν ὑπέρ την ψυχήν. The aorist ὑπερηγάπησαν in contrast to the imperfect ἐκήρυσσον indicates a unique ActsThis is the conclusion of the teaching activity (first comes ἐκήρυσσον, then ὑπερηγά¬πησαν) the devotion of life out of love to the Lord. Accordingly, we have here a chronological point of reference for the composition of the epistle, insofar as the apostles had already died at that time.

[100] The view that in Chap. 5 ff. out of opposition to Judaism the meaning and validity of the New Covenant should be proved. Hefele overwrites chap. 5: "The new covenant established in the blood of Christ brings us salvation, the Jews to destruction." Funk p. XXVII: Dominum prophetis praenuntiantibus, Judaeis vero non intellegentibus, propterea passum

A great development of sinful power cannot offer any obstacle to the Son of God who has become man, but rather helps to reveal his divinity.[101] So it can now be understood that Christ even lowered himself to suffering in human nature for the very purpose of bringing evil to its highest form. "So the Son of God appeared

---

esse, ut nos per sanguinem ipsius sanctificaremur, peccata Judaeorum autem consummarentur." Likewise Hilgenfeld p. XXXI; the same "Apostle Fathers" p. 17. Harnack p. LVIII f. — Barnabas also wanted to counteract docetical errors. So Hefele p. 138 (cf. p. 182 f. and 249 f.). Müller p. 128 writes about chap. 5: "The emphasis is on the appearance in the flesh ... This now points quite clearly to docetistic views, which are fought here and elsewhere in the letter." A writer who aimed to combat docetism could have written 5.6 and 7 with this intention, and the fact and meaning of the bodily resurrection and would have had to emphasize that Christ wanted to fill up the measure of the sins of his enemies in his bodily suffering. But by mentioning his teaching and his miracles (8) he would not have proved anything to a doctor. Furthermore, Barnabas would abandon the argument once taken in 9 and 10, where he shows that Christ is the Son of God and declares that Christ could not possibly have manifested himself in His divine splendor. This 5:10 pronounced impossibility does not yet require any revelation in the flesh in the form of an actual incarnation. Hilgenfeld raises the following objection to Müller's statement: verum enimvero Barnabas non demonstravit, Christum in carne venisse, sed eum, qui in carne venit et ipsam mortem perpessus est, esse filium dei (p. 84; cf. Ap. V. p. 37 f.) . This objection is not precisely formulated. It should read: Barnabas showed that Christ, despite his incarnation and suffering, was the Son of God and as such had supreme power, having dominion over life and death. Weizsäcker rightly writes p. 15 f.: "In the exposition about the person of Christ in c. 5 the main thing is not the appearance of Christ in the flesh, but his suffering in death. Here, however, the phenomenon (ν σαρχί) is also discussed, but not according to its reality, but according to its necessity." Ibid. p. 17: "The voluntariness of this suffering and the divine purpose of it was to be asserted: consequently to contest the opinion that his suffering was a human shame and a testament to the power of men over him."

101 The harsh judgment on the apostles (αποστόλους . . . όντας υπέρ πάσαν αμαρτίαν άνομωτέρους) is viewed as evidence against the writing of the letter by the apostle Barnabas by Hefele, p. 160 f., J. Kayser, "About the so–called Letter of Barnabas" (Paderborn 1866) p. 77 f., Müller, p. 17, 144, Riggenbach p. 33 f., Harnack, History of the Altchr. L. II. 1. P. 411. Braunsberger, on the other hand, does not want this reason for the inauthenticity of the writing to be considered valid, Jassen (pp. 229–232). If the purpose pursued by the author in sentences 5:6–13 is taken into account, then that statement about the apostles will in no way cause particular offense. — Weizsäcker p. 37 comments on 5:9: Here "the author mentions the moment from which Jesus revealed himself as the Son of God during his earthly life. "He wants to give very precise information here." This claim is incorrect. As the context shows, the letter does not say in 5:9 that Jesus revealed himself as the Son of God from a certain point in time, but rather it offers a new moment that shows us that Christ was not just a man.

in the flesh for the purpose of filling the measure of sin for those whom his prophets had persecuted to the death. For this purpose he took it upon himself (to suffer)."[102] With the words 5:13 "But he wanted to suffer like this; because it was necessary that he, "suffering on the cross"[103] already leads to the development of the theme. But they also emphasize once again the independence and power of Christ in relation to the enemy power by explaining in the second part that no unforeseen obstacle that was not of his own will was put in the way of the Son of God.[104]

---

[102] 5:11 and 12

[103] ἔδει γάρ, ἵνα. . . Harnack p. 24 adds the infinitive παθεῖν to ἔδει. Sensus: Ut in ligno pateretur, pateretur necesse erat. But now the meaning of these words probably needs an explanation. Funk (p. 53) follows Harnack, as does Veil in the translation: "For this (i.e. suffering) he had to understand himself in order to suffer from the tree." The thought would certainly be understandable: Jesus suffered on the cross in order to suffer at all. But the claim is probably pointless: Jesus suffered in order to suffer on the cross. There is nothing left but to explain " ἵνα" here not as a final conjunction, but to make it dependent on δεί, since in the N.T. ἵνα follows synonymous expressions like this after χρείαν ἔχεις (Jo. 2:25; 16:30; 1 Jo. 2:27) or after expressions like συμφέρει (Mt. 18:6; 5:29–30; Jo. 11:50; 16:7). λυσιτελεῖ (Lk. 17:2), ἀρκετὸν ἐστιν (Mt. 10:25), ἄξιος (Jo. 1:27), ἱκανός (Mt. 8:8; Lk. 7:6), ἐλάχιστόν μοί ἐστιν (I. Cor. 4:3) See, for example, Grimm, Lexicon Graeco–Latinum in libros Novi Testament! 1888, p. 211. Blaß, Gramm, of the New Testament. Greek, 1902, p. 232 f.

104 There is a widespread view that in Chap. 5 ff. The meaning and validity of the New Covenant should be proven out of opposition to Judaism. Hefele writes about chap. 5: "The new covenant established in the blood of Christ is for our salvation, for the Jews it is for destruction." Funk p. XXVII: Dominum prophetis praenuntiantibus, Judaeis vero non intellegentibus, propterea passum esse, ut nos per sanguinem ipsius sanctificaremur, peccata Judaeorum autem consummarentur." Likewise Hilgenfeld p. XXXI; the same "Apostolic Fathers" p. 17.. Harnack p. LVIII f. and others. — Barnabas also wanted to counteract docetic errors. So Hefele p. 138 (see p. 182 f. and 249 f.). Müller p. 128 writes about chap. 5: "The emphasis is on appearance in the flesh. . . This clearly points to docetic views that are combated here and elsewhere in the letter." A writer who aimed to combat docetism could also have written 5:6 and 7 with this intention and the fact and meaning of the physical resurrection and would also have had to emphasize that Christ wanted to fulfill the measure of the sins of his enemies in his physical suffering. But by mentioning his teaching and his miracles (8) he would not have proven anything to a Docetist. Furthermore, when confronted with a Docetist, Barnabas would again abandon the course of argument he had once taken in 9 and 10, where he shows that Christ is the Son of God and declares that Christ could not possibly have revealed himself in his divine splendor. This stated impossibility in 5:10 does not yet require revelation in the flesh in the form of an actual incarnation. Hilgenfeld raises the following objection to Müller's statement: verum enimvero Barnabas non demonstravit, Christum in carne venisse, sed eum, qui in carne venit et ipsam mortem per-

b) The Death of Jesus (chap. 5:13–7:2).

The basic idea of chapter 5:1–13 is according to what has been said: The suffering of Jesus warns against sin and teaches that the fight against the power of evil is not fruitless, that with perseverance despite various seemingly insurmountable obstacles it must and finally leads to victory, since the highest display of evil power could only humble the Savior for a certain time and to a certain degree. This teaching is repeated and confirmed from 5:13 to 12:11, following facts of the Lord's passion insofar as they were already predicted in the Old Testament, in such a way that reference is made

1. on the manner of death in general: 5:13–7:2;

2. on the soaking with gall and vinegar: 7:3–10:12;

3. to the spilling of water: 11:1–11;

4. on the cross: 12:1–11.

Chap. 5 suggests what the theme of the following discussion must be; but the same is not always expressed clearly and distinctly enough in what follows. What is certain is that in section 5:13–12:11 different facts from the passion of Christ are reported following the OT. Various other remarks from prophets are connected with these reports, but the writer does not always emphasize their relation to those facts sharply enough. It is now impossible to assume that Barnabas only wanted to loosely juxtapose a very varied series of different passages from the prophets. If he wanted to work seriously at all and not just play around with all sorts of quotations from the OT, he must have been guided by a very specific intention. A unified idea must govern both the passage mentioned as a whole and all its individual parts. But it is such a guiding principle; If an idea that summarizes and organizes everything down to the final detail is not expressed clearly enough in a section, then you have to look hard for such an idea. But there is a great danger that something will be artificially read into the text that is not there.

---

pessus est, esse filium dei (p. 84; cf. Ap. V. p. 37 f.) . This objection is not precisely formulated. It should read: Barnabas showed that, despite his incarnation and his suffering, Christ was the Son of God and as such had supreme power, dominion over life and death. Weizsäcker rightly writes p. 15 f.: "In the exposition about the person of Christ in chap. 5 the main thing is not the appearance of Christ in the flesh, but his suffering of death. Here, however, the phenomenon (ἐν σαρκὶ) also comes up for discussion, but not according to its reality, but according to its necessity." Ibid. S, 17: "It was necessary to assert the voluntariness of this suffering and the divine purpose of it: therefore to dispute the opinion that his suffering was a human disgrace and a testimony to the power of men over him."

But I think I have escaped this danger. Because there will still be enough evidence to prove the correctness of the train of thought I claim, even if the way-marking between here and there leaves a lot to be desired. It often took a long time to search. Some conclusions can only be reached indirectly. But indirect conclusions can also be certain, and they become more certain if, as in the present case, even four times in succession in four different parallel discussions 5:13–7:2; 7:3–10:12; 11:1–11; 12:1–11 the same conclusions can always be drawn about the same intentions of the writer.

But indirect conclusions can also be certain, and they gain in certainty if, as in the present case, even four times in succession in four different parallel discussions 5:13, 7:2: 7:3–10, 12, 11:1–11; 12:1–11 the same conclusions can always be drawn about the same intentions of the writer. Furthermore, the recurring basic ideas highlighted throughout the entire section are supported and confirmed by the introductory remarks in Chap. 5.

The remarks already given here may have been the reason for the author not to specify his intended teachings in the following explanations and to content himself somewhat superficially with the reference to such OT revelations from which the conclusion about his intentions could be drawn. However, for those who want to subject the Epistle to Barnabas to a thorough interpretation, it will be necessary where possible to treat the introduction and exposition separately, and to examine them separately for their conceptual content. In this way, the investigation of the executive part can confirm that of the introductory part and vice versa.

5:13–6:7. — That the suffering of Jesus was not primarily caused by the will of those who persecuted the prophets to the death (5:11) and beat the shepherd (5:12), but rather the eternal plan of God had to take place, is shown by the divine will, which is revealed in Ps. 21:21; 118, 120; 21:17; Is. 50:6, 7. These passages indicate the manner of suffering and death of the Lord and justify the explanation 5:13: "For it was necessary that he should suffer on the cross." The intention, Jesus' superiority to show the power of evil becomes clear following the passage from Isaiah mentioned in 6:1–4. 6, 1: "When he (= the Lord in Isaias 50:6 and 7) has now given the order, he says (Is. 50:8 and 9): 'Who is it that argues with me? What does he want? Let him me! Or who is it that wants to justify himself to me (= wants to be right)? He approaches the Son of the Lord! Woe to you, for you will all grow old like a garment, and the moth will eat you up.[105]"

---

[105] ὅτε οὖν ἐποίησεν τὴν ἐντολήν. εντολή = the ordinance regarding suffering. Müller p. 154 f. explains that ποιεῖν is = τηρεῖν, φυλάσ– σειν, and must therefore take ἐποίησεν in the future tense, exactly, and translate: "For the time when the Son of God will have carried out the command of his Father, says he himself through the prophet of himself, de tempore, quo patris mandatum exsecutus erit, ipse, dicit." He follows Harnack p. 25, Funk p. 53. Veil:

The mentioned intention of Barnabas also speaks from the quotations of the OT cited in 6:2b–4, in which Christ is compared to a stone. As a crushing stone and as a man of strength,[106] Christ is a precious, exquisite, valuable cornerstone that gives life,[107] a strong rock.[108] His humiliation and power at the same time speaks from Psalms 117:22 & 24, according to which the very stone which the builders rejected became the cornerstone of the great and wonderful day which the Lord made (6:4). Once again the exalted position of the Savior in relation to the evil powers is emphasized in 6:6 & 7, but more briefly and concisely than was previously done in 5:13, 14 and 6:1–4, following other OT Scriptures.

In the transitional sentence 6:5 Barnabas explains: "In a still simpler way (ἁπλούατερον) I write to you that you may understand (ι'να ουνιήτε), I, the submissive servant of your love"; that is, I want to speak to you in a way that you will understand even better, namely briefly and succinctly. And now in 6:6 and 7a

---

"And what does he say in relation to the time Completion of his mission?" In noulv τήν ἐντολήν, Hefele also sees p. 60 and Hilgenfeld Ap. V. p. 18 a fulfillment of the order. But ποιεῖν does not only mean "perform, achieve" and the like (= πράττειν), but also and initially "do, cause". And the latter meaning ("to give the order") is only appropriate, since shortly before that in various places God's commissions and orders were spoken of with regard to his suffering, and there is the grammatical difficulty recognized by Müller himself when accepting this meaning ¬erity in omission. Riggenbach: "Since he gave the commandment, what does he say?"

[106] ἐπεί ὡς λίθος ἰσχυρός ἐτέϑη εἰς συντριβήν (6:2b). Hefele and Weiss take exception to the conjunction εηεί. The former p. 60 note 3: "In Greek the sentence begins with ἐπεί, this either cannot be translated at all, which the old Latin interpreter noticed and followed, or one must assume an ellipse, = επει Ιησούς τήν εντολήν τού ια τρός ἱποίησεν, ἐτέϑη ὡς λίθος ἰσχυρός εἰς συντριβήν πει ... First, how can the author say that the prophet spoke after the exaltation of the Lord (λέγει επεί); secondly, when he is speaking of the stumbling block against which one is ground (συντριβή), how can he cite a saying in which the very valuable, precious part of the stone is praised? The quote is supposed to be the sentence επεί ... συντριβήν illustrate. It cannot have been written by one and the same person." However, these doubts disappear for anyone who finds in the sentence ἐπεί (= there) ... the explanation for the following passage from Isaiah and a basic idea that is closely related to the purpose of the Scripture. See Ad. Link in Theol. Literaturzeitung 1889, column 597.

[107] ἐν ἰσχῦ τέϑεικεν τήν σάρκα αὐτοῦ κύριος (6:3b)

[108] 6:2b f. Is. 28:16. At this point, Kayser p. 11 does not understand λίθος to mean Christ, but the kingdom of Christ, the spiritual building in contrast to the physical temple of the Jews. Such a juxtaposition of the Old and New Covenant is unthinkable. From the preceding words λίθος ἰσχυρός ἐτέϑη εἰς συντριβήν it follows that λίθος is meant to explain the position of Christ. In these words λίθος is a predicate and as such gives an explanation of something that must have been mentioned shortly beforehand. But in 6:1 there is no talk of a kingdom of Christ, but of the Lord himself.

according to the procedure in 5:13 and 14, citing Psalm 21:17; 117:12; 21:19 again first emphasizes the prophecy of the suffering of Jesus, from which the reader can again recognize that the suffering of the Lord is not the proof of the omnipotence of an evil power, but is based on the divine plan, which is announced in advance in the OT, and only then in 6:7b, in order to make the already given teaching of the ultimate powerlessness of evil even more understandable[109], is Is. 3:9, 10 and Wisdom 2:12 is quoted: "Woe to their souls, for they have one another devised an evil plan against themselves, saying: Let us bind the righteous, since he is inconvenient to us."[110]

6:8–7:2. — After Barnabas 5:13–6:7 showed in the suffering of the Lord that the dominion of evil must have its limits, he demands in 6:8–7:2 something moral a walk in the spirit of Christ by referring to Exodus 33:1, 3 (Lev. 20:24): "Behold, this is what the Lord God says: Enter into the good land which the Lord has swore to Abraham, Isaac and Jacob, and possess it, the land flowing with milk and honey, and rule it!" This passage is interpreted allegorically. It is expressly stated that the readers are to receive Gnosis with it. 6:9: "But what Gnosis says, learn! Hope, she explains, in Jesus, who wants to reveal himself to you in the flesh!" And now the same verse continues: ἄνθρωπος γὰρ γῆς ἐστιν πάσχουσα· ἀπὸ προσώπου γὰρ τῆς γῆς ἡ πλάσις τοῦ Ἀδὰμ ἐγένετο. Usually γῆ is related to Christ. "For the promised land signifies the one in the flesh, i.e., Christ revealing himself, dwelling in man and transforming him into God's temple."[111]

The interpretation of γῆ to the human nature of Christ would be correct if ἄνθρωπος = γῆ ἄνθρωπος were to be related to the aforementioned Jesus. However, the probability initially speaks in favor of this, since when Jesus is mentioned, his human nature is expressly emphasized and the suffering of this nature is repeatedly referred to in the preceding sentences. And yet this relationship is incorrect. The sentence ἄνθρωπος γὰρ . . . initially only says in general terms, without regard to specific persons, that the earth symbolizes human nature as something suffering. But who is to be understood by ἄνϋρωπος is to be answered in the following sentences. In 6:10 and 11 it is further built on the knowledge that γῆ = ἄνθρωπος and

---

[109] 6:3. Is. 50:7. Völter p. 417 f. sees in the prophetic comparisons of Christ with a stone only a reference to his resurrection caused by divine power and in the quotations 6:1 and 2 a reference to Christ as the Son of God. But that Barnabas intends more than just this Christological teaching is shown above all by the explanation given by him in Is. 28:16. This introduces Jesus as the judge of the evil powers, just like 6:1 with the words: οὐαὶ ὑμῖν, ὅτι ὑμεῖς πάντες ὡς ἱμάτιον παλαιωθήσεθε . . . and 6:4 by the designation κεφαλὴν γωνίας.

[110] With γάρ in 6:7b the new proof of the final victory of Christ over the powers hostile to God is to be introduced, as promised in 6:5 (ἀπολούστερον ὑμῖν γράφω...).

[111] Veil in NT apocr. p. 145. γή also point to Christ, Hefele p. 62, note 23; Hilgenfeld, Ap. V. p. 18 f.; Harnack p. 27; white p. 17; Völter p. 345 and 419.

from this a corresponding conclusion is drawn, namely that we, following the commandment to move into the good land, become new people, one takes on a second form, transforming us into children of God. "What then is meant by 'into the good land that floweth with milk and honey?'... "So after he renewed us through the remission of sins, he made us in a second form, so that we might have the souls of children, as if he created us again from now on." So the Christian who has been renewed inwardly is "the land", "the man" in 6:9.

The particle γάρ in this verse 6:9 can therefore have no purpose in Ex. 31:1, 3 to justify why the Lord appeared in the flesh. The words of 6:9 do not want to draw a conclusion from the Exodus passage quoted above about the incarnation of Jesus. The incarnation of Jesus is only mentioned as the cause of the spiritual and moral rebirth, which is discussed in the following verses and which is only taught by the exodus quotation. In 6:12 this is paralleled and set to the words of creation in the formation of the first man Gen. 1:26 and 28. The renewal through Christ is compared with the first creation,[112] in order to state in 6:13 that a new creation actually takes place through Christ. "A second creation he (the Lord) has wrought in the last days. The Lord says: Behold, I make the last like the first."[113] This new creation is the "land".

---

[112] But that Barnabas already 6:12 through Gen. 1:26 (Ποιήσωμεν κατ᾽ εἰκόνα καὶ καθ᾽ ὁμοίσιν ἡμῶν. . .) teaches the new creation through Christ and therefore does not want to speak at all of the first creation as such, expressly accept Kayser p. 11, Harnack p. 29, Völter p. 420. But such an intention is far from the author's mind. By ἄλλον τύπον in 6:11 he recalls, albeit indirectly, the first creation. That is why he cannot want to have the Generic Authority, through which we primarily have knowledge of the primeval creation, already applied to the later transformation without further ado. It must refer to the creation of which it first speaks. Otherwise, Barnabas would have previously had to focus solely on the renewal of man, without giving a glimpse of prehistory, which is also offered by the words ὡς ἂν δὴ ἀναπλάσσοντος αὐτοῦ ἡμᾶς (= as if he were creating us again), or else Barnabas should have expressly stated at the beginning of 6:12 that he now wanted to accept the quotation from the rebirth in Christ.

[113] The words " Ἰδού, ποιῶ τὰ ἔσχατα ὡς τὰ πρῶτα " are never found verbatim in Scripture. Some think of Matthew 20:16 (ἔσονται οἱ ἔσχατοι πρῶτοι καὶ οἱ πρῶτοι ἔσχατοι.) like Müller S,. 172, Funk p. 56 f., Veil in NT apocr. p. 155. Others recall 2 Cor. 5:17 (ὥστε εἴ τις ἐν Χριστῷ, καινὴ κτίσις· τὰ ἀρχαῖα παρῆλθεν, ἰδοὺ γέγονεν καινά.) or to Apoc. 21:5 (Καὶ εἶπεν ὁ καθήμενος ἐπὶ τῷ θρόνῳ· ἰδοὺ καινὰ ποιῶ πάντα). The passage Alfr. Resch, Agrapha 1889, p. 261, compared to James Hardy Ropes in a critical treatment of the material collected by that aut Ez 36:11 resp. Matthew 20:16 and Apoc. 21:5 refers ("The sayings of Jesus, which are not handed down in the canonical gospels." Lpz. 1896.Texts and investigations into the history of the ancient Christians. Lit. XIV, 2). Also in the second edition of the Agrapha (Texte und Untersuch, z. Gesch. der Altchr. Lit. Neue Folge, XV, 3 and 4, Lpz. 1906)

"Therefore the prophet proclaimed: Enter the land that flows with milk and honey, and rule it!" According to 6:14–16, the new creation consists in the removal of hearts of stone and the planting of hearts of flesh, in indwelling of the Lord in us.[114] "So we are the ones whom he brought into the good land." The words "milk and honey" of the Exodus passage mean, according to 6:17, that the new life comes through believing in the promise (= honey) and awakened by the word[115] (= milk). In 6:18 and 19 a view is opened into the glorious future that is certain for the newly created. 7:1 and 2, as the conclusion of 5:13–6:19, corresponds to the content of this section. 7:1: "Consider then, ye children of joy, that the good Lord has revealed everything to us in advance, so that we may know whom in all things we ought to praise out of gratitude."

Resch explains the passage as an agraphon (p. 167) and at the same time refers to it the Syriac Didascalia (translated by Achelis and Flemming, chap. 26, p. 136) and to the Didascalia Apostolorum (Fragmenta Veronensia Latina ed. Hauler, chap. 53, p. 75). But neither to an agraphon nor to an NT This passage is to be considered, since Barnabas fundamentally bases his proofs on only OT passages in the execution of his theme. The decision as to which passage of the OT is alluded to depends on the meaning attached to the words Ἰδού, ποιῶ . . . in Barn. 6:13. Their purpose is to compare the primal creation and the "entry into the promised land". But if with that quotation, as some explainers want, on Ez. 36:11 or Jer. 40:7, where the Lord tells his people the happy possession of Holy Land in prospect, then the citation in question with the words εἰς ἐλιαζε εἰς τὴν γην would correspond completely in terms of content, and no relation to creation would be taken. If a passage of OT is to be thought of at all, then only Is. 43:19 comes into consideration, but only insofar as this passage is taken on its own and the closer context in which it stands is not taken into account. It reads: ἰδοὺ ποιῶ καινὰ ἃ νῦν ἀνατελεῖ καὶ γνώσεσθε αὐτά..

[114] The reason given for the deletion of 6:14 ff. by Weiss Chap. 16:8 Christ does not dwell in our hearts, as is said here (= 6:14 ff.), but God himself, and this latter is such an important thought for the author that the exposition of the letter culminates in it. So he cannot very well claim the indwelling of Christ at the same time."

[115] λόγος in 6:17 is probably in contrast to the previously mentioned πίστις τῆς ἐπαγγελίς, the promise, the promised Self, Christ, and this is already because faith in the promise, or rather, faith in the promise. the honey is the first, the word bezw. the milk that is called the later. White p. 19: "since λόγος has no other additions (neither θεοί nor αττού), it will hardly be possible to relate it to the proclaimed Word of God, but only to the Greek λόγος, so dal" also from this side the sentence reveals itself as a later element." On the other hand, Hefele understood by λόγος the preaching of the Gospel (p. 65). — If Barnabas can say that we were awakened to life first by faith in the promise and then by Christ, he probably belongs to a generation that — if perhaps only to the very least part — still had a part in the old covenant or was still very close to it.

The words τέκνα εὐφροσύνης refer to the new creation and Sonship of God is referred back to and in the call to praise the Psalms quoted in 6:16 alluded to: "I will praise you in the congregation of my brothers and in the congregation of the saints I will sing praise to you." In 7:2, the intention of the Lord becomes clear, to enliven spiritually and morally through his suffering, proved that he himself was only temporarily handed over to evil power. "If therefore the Son of God, although he is Lord and will judge the living and the dead, suffered that his suffering might give us life, let us believe that the Son of God could not suffer except for our sake." Meaning: let us believe that only our salvation, and not the superiority of enemy powers, could cause the suffering of the Lord.[116] The relationship to the incarnation of Jesus and his suffering is generally secondary in 6:8–19, but apart from the passage 7:2 just mentioned, there are also references to it in 6:9 and 14. The terms αὐτοῖς, ἐπιστήμη, γνῶσις from 2:3 return in 6:9 and 10: τί δὲ λέγει ἡ γνῶσις; . . . τίς νοήσει, εἰ μὴ σοφὸς καὶ ἐπιστήμων καὶ ἀγαπῶν τὸν κύριον αὐτοῦ; since the view has already suggested that, according to barnabas, wisdom, knowledge, gnosis life, love, may be assumed that the composition οοφόςἐπιστήμων–ἀγαπῶν should be explained as related terms.[117]

c) The Soaking of Jesus with Vinegar and Gall (Chap. 7:3 — 10:12).

The same teaching that section 5:13–7:2 contains is also presented in 7:2–10:12. Barnabas repeats this teaching in connection with the fact that after Christ was crucified he was given vinegar and gall to drink. The disposition is again the same as in the previous discussion: first 7:3–8:6 Barnabas tries to suppress the doubts that arise from the rule of evil and make him timid, on the one hand 7:3–5 by pointing out that God himself this dominion foretold and preordained, and on the other hand 7:6–8:6 by the doctrine of the final victory of the good. Then, after an excursus 8:7–9:9, in Chapter 10 there are admonitions on moral life. Of the OT passages on which these teachings are based, only those that serve to prove the foreknowledge of God refer directly to the aforementioned privation of the thirsting Saviour. The Bible passages otherwise used, on the other hand, are not directly related to it. The introductory words ἀλλὰ καὶ σταρωθεὶς ἐποτίζετο ὄξει καὶ χολῇ are to be regarded more as a preface to the following treatise or — perhaps better — a

---

[116] 7:2, therefore, does not contain an "empty tautology", as White asserts: "according to the premise εἰ ὁ νιος τοῦ θεον επαθεν, (ἵνα ... ζωοποιήση ημάς is the author's invitation to believe in dal! he could only suffer for our sake, actually superfluous" (p. 62).

[117] According to Weiss p. 16, it is to be shown in 6:8 et seq. that "the salvation or possession of the promised land, which was intended for the Jews, did not fall to them, but to the Christians". Likewise Hilgenfeld p. XXXI; Ap. V. p. 18. But nowhere is there a comparison between the old and the new covenant.

homily. They do not contain, and do not even suggest sufficiently, the theme and main ideas of the whole section.

7:3–5. — The new section is introduced by ἀλλά καί. This emphatically introduces something that should now be added to the previous discussion. The strong emphasis in this transitional formula is explained by the fact that important parts are related to one another. It therefore not only connects individual sentences that are subordinate in content, it also connects basic ideas. It suggests that the same teachings that have just been thoroughly appreciated can be illuminated and proven from another perspective. The introductory sentence is followed by two attitudinal prophecies, which have the purpose of showing that the Lord necessarily had to suffer in the manner mentioned, and that this suffering did not have its ultimate cause in the will of the enemy power.

The purpose of the two quotations is given twice by the author himself at the appropriate place to explain each of the two prophecies. In connection with the first of these, it says in 7:3: "The Lord gave the order, since he also himself . . . wanted to offer the vessel of the spirit as a sacrifice. . .", i.e., the Lord intended his will to make sacrifices to be made known through the commission. On the other hand, the author remarks in 7:5: "The Lord intended to show that he had to suffer at their hands."[118] — The first prophecy reads: "Whoever does not observe the fast shall surely die" (Lev. 23:29). In the "fast" lies the reference to the bitter, self–sacrificing renunciation of the thirsting Saviour.

The other prophecy, the origin of which is questionable,[119] says: "And they shall eat of the goat, which is offered in Lent for all sins. And the priests alone

---

[118] ἵνα δείξῃ (sc. κύριος), οτι δει αυτόν παϑειν ὑπ αυτών. This final set is drawn by some to 7:6 (ά ἐνετείλατο, προσέχετε). Veil: "Notice what commandments he gave to indicate what he should suffer from them." Likewise Hefele, Chr. Mayer, "The Writings of the Apostolic Fathers" (Library of the Church Fathers I. Kempten 1869). But the content of the final sentence fits only to the preceding, but not to the following section, which no longer has the purpose of proving the necessity of Jesus' suffering, but, as will be shown, pursues the purpose of showing the final victory of Jesus over the evil forces. "να δείξῃ . . . also already belongs as the answer to the 7:5 introductory question πρoς έι; to 7:5. — S reads αττίν πολλά παοείν πολλά but is superfluous; for the author is not concerned with proving that Christ had to suffer a lot, he just wanted to show that he had to suffer, πολλά has probably been inserted here with regard to 7:11 δει αυτόν πολλά παϑεεν.

[119] According to Güdemann, "Studies in the History of Religion" (Schriften des Israel-itischen Literaturvereins. 2nd year., 1876, p. 108) is the "prophetic passage" καὶ φαγέτωσαν εκ τον τράγον . . . artificially adjusted "with the intention of being able to link the following interpretation to it". "What this passage says is nothing other than the good Talmudic commentary on the verse Num. 29:11." The following words introduced by προσέγετε ακριβώς are the "interpretation of the quoted alleged prophetic word in the Midrash style". Hefele

shall eat all the entrails unwashed with vinegar." The goat to be eaten with vinegar is the Saviour soaked with vinegar, who is subject to the evil doings of the priests, and who must fast with his people while they indulge in food. This is the meaning of the statement 7:5 attached to that quotation and put into the mouth of the Lord: "Since you want to give me, who want to sacrifice my flesh for the sins of my new people, to drink gall with vinegar, you eat alone, while the people[120] fast and mourns in sackcloth and ashes."[121]

7:6–11. — The second proof, which is conducted against the misgivings arising from the reign of evil, begins with 7:6: "Whatever he commanded, take heed to it. . ." According to H, S and L, there is no connecting or connecting particle, which is precisely because a new part of this section begins at this point. The scripture, which 7:6f. is used for the purpose mentioned, reads: "Take two beautiful and similar goats and offer them, and the priest take one as a burnt offering for sins . . . Cursed be the other.[122] 7:8, follow the words, which again are questionable in terms of their origin:[123] "And spit on him all and pierce him and put the scarlet wool

---

p. 67, note provides detailed discussions on the origin of the quotation. 6; ßraunsberger pp. 253 et seq.; Hilgenfeld pp. 88 et seq.; Völter pp. 423 et seq. — Braunsberger pp. 260 et seq. advocates the credibility of the report given by Barnabas in a detailed investigation.

[120] At first it may seem questionable whether λαος in the words τοῦ λαοῦ νηστεύοντος is to be understood as the Jewish people or the people of the new covenant. One could conclude that from ιερεῖς μόνοι, to which the Jewish people initially form the contrast. But the Christian people must be remembered, because we are talking about them shortly before (τοῦ λαοῦ μου τοῦ καινοῦ).

[121] Veils in Hdb. Z. D. NT Apokr. P. 219: in 7:3–5, it would be important for the author to "show that the Jewish priesthood and with it the Jewish people, through their mistreatment and killing of Christ, have deprived themselves of all share in the high priestly atonement performed by him and have pronounced the death sentence according to the law: Whoever does not fast on the day of Fasting (Day of Atonement) should be exterminated by capital punishment." There is no mention of the Jewish people alone at all, and only the second quotation is directed against the Jewish priests. — White p. 63 claims that in the abominable food, which the priests are to eat alone, there is a temporary punishment for them as the instigators of Jesus' suffering.

[122] Lev. 16:7–10. Although the predicates "beautiful, similar" used in holy Scripture is not mentioned, but find confirmation elsewhere (Mishnah Joma 6:1; Justinus Dial. c. 40; Tertullian adv. Mark 8:7; cf. Bähr, Symbolism of the Mosaic Cult II. 679). The passage is quoted very freely at all.

[123] Güdemann S. in writes about these words: "Here, too, it is not a quotation, although the form of it has been retained, but a wickedly exaggerated description of a real event." Braunsberger p. 260 et seq. deals in detail with the reports about the scapegoat and the various views on it. There is no contradiction with the Bible and the Talmud. The report is recommended

around his head, and so he will be driven into a desert!" The explanation is made in these words: "And when this has happened, the one who has to lead the goat brings it into the desert, takes away the wool and places it on the so–called blackberry bush." A relationship of the quoted passages to the preamble of the section is only given indirectly. It is conveyed through the passages 7:3 and 4 mentioned. The drinking of the suffering Lord was found directly represented in the sacrifice of the goat, prefigured in the sacrifice of the goat, which the priests were to enjoy with vinegar alone on the fasting day.

And this sacrifice is now reminiscent of the sacrifice of the two goats mentioned in 7:6, as well as that of the red heifer in Chap. 8. In the report about the two goats, the similarity between them and the placing of the red wool on the previously cursed and mistreated goat are of particular importance to the author. According to Barnabas, the lesson that follows from the Jewish custom mentioned is: Christ will first be insulted, pierced, spit on, crucified, but on the day of judgment he will appear in a scarlet cloak reaching down to his ankles, that is, in the robe of princes and lords, the magnificent talere (robe) of the high priest.

7:9: "They will see him on that day when he has the long purple robe[124] on his body, and they will say, "Isn't he the one we insulted, pierced, spit on, and crucified? Truly it was this one who then presented himself as the Son of God." By pointing out the similarity of the goats in 7:6, it is intended to emphasize that in a very special way that the very one who sacrifices himself is also glorified, that he can actually be a suffering Son of God.

7:10, the author asks: "For how is he similar to that one?" The objects of comparison arise from 7:9: 'Take heed: one (of the goats which the priest is to take) is destined for the sacrificial altar, the other, the cursed one, for the crowning."[125]

---

by internal probability. See, inter alia, Hefele p. 69, note. 12; p. 71, Note. 14; p. 72, Note. 15; Hilgenfeld p. 92 et seq.; Völter p. 426 et seq.

[124] τότε (H, Hilgenfeld) probably deserves preference over ποτέ (S V, Gebh., Funk, Heer) in consideration of the following δ τότε λόγων.

[125] I am following H: τον δε άνα, and also being able to give a different kind of feedback, I am following H: τον de, and being able to give a different kind of feedback, and being able to give a different kind of feedback, and being able to give a different kind of feedback. On the other hand, it reads as follows: κπικατάρατον: και άτι τον, but it reads as follows: ἀστεφανιμμενον, but it reads as follows: V and L have instead: και στι τον ἀπικατάρατον ἀστεφανωμενον. The type of reading: και στι .. . as a rule, it is preferred and considered to be the subject of a question, the subject of which is the subject of a question, the subject of a question.

After that, the cursed goat, provided that he is already distinguished by the imposition of scarlet wool, is similar to the one who is sentenced to sacrifice.[126] This similarity now indicates the amazing similarity, i.e.,equality, of the suffering and the glorified Savior. 7:10: "For this purpose, the goats should be similar, beautiful, the same,[127] so that when one sees him (Christ) coming then, one is amazed at his similarity." The lesson that emerges for the readers of the letter from the glorious victory and the final reign of the Savior is that they too need not be afraid of the evil, hostile powers, their sufferings and tribulations, and that they should patiently endure in the good hope of better times.

Barnabas takes the opportunity here to make this application explicitly and to point out the Christian's present sufferings and at the same time his future victory over them. The reason for this is the Jewish custom, mentioned in 7:8b, of placing the scarlet wool taken from the goat on a thorn bush. An interpretation of this custom follows in 7:11. Let there be a teaching given in the example of "The Church of Jesus".[128] The union of the rough thorns with the red wool indicates the close relationship between the sufferings of the Christian and his glorification; only through affliction and suffering can the Christian come to the view of God and enter the kingdom of heaven. "Thus, he says,[129] those who want to see me and gain my kingdom should only find me after tribulation and suffering."

---

[126] Müller p. 202 assumes that the cursed goat as such is compared to the sacrificed one. "But the equality with the sacrificed is emphasized, because the latter is consecrated to God, holy and pleasing to God, and therefore can be considered as a type of the victorious Jesus." This idea alone is in no way indicated in the text.

[127] Müller, p. 202, comments on ἴσους: "Our author felt that comparison alone was lagging behind similarity, he had to at least emphasize equality. After all, he could not talk about the identity with the Goats."

[128] τύπος ὑοτιν τον Ἰησον τζ ἐκκλησία κείμενος. As a rule, Ἰησον is related to τύπος. But according to the following explanation, the laying of wool on the thorn bush is understood only from the suffering of the believer, but not from the suffering of Jesus. The presupposition of the genitive case is justified by the train of thought described by the person of Jesus in 7:9 and 10 transferred to his congregation. — Sprinzl p. 57, note. 2 through these words, he wants to make Barnabas the defender of the church's teaching authority.

[129]The thought that is put into the mouth of the Lord here is not to be understood as a direct utterance of Jesus. It is the interpretation and translation of the ot mentioned in 7:6–8. Orders of God, but l a new quote. Ropes rightly explains "The Sayings of Jesus" p. 17 f.: "But it seems to me certain that the sentence should only give the summary of the spiritual thought of the picture... Resch (Agrapha 1889) seeks, however, to prove, that κτλ the frequent echoes of the words ὀφείλουσιν θλιβέντες χτλ IIA category& ὄντες. there is only one logion of Jesus. But this evidence is not very convincing. To assume that the Christians of the first two centuries could only speak of persecution and tribulation on the basis of a word

That the sufferings and tribulations of various kinds are not an offense and annoyance to the disciple of Jesus, but rather a means of bliss and in this respect sweet fruits, the writer already hinted at the mention of the laying of the red wool on a thorn bush 7:8 by the remark: "From him (= the thorn bush) we even tend to eat the fruits that are still in the first development (βλαστοί) and growing wild[130]; so are the fruits of the blackberry bush[131] (?) alone, sweet." Apparently the author was thinking of the arduous earthly life of Christians, which, although it produces unripe and ignoble fruits as a result of his sufferings, but which, with regard to the better eternal future, already makes the bitterness and imperfections of the present seem sweet fruits to the true Christian, since this life grants him happy prospects only in the effort.[132]

---

of Jesus seems to me almost heartlessness." Resch alone still holds the title in the second edition of his Agrapha (Texte und Untersuchungen z. Gesch. d. altchristl. Lit. N. F. XV, 3 & 4, Lpz. 1906) is determined by the probability that a gentleman's word is quoted because of the kinship with Akt. 14, 22 and da Prochorus (Acta Ioannis ed. Zahn, Erlangen 1880, p. 83) Acts14:22 as a logion.

[130] Actually: which we find in the field, so = ungrafted fruits.

[131] = in such an immature and not refined state.

[132] The purpose of Chap. 7, according to the usual view, is to call from the OT types on the suffering of Jesus. So Hefele p. 66; Kayser p. 12; Funk p. XXVII. Völter p. 347 looks at Chap. 7 as well as 8 types on the passion of Christ, His gospel and His kingdom. According to Harnack, the purpose of ch. 7 to show that Jesus' suffering is preformed. But he is also aware that he has disregarded some thoughts through this content determination. He reproaches the author for the fact that, similarly to 6:11–19, he is also mentioned in 7:11 and 8:3 et seq. of OT Prophecies offer a double interpretation and thus deviate from the established topic (see LIX, note. 5). Even the thorn bush mentioned in 7:8 is said to be a type on the crown of thorns of Christ. . So Hefele p. 72, note. 15; Völter p. 429. Also Müller p. 197, not on the other hand p. 202 f. But for such an interpretation of the thorn bush not only every clue is missing, it is also contradicted by the explanation of the rite in 7:11. But speaking of the sweetness of the fruits of the thorn bush — so Müller p. 198 — Barnabas only claims that he explains the τρώγειν. As if the author, who claimed that he could hardly discuss the most important religious teachings sufficiently due to lack of time, wanted to draw a pure stomach question into his topic here! Müller rightly declares, p. 181, that it is in the Chap. 7 and 8 expressed the thought that "the New Covenant triumphs through suffering". But this triumph is not for him the arduous and combat–rich victory over sin and suffering, but the victory over the Old Covenant. — Zahn, "Geschichte des NT Canons" I. 2. p. 955: "A reference to the Apocalypse alone seems sufficient to explain to some extent the whimsical and, according to the manner of this writer, highly unclear typological interpretation of the two goats of the Day of Atonement."

In order to stop the fearless endurance in the good, it is mentioned in Chap. 8 mentions the sacrifice of the red heifer.[133] According to 8:1, the commandment was given to Israel: "The men, in whom the measure of sin is full, should offer a young cow, slaughter it and then burn it, and then boys should pick up the ashes, pour the scarlet wool into vessels, around a wood — see again the model of the cross and the scarlet wool! — and lay the hyssop, and so the boys should sprinkle the individual people, so that they will be cleansed of their sins."[134] — By the difference in the persons of those who were to slaughter and burn the cow, and of those to whom it was incumbent to collect the ashes and to carry out the sprinkling, it should be taught that the credit is due to the good. The former are called completely sinful men[135], the latter (innocent) boys (παιδία).

8:2: "Here no more men appear, no more sinners have the honor."[136] These words briefly express the basic idea: after all, victory and honor are due to the good.[137] The "honor" is what is mentioned in Chap. 7 and 8 is symbolized by the

---

[133] δάμαλις 8:1, ὁ μόσχος 8:2. Τὸ ὁ μόσχος cf. Müller p. 210; Hilgenfeld p. 95: „Iesu congruere non videbatur femin. δάμαλις"

[134] On 8:1, Güdemann, p. 114, says: "In B.'s account, a too precise knowledge of even tradition emerges that one should not consider him to be a born and educated Jew, and the errors and inaccuracies to be deliberate typological changes." — Braunsberger p. 278: "What the Epistle of Barnabas states about the red heifer does not contradict either the holy Scriptures or any other ancient witness. Rather, the letter complements the other reports ..." Cf. still and a. Hefele p. 74, note. 1; p. 76, Note. 2; Theol. Quarterly. 1852, pp. 615 –627; Hilgenfeld p. 94 f.; Völter p. 429 fr. — "Due to the extensive distortions of the Jewish rite of sacrifice and priesthood," Güdemann believes himself prompted to the assertion that "the letter was an anonymous letter of denunciation directed against the Jews, issued at the time of Hadrian, when on the Roman side a mood favorable to the Jews and the reconstruction of the temple made itself felt, and calculated on the intention to convert it into the opposite. That is why the sacrifices, the priesthood and the ceremonial law are given such a detailed description, exposing them to ridicule.' (p. 130). In contrast, Funk in Theol. Quarterly. 1878, pp. 150 f.

[135] ἄνδρας, ἐν οἷς εἰσὶν ἁμαρίαι τέλειαι

[136] εἶτα οὐκέτι ἄνδρες, οὐκέτι ἁμαρτωλῶν ἡ δόξα. The editio Οχοη. and following her Hefele: εἶτα ονκέτν ανδρες αμαρτωλοί, ... The addition is a later, appropriate explanation. In L, the sentence is missing.

[137] Hefele explains these words for a marginal glossiness. He translates: "Then they are no longer sinners, nor are they considered sinners anymore" (p. 77). Harnack p. 39: "verba εἶτα οὐκέτι δόξα omni sensu carent." Müller p. 211: "And really mock all attempts at an explanation... The words are, where not spurious, so definitely mutilated and critically suspect." Völter p. 430, note 1.: "Those words simply want to transfer from the sinful men and their work to the innocent boys and their work." Veil im Handb. Z. D. NT Apokr. p. 220: "These words, on the interpretation of which the interpreters have all failed so far, were originally,

"scarlet wool". The mentioned custom of the sacrifice of the red heifer is considered a type. The sacrificial animal points to Jesus. The slaughterers are the ones who killed Jesus.[138] Boys are to be understood as the preachers of the gospel. Barnabas, however, does not intend to just present types from the O. T. since he expressly emphasizes that the honor of sprinkling and purification belongs to others than the sinful sacrificial men, in the typological interpretation he pursues only the purpose of teaching his readers that the honor, fame and glory of Jesus' apostles is assured.

This fact is important for readers who are oppressed by suffering and sin and want to take offense at the currently still victorious power of a world hostile to God and Christ. Barnabas wants to influence morally. This is also shown by the remark that these apostles proclaim to us the good news of the remission of sins and the sanctification of the heart. Probably with the intention of contributing to the honor of the apostles, he compares them with the twelve tribes of Israel and claims that their role models, the sprinkling boys, are reminiscent of Abraham, Isaac and Jacob by their number of three, "for these were great before God". The Old Covenant must therefore lend its reputation to the apostles in order to honor them.[139] Chapter 8 concludes with the same thought as the previous chapter. 8:5 and 6 contains the teaching that the kingdom of Christ on earth is not yet a kingdom of perfect bliss. The laying of the wool on the wood indicates that the cross belongs to the kingdom of Jesus. 8:5: "But it is said that the scarlet wool is to be put on the cross. For the rule of Jesus is based on the cross, and those who hope in him will live forever."[140]

According to 8:6, the imperfection in Jesus' earthly kingdom is expressed by the fact that hyssop was attached to the rod of sprinkling at the same time as the red wool. "But why the hyssop in addition to the wool? Because in his kingdom there will be bad and gloomy days through which we will achieve salvation, especially since the physically sick will also be healed through the murky juice of hyssop."[141] The bad and gloomy days might perhaps at first remind of physical sufferings and tribulations of persecutions. Remember the consequences. But the preceding admonition to cleanse oneself of sins and the teaching that honor is not due to sinners, as well as the contrast to the physically suffering person, in contrast

---

in my opinion, like 1:6, a marginal glossary, in which a sensitive reader of the following time (but probably certainly before 350 AD.He expressed his satisfaction with the decline of Judaism."

[138] 8:2. Hilgenfeld, Apost. V p. 22: "The anti–Jewish intention . . . this is especially evident in the alleged sinfulness of the slaughterers."

[139] 8:3: οἱ ῥαντίζοντες παῖδες οἱ εὐαγγελισάμενοι (H V; on the other hand S and L εὐαγγελισάμενοι). The reading of H and V points to an older time, still closer to the apostles.

[140] For this reason, one cannot speak badly of an anti–Jewish tendency of Barnabas.

[141] Add: whose rule is based on the cross.

to 7:11, which speaks of the necessity of physical suffering for the Christian is to think of the mental suffering of temptation through the richly developed power of sin. Just as the bitter medicine of the Hyssop gives health to the sick body,[142] so it is precisely those bad and gloomy days that give health and eternal life to the soul.

According to 8:6, the imperfection in the earthly realm is expressed by the fact that hyssop was also attached to the rod of blasting at the same time as the red wool. "But why, besides the wool, also the hyssop? Because there will be bad and gloomy days in his kingdom, through which we will reach salvation, especially since the physically sick person will also be healed by the turbid juice of the hyssop."[143] The bad and gloomy days might perhaps at first remind of physical sufferings and tribulations of persecutions. But the previous admonition to cleanse oneself from sins, and the teaching that it is not sinners who deserve honor, as well as the comparison with the physically suffering one, requires, in contrast to 7:11, where we are talking about the necessity of physical suffering for the Christian, to think about the mental sufferings of temptation through the richly unfolded power of sin. Just as the bitter medicine of the Hyssop gives health to the sick body,[144] so it is precisely those bad and gloomy days that give health and eternal life to the soul.

Even if Barnabas did not emphasize his intentions clearly and clearly enough in 7:3–8:6, the same thoughts could still be found, which are known from the earlier sections of the letter.[145]

---

[142] 8:5: ὅτι δὲ τὸ ἔριον ἐπὶ τὸ ξύλον; ὅτι ἡ βασιλεία Ἰησοῦ ἐπὶ ξύλου, καὶ ὅτι οἱ ἐλπίζοντες ἐπ' αὐτὸν ζήσονται εἰς τὸν αἰῶνα. Of these three phrases with οτι, the first refers to a part of the ot mentioned in 8:1. Areas, the second and save explains the first sentence. L: quarc ergo et Jana in ligno est? In accordance with this, explain the first ὅτι as a question word: Hefele p. 77; Müller p. 213; Mayer p. 93; Riggenbach p. 13; Veil in NT Apokr. P. 157; Funk p. 61. — Hefele on 8:5: "In this comparison, the wood corresponds to the throne, the wool to the royal mantle."

[143] See the translation of Veil!

[144] διὰ τοῦ ῥύπου τοῦ ὑσσύπου ἰᾶται. Hefele p. 78: τοῦ ῥύπου διὰ τοῦ ὑσσύπου ἰᾶται — "the physically ill person is indeed healed of uncleanness by the hyssop." According to Kayser p. 12, the hyssop is a ..Symbol of the soul–cleansing power of the passion of Christ". Müller p. 214: "Wool and hyssop are therefore connected in order to serve as a type of purification from the t'bdn, from which we are freed in the kingdom of God." Hilgenfeld: διὰ τοῦ ῥύπου τοῖ–ὑσσύπου τονσσούιπον (cf. Zeitschr. F. wiss. Theol. 1879, pp. 137 & 268).

[145] White: Chap. 7 and 8 offer "an extremely complicated discussion, of which probably no interpreter will dare to have given an exhaustive explanation" (p. 62). They are supposed to contain "a tangle of thoughts", so that he "did not find any advice among the interpreters in this complicated matter" (p. 64). — P. Heinisch, "The influence of Philo on the oldest Christian Exegesis" (Alttest. Abhandlungen, ed. by J. Nikel, I. 1 and 2. Münster I. W. 1908) claims that Barnabas rejects regulations and ceremonies of the OT (p. 58). But he does it in

8:7–9:4. — A digression begins at 8:7. He extends over chapter 9 and aims to give information why some people lack an understanding of the teachings of the OT 8:7: "And it is clear to us that it must therefore take place, but it is dark to those, because they have not listened to the voice of the Lord." For anyone who has listened to the voice of the Lord understands that — these are the preceding sentences — because of OT teachings contained in the ordinances which must still be mixed with sorrow and joy in this life. The reason why the historical appearance of the divine kingdom remains incomprehensible to some will be explained in more detail below. The fault for the spiritual blindness lies in the fact that the ears were not circumcised, i.e., that one remained uncircumcised at heart.

Namely, Barnabas writes 9:1: Λέγει γὰρ πάλιν περὶ τῶν ὠτίων, πῶς περιέτεμεν ἡμῶν τὴν καρδίαν. The meaning of these all–too–succinct words is this: Elsewhere the Lord speaks of the ears and their circumcision,[146] and by requiring willing hearing by circumcision of the ears, he wants circumcision of the heart. The blame for the poor understanding of the OT types and prophecies lies with the failure to circumcise the heart. The following passages of Scripture, 9:1, show how one must listen to God. Ps. 17:45: "By listening with their ear they obeyed me"; Is. 33:13: "Those who live far away will hear with their ears what I have done and will recognize it." The teaching intended with these passages is: one must not only listen externally with the ear, but at the same time must also obey (ὑπακούειν) and have understanding (γιγνώσκειν).

Now, in 9:1, from Jer. 4:4 the word of the Lord is mentioned: "Circumcise your hearts", so the commandment of obedience and knowledge, which results from the commandment to hear and to circumcise the ears, is related to that of circumcision of the heart. The fact that the latter commandment falls under the others, and that ear circumcision means obedience and knowledge and thus heart formation, is intended to be taught by this compilation of the three quotations. At

---

chapters 7 n. 8 is an exception. "At least he recognizes the rite of the Feast of Atonement with the sacrifice of the goats and the sacrifice of the red heifer in the literal sense" (p. 59 f.). If there is now no negative position towards the at in Chapters 7 and 8. If regulations and ceremonies are found, then the conclusion should be drawn that the Barnabas letter also does not want to deny their relative "'right" to the ceremonial laws of the Old Testament in any other way. Similar to Heinisch, Völter, among others, judges. While in the Cape. 2–4 the Jewish customs of fasting and sacrifices have never been valid at all, ch. 7 and 8 contain customs which always remain of importance as pre–revelations of Christianity (p. 347). The aforementioned contradiction exists in the view of OT Then Völter is right when he declares one part to be interpolated.

146 The term περιέτεμεν of the subordinate clause must also be transferred to the main clause: Cf. 9:3: οὐκοῦν περιέτεμεν ἡμῶν τὰς ἀκοάς.

the end of 9:3[147], after 9:2, there are some Bible passages are addressed to Israel (Jer. 7:2 f.), to all those desirous of salvation (Ps. 33:13) Ex. 15:26), in heaven and on earth (Is. 1:2), to the mighty (Is. 1:10), as to children (Is. 40:3) the invitation to listen to the Lord is directed, thus the ear circumcision is explained. "Therefore he circumcised our ears, so that when we heard the word we might believe."[148] However, a circumcision of the ears according to these words requires faith, but the πίστευεω, in terms of context, can mean nothing other than obeying, recognizing, circumcising the hearts, which is required in 9:1, and to which the following οὐκοῦν refers back in 9:3.[149]

9:4–9:9. — The admonition to the attitude that follows from the circumcision of the heart and ears, from which the understanding of the books of the Old Covenant and its various statutes grows, and light into the darkness the purpose of the commandment is to circumcise the foreskin. The deeper meaning of the circumcision commandment, aimed at promoting spiritual life, is set out in 9:4–9. The explanation begins 9:4 thus: "But also the circumcision on which you have placed your (special) trust has been rejected. For he did not say that there should be a circumcision of the flesh. But they transgressed (his commandment) because an evil angel beguiled them."[150] The connection ἀλλὰ καί[151] shows that Barnabas 9:4 wants to speak of the circumcision of the foreskin in the same sense as before of the

---

[147] The sentence ονκονν περιέτεμεν . . . is put by Funk, Veil and Völter at the end of 9:5, but usually drawn to 9:4 as by Riggenbach, Müller, Gebhardt, Weiss, Heer.

[148] S: ἵνα ἀκούσαντες καί μη μόνον πιστεύσωμεν. According to this, as in 1:5, faith is what readers already possess.

[149] ἀλλὰ καὶ ἡ περιτομή, ἐφ᾽ ᾗ πεποίθασιν, κατήργηται. περιτομὴν γὰρ εἴρηκεν οὐ σαρκὸς γενηθῆναι· ἀλλὰ παρέβησαν, ὅτι ἄγγελος πονηρὸς ἐσόφιζεν αὐτούς.

[150] V. and Müller: εἰ γάρ.

[151] 9:1–3 should also already be taught the importance of the circumcision of the foreskin. This is the ordinary view. But since the beginning of something new, which has not been mentioned before, begins with the fact that it starts with the fact that it starts with the fact that it starts with the fact that the assumption of interpolation is necessary. Weiss writes 9:1 & 3 (οὐκοῦν περιέτεμεν . . .) to the interpolator (p. 22). According to Völter, 9:4 et seq. "is the direct continuation of the execution via the covenant in 4:1–5:4 . . . Originally, the discussion of the Federal sign, i.e.,followed by circumcision" (p. 349)" — Of course, in the phrase περιέτεμεν ἡμῶν τὴν καρδίαν in 9:1 and 3 the verb is used figuratively and in its literal meaning indicates the well—known circumcision law, but from this it follows at most so much that the author wants to prepare and initiate the discussion of this law in 9:1–3, but not that he has the intention to explain the same here already. It is to be assumed that in the above turn he wants to distract his readers from a literal conception, from the thought of an actual circumcision of the flesh, so that even when he mentions the περιτομή, ἐφ᾽ ᾗ πεποίθασιν, they will think of the higher moral meaning of the περιτέμνειν and now just as little as the περιέτεμεν τὰς to take περιτομή τις σαρκός literally.

circumcision of the ears.[152] As he has therefore just spoken of a circumcision of the ears in the sense of a circumcision of the heart,[153] so he now explains that the Scriptures also do not speak of a circumcision of the foreskin in the last resort in order to prolong a circumcision of the flesh. The order of God in this regard reaches deeper.

True, the carnal circumcision is also initially willed by God; for Abraham, who was "great before God" (8:4), actually made such a circumcision (9:7), "also, in fact, the people were circumcised for sealing" (9:6), i.e., by circumcising the flesh, the covenant with God was actually sealed. That "but also" circumcision of the foreskin requires a circumcision of the heart is shown by the immediate reference to the fact that "circumcision has been abandoned". Barnabas is very likely thinking about the ban on circumcision issued by Emperor Hadrian in 131.[154] But if fleshly cir-

---

[152] Since it is not said that circumcision has been abolished for Christians or by the new law or the like, the words ἡ περιτομή indicate. . . κατήργηται in its generality refers to an actual, historical, general abolition of circumcision, not to a mere declaration of invalidity within a certain confession. (Compare, in contrast to the perfect κατήργηται, the aorist κατήργησεν in 2, 6). Emperor Hadrian issued a comprehensive ban on circumcision for Jews and Samaritans, which prohibited them from circumcising proselytes as well as their own children (cf. A. Schlatter, "The Days of Trajan and Hadrian", pp. 6 and 7, Gütersloh 1897). Barnabas certainly remembers this imperial edict, which was repealed by Antoninus Pius. — Other historical circumstances seem to exist for L, since he wrote the omitted sentence ἀλλά καὶ . . . κατήργηται.

[153] Bardenhewer, "Gesch. d. old church. Lit." I, p. 88: according to Barnabas, "the Jewish use of circumcision was not based on divine institution, but on a deception of the Jews by an evil angel". The fact that circumcision was against the will of God from the beginning can also be concluded from 9:4, among other things. Hilgenfeld, Apost. V. p. 22; Müller p. 218 u; 223; Harnack p. 41; Funk p. XXVII and 65; Veil in N.T. Apocr. P. 145. It was precisely this view of 9, 4 that was usually the reason for denying the letter to the apostle Barnabas (Braunsberger p. 222; Funk. Kirchen–gesichtl. Abhand, und Untersuch. II, p. 81 f.). Ferd. Chr. Baur, "The Christian. Gnosis or the Christian Religious philosophy in its own right happens!». Development" (Tüb. 1835) compares the ἄγγελος πονηρός, who is the cause of the Jews' delusion, with the Gnostic demiurge (p. 89, note). Judge correctly about 9, 4 Sprinzl p. 185, note 2.

[154] Weiss p. 23 and Völter p. 350 and 433 admit that in 9, 7 the physical circumcision is found quite in order, and that Abraham cannot have been seduced by an evil angel after 9, 7. But both of them, on the basis of this correct knowledge, also refrain from looking for a corresponding explanation of the preceding sentences 9,4—6. They too join the general view about the content of these sentences and teach that God never wanted a carnal circumcision afterwards. In order not to disturb the uniformity of the train of thought, declare 9, 7–9 interpolated.

cumcision is now abolished and thus made impossible, then it can also be impossible for the time for which Barnabas is writing, according to the intended will of God. The commandment of circumcision is only valid if it is understood spiritually.[155]

Its deeper meaning and its final purpose are expressed according 9:5 Jer. 4:3f.: "Do not sow thorns, circumcise yourself for your Lord!" Deut. 10:16: "Circumcise your hardness of heart and do not harden your neck!" Jer. 9:25 — the third passage of the prophets quoted in 9:5 — is intended to show what the Lord intended by this commandment: "Behold, says the Lord, all nations are uncircumcised on the foreskin, but this people is uncircumcised on the heart." From these quotations it can be concluded that the law of circumcision demands devotion to God, overcoming of hardness of heart and formation of heart from the very beginning in its ultimate purpose. If from some quarters this purpose of the divine commandment was not recognized and the regulations contained in it were not observed, then knowledge and wisdom were displayed which do not come from God, but were bestowed by "an evil angel". . . In order to justify that God requires more for a covenant than external circumcision.

It is pointed out in 9:6 that "all Syrians and Arabs and all idolatrous priests" as well as the Egyptians[156] have the custom of circumcision.[157] What is the final purpose and meaning of carnal circumcision is also precisely taught by its execution by Abraham.[158] The fact that Abraham circumcised "eighteen and three hundred of his household" is especially instructive according to 9:7.[159] "In the Spirit" and, since Gnosis is given to him,[160] he points to Jesus the Crucified, since the number 18 — ιη reminds of Jesus, the number 300 = τ reminds of the cross. This declaration is concluded 9:9 with the remark: "He possessed knowledge, who has placed in us the gift of his covenant inscribed in the flesh."[161] The ἔμφυτον

---

[155] Barnabas combines two very different Biblical passages here: Gen. 17 23. 27; 14, 14. Cf. Hefele p. 82, note. 21; Braunsberger p. 214 f.; Völter p. 433.

[156] τίς οὖν ἡ δοθεῖσα αὐτῷ γνῶσις;

[157] οἶδεν ὁ την ἔμφυτον δωρεάν τής δια&ήχης αυτοῦ τέμενος ἐν ἡμῖν. Instead of δια&ήκης (H, S) read V and L: διδαχής (cf. Heer p. LXVI).

[158] So Hilgenfeld, Apost. V. p. 23.

[159] So Hilgenfeld ibid. and Hefele p. 83.

[160] Instead of Abraham, one usually thinks of oneself as a subject to οἶδεν God or God. Christ. Hefele p. 83, note. 26: "Barnabas attaches such importance to his typological interpretation that he calls Christ himself to witness to its correctness and truth." Cf. Hilgenfeld, Apost. V. p. 23; Rraunsberger p. 215; Harnack p. 45.

[161] οὐδεὶς γνησιώτερον ἔμαθεν ἀπ' ἐμοῦ λόγον. Veil still connects these words with the preceding sentence and translates: "He who has placed the implanted gift of his teaching in us

δωρεὰν, spoken of here is not the gift of penetrating into the deeper meaning of Scripture and interpreting it typologically,[162] not just the "deep–rooted gift"[163], but rather the gift incised into the nature of the flesh at circumcision. The meaning of these words is: Abraham had an understanding, because he not only carried out the circumcision of the flesh on his own, but also because, by performing the physical circumcision and pointing us to Christ and the cross precisely through it, but because he also performed the circumcision of the body and through it pointed us to Christ and the cross, he also worked the circumcision of the heart in us.[164] Chapter 9 concludes with the words:

"No one learned from me a more heartfelt instruction.[165] But I know that you are worthy." What the readers of Barnabas learned is called λόγος γνηοιωτίρος.[166] It is not to be assumed that this is intended to explain the interpretation of the number 318 as a more appropriate, more correct, closer to the truth teaching than other teachings that are otherwise presented by him.[167] For with this assumption, the impossible assertion would be expected of Barnabas: "That which I am able to read from the number 318 has more value and greater claim to truth than, for example, the Bible quotations in 9:5 mentioned just before, which directly express the will of God." It is necessary, to adhere to the original meaning of γνήοιος and to see in the λογος–γνησιώτερος a teaching that is particularly peculiar to the author, comes from his deepest heart.[168] λογος is to refer to the instruction on the necessity

---

knows: no one has received a more genuine instruction from me." So, as a subject to οἴδεν, God is meant.

[162] γνησώιερος λόγος translated L: artius verbum. The editio Ox., Hilgenfeld et al. correct in aptius verbum.

[163] Harnack p. 45 explains the Greek texts: auctor. . . aptissima gioriatur expositione.

[164] Güdemann p. 121 also sees in λόγος γνησιώτερος the intention to confront one's own views with strangers. ..This fact, that he (= Barnabas) has, as it were, struck a sniff at the Hagada, is confirmed by the self–satisfied remark ονόεις γνησιώ– τερον . . . more confirmed than denied."

[165] Cf. the praise to the addressees in 1:2. — Sprinzl, p. 80, note. 1 view 9:9 as a satyric conclusion.

[166] 10:1: τρία ἔλαβεν ἐν τῇ συνέσει δόγματα. 10:2 and 9 ἐν πνεύματι ἐλάλησεν.

[167] Cf. 2:1 and 1:6

[168] Also Hefele p. 85, Anni. 7 claims that Barnabas does not want to protest against a literal interpretation of the dietary commandments at all, and refers to Clement of Alexandria, who gives the allegorical interpretation almost entirely using Barnabas's words, although he speaks out against the natural–historical inaccuracies of his letter, but claims a violation of the OT doesn't mean anything. Hefele reads 10:2: ἄρα οὖν (nun) ἔστιν ἐντολὴ θεοῦ τὸ μὴ τρώγειν; Völter explains p. Chapter io should therefore not be assigned to the original letter writer. Most people see the treatise on dietary laws as anti–Jewish polemics. So Riggenbach

of circumcision of the heart for the sake of the Cross of Jesus. With the reference to the worthiness of the readers at the conclusions of 9:9, the author wants to explain that this instruction is not based on mistrust.[169]

10:1–12. — As in sections 5:13–7:2 following Ex. 33:1, 3 has been concluded with the admonition for spiritual and moral renewal, so also the section beginning with 7:3 in chapter 10 is followed by Lev. 11 and Deut. 14 concluded with admonitions on moral life. Barnabas quotes 10:1 the words of Moses: "You shall not eat the pig, nor the eagle, nor the hawk, nor the raven, nor any fish that does not bear scales." That these regulations are not meant literally in their final purpose, but have a deeper, spiritual content, that Moses, when he received and gave these commandments, showed understanding and spirit[170], follows after 10:2 from his explanation Deut. 4:1–5: "And I want to explain to this people my legal statutes (δικαιώματα)."Since these dietary laws are hereby designated as statutes that are intended to give righteousness to man, God's last intention was therefore not to issue only dietary regulations: "Therefore it is not God's command not to eat, but Moses spoke in the Spirit" (10:2b). Barnabas does not care about the literal interpretation of the regulations observed by the Jews at that time. We do not know how he judges them. Since he writes for Christians, he is only interested in their moral sense.[171]

---

p. 25; Weizsäcker p. 44; Müller p. 255; Braunsberger p. 226; Harnack p. 45; White p. 24; Bardenhewer, Gesch. d. oldk. Lit. I, p. 88.

[169] Since Barnabas clearly distinguishes the beings of the three animal kingdoms, the connection of the five members, as handed down by H, deserves preference in the quotation 10:1. While S writes ηυτε four times and thereby equates all members, H only connects the three species of birds with οντε and prescribes πάντα ἰχθύν; συδέ. — The above interpretation of the τρία δόγματα escapes the difficulties in which the explainers of the expression usually find themselves by assuming that in 10.9 Barnabas only thinks of the first three of the six different animal species mentioned above, viz 1. the pig, 2. the hawk, eagle, vulture and raven, 3. the conger eels, polyps and squids are taken into account, but hares, hyenas and weasels are ignored. Müller writes on page 250: "Our author likes to highlight three dogmas. 1:6; 9:7; 10:1, 10. Here this is all the more sought after, since he has to omit some of the provisions listed and explained above in order not to exceed the number of three." P. 251: "Our author limits himself here to three cases out of six by which leaves out rabbits, hyenas and weasels as being too dirty.1' According to Hilgenfeld p. 106, in 10:9 and 10, section 10:6–8 is completely ignored. Funk writes p. 71: Auctor tria animalia vel genera animalium praecipue respicit: suem, aves rapaces et pisces in profundo maris degentes. Accedunt v. 6–8 tria alias. Weiss p. 24 f. and Völter p. 351 help themselves out of the difficulty by attributing 10:6–8 to a later, revised hand.

[170] 10:11: Φάγεσθε πᾶν διχηλοῦν καὶ μαρυκώμενον (Lev. 11:3; Deut. 14:6).

[171] κολλᾶσθε . . . μετὰ τῶν φοβουμένων τὸν κύριον,
μετὰ τῶν μελετώντων ὃ ἔλαβον διάσταλμα ῥήματος ἐν τῇ καρδίᾳ.

10:3ff. the deeper meaning of the dietary laws is explained, with several other commandments from Lev. 11 come up. In more detail, their content is as follows. One should not join those people who, like the pigs, only know their master in times of need (10:3) or, like the eagle, hawk, vulture and raven, do not want to laboriously get their livelihood (10:4). One should not, like the sea eels, polyps and cuttlefish, stay only in the depths of the sea, get stuck deep in vice (10:5) furthermore, one should not become like the hare through the sexual abuse of boys (10:6), like the hyena by fornication and seduction (10:7), like the weasel by unchastity (10:8). According to 10:10, the teaching of the dietary laws presented here also results from Ps. 1:1. David also had "the knowledge of the three same teachings": "David receives knowledge (γνώσι) of the same three teachings, and he says in a similar way: 'Blessed is the man who did not walk in the counsel of the wicked', as the fish also walk in darkness through the depths, 'and did not enter the path of sinners', like those who sin like the swine, fearing the Lord only for appearances, and did not sit on the seat of the rogues, like the birds, like birds lying in wait for prey." When Barnabas writes of three doctrines (10:1. 9:10), he certainly refers to the beings belonging to the three animal kingdoms; for the three propositions in Ps. 1:1, he separates one from the other precisely for the purpose of giving one of

---

μετά τών μελετώντων ο ελαβον διάσταλμα ρή¬ματος έν τή καρδία. διδαιώμα is ἅπαξ λεγόμενον. The word is probably formed from διαστέλλομαι = I arrange and points to the preceding εντολή and the following parallel δικαιώματα (see Müller p. 255). Some derive the word from διαστέλλω = I split, distinguish. You will find a partial allusion to the Aristeas letter (published by Mendelsohn–Wendland, "Aristeae ad Philocratum epistula" Lpz. 1900; translated by Wendland in Kautzsch, Apocr. and Pseudep. des Λ. T. II. S 1 ff. cf. esp. p. 17 f.). Aristeas chap. 37: τὸ γάρ διχηλενειν και διαστίλλειν οπλής ουνγας σημείον εστι τον διαστίλλειν εκαστα τών πράξεων επ! τὸ καλώς εχον ... μετά διαστολίς ἅπαντα επιτελεῖ προς δικαιοσίνην αναγάάε τώ σημειοῦσ & α διά τούτων, ετι δι π π ά ά νἱλρώπονς ὁεστάλμεδα. Others also find a reference to Philo, de concupiscentia chap. 5: ἀλλ' ουδέν, ιός ἴοικεν, δηελος ἡ τών νοημάτων βέβαια κατάληιἵΐς, εἰ μὴ προσγένοιτο διαστολή τούτων καί Αιαίρεσις εις τε αἱ'ρεσιν ών γρή καί φυγήν τών εναντίων, ἡς τὸ διχηλονν σύμβολον (p. 107) . The second meaning of διάσταλμα is followed by the Latin: distinctum sermonem. Also Riggenbach p. 16 translated: difference of the word. Harnack p. 48 f. explains the word in question: Alludit auctor ad Iudaeorum et Christianorum differentiam, while Funk p. 71 remains undecided: verti potest praeceptum aut differentia. Völter p. 456 writes of the "distinction teachings" and Veil translates: "Cling to them ... who meditate in their hearts on the difference in doctrine." However, the fact that Barnabas did not think of the term διάσταλμα when he used the expression διχηλίύειν, results from the fact that of the two predicates διχηλοίς and μαρυχώμενος he initially only explains the latter and only deals with the former when he asks the question: τί δε το διχηλούν:

the three thoughts to one of the three animal kingdoms, respectively, or a creature taken from the same.[172]

After discussing the forbidden foods, Barnabas also gives an interpretation of the commandment: "You shall eat all ungulates and ruminants."[173] In μαρνκώμενος and δίχηλούς he finds a special moral teaching pronounced in each case: "Join those who fear the Lord, take to heart the decreed word that they have received,[174] preach and observe the orders of the Lord, know that contemplation (according to the teachings of the Lord) is a work of joy, and regurgitate the word of the Lord. But what does the two–hoofed ungulate mean? That on the one hand the righteous man walks in this world and on the other hand awaits the holy eternity (10:11)." At the conclusion of the chapter, it should also be noted that the ears and hearts of those who have an understanding of the Mosaic dietary laws are circumcised. "To do this, he circumcised our ears and hearts so that we could understand these things. But of those who did not properly understand the commandments of Moses, it has already been said in 10:9 that they accepted them "according to the sensuality of their flesh, as if it were food". So there were ignorant people who only understood these laws literally because their sensuality did not allow them to accept the moral teachings contained in the dietary laws.

d) The Water (Chap. 11).

The new section is thus introduced: "Let us examine whether the Lord was concerned to give revelations about the water and the cross!" While in the previous section the author assumed that Jesus was given vinegar and gall to drink, in chapters 11 and 12, in which the theme begun in chapter 5 is continued and concluded, following the Cross of Christ and the fact that water flowed from the side wound at Christ's suffering, teachings are given which pertaining to life, and refuting those thoughts which could be held against the observance of moral teachings. Chapter 11 is about the water, Chapter 12 is about the Cross. For this classification, 11:8 is not an obstacle. Although reference is already made here to a model of the

---

[172] Cf. 1. Jo. 5:6: οὗτός ἐστιν ὁ ἐλθὼν δι᾽ ὕδατος καὶ αἵματος, Ἰησοῦς Χριστός. In Luke 12:50 the suffering of Christ himself is called baptism.

[173] In general, however, baptism is understood under the water in the various places of the chapter.

[174] LXX reads Sion instead of Sinai. Harnack p. 50 supposes that Barnabas with special intention calls Sinai instead of Sion: probare enim voluit montem Sinae aquarum i. e. baptismi expertem esse. He seems, therefore, to find in the quotation a tendency pronounced against the Mosaic law. But the Prophet says, as the question particle μή shows, just that the mountain is not waterless.

Cross, the discussion on the Cross announced in 11:1 is only to be found in chapter 12. Occasional remarks about the cross can also be found already in 8:1 and 9:8.

Chapter 11 is about the water, chapter 12 about the cross. 11:8 is not an obstacle for this classification. Although an example of the cross is already pointed out here, the discussion about the cross announced in 11:1 can only be found in chapter 12. Occasional comments about the cross can also be found in 8:1 and 9:8.

First of all, in 11:1a the author speaks only in general terms of the water, without specifying it in more detail. However, it is not difficult to understand that there is a difference in the context. The connection of ὕδωρ with σταυρός and the whole train of thought of chapters 5–12, according to which the author likes to link his teachings to individual moments from the suffering of Jesus, are reminiscent of the Jo. 19:34 mentioned an incident according to which "one of the soldiers pierced his side with a lance, and immediately blood and water came out".[175] However, the author does not speak explicitly and unequivocally about the water of the Lord's side wound. It is less the text than the context that demands this interpretation of τό νόωρ.

The explanation of Chapter 11 will be based on the assumption that this interpretation is intended by Barnabas. If then, precisely on the basis of this presupposition, the same thoughts that are already well known from previous chapters recur in detail in the chapter, then the correctness of that presupposition is confirmed. And in fact, under this premise, we again encounter in chapter 11 the same teachings that have already been presented to readers earlier. These teachings of the chapter are: 1. God foreknew and foretold how the power of evil would be revealed in the suffering of the Lord: 11:1–3. 2. Christ triumphs over the power of evil: 11:4 and 5:3. The Christian will also become master over them: 11:6–8:4. After cleansing himself of sins, the Christian should manifest his Christian attitude in active love: 11:9–11. The last three teachings are introduced with the same formula καὶ πάλιν λέγει ὁ προφήτης (4), καὶ πάλιν ἐν ἄλλῳ προφήτῃ λέγει (6), καὶ πάλιν ἕτερος προφήτης λέγει (9).

11:1–3. — The first of the four teachings is proven to be taken from Jer. 2:12, 13 and Is. 16:1, 2. Barnabas himself gives 11:1b the purpose of the two passages of the prophets only with the meager words: "Concerning the water it is written to Israel that they will not accept the washing that cleanses them from sins, but will build for themselves."

---

175 Weiss P. 30: As punishment for the fact that Israel had left the living God, Jerusalem had been destroyed, or, as the Prophet says, the nest had been taken away from the little ones. In order to be able to find such thoughts, which should be peculiar to the whole original step, Weiss explains 11:1 and 4, and also parts of n, 8:9, 11 for interpolated.

Under the assumption that this water is that of the side wound[176] of Jesus, it is to be proven by the two quotations that Jesus will wash away sins in his suffering by shedding water, but an evil power will resist this grace in selfishness. — Jesus, from whose side wound water flows, is now referred to by Jeremias as a "living spring". Isaias points to him with the words: "Is my holy mountain Sinai a barren (waterless) rock?"[177] According to Jeremias, the evil power that opposes the grace of salvation are those who "left the living spring and made themselves a watery pit of death". According to Isaias they are like the "young birds which fly away after the nest is taken away."[178]

11:4 & 5. — In the long run the power of the evil one cannot harm Christ. This is the content of the prophetic words quoted in 11:4 and 5. The victory of the Savior over the hostile forces is not pronounced indistinctly in them. Barnabas contents himself with communicating Is. 45:2, 3 and 33:16–18. Barnabas, who is always in a hurry, saves himself from having to interpret its meaning. The first passage of Isaiah reads: "I will go before you and I will level mountains and crush iron gates and break iron bars, and I will give you secret, hidden, unseen treasures, so that they may know that I am the Lord God."

While in the two previous quotations from the prophets, according to the explanation given by Barnabas himself 11:1b, the self–confident power of evil was announced, the purpose of these words is to show the limitations of the evil power compared to the glory of Jesus. The power hostile to God is compared to mountains, iron gates and iron bars. The glory of God is manifested by the fact that he levels the mountains, breaks down the gates and bars. But this is revealed even more after the destruction of these powers in the fact that the Lord will then freely distribute the treasures that previously had to be kept hidden from the influences of

---

[176] Müller p. 262 explains at 11, 4: "These hidden and locked treasures in the mountains are the water sources hidden in the rock, the baptism." However, if it is about the treasures, since they are hidden in the mountains, one might think of water sources, because previously there is talk of a "not desolate rock" and immediately afterwards of the water in the cave of a strong rock. Hefele believes that the effects of the divine water of baptism were described to dali through the Isaiah passage. "The Prophet, more precisely Christ proclaimed through the Prophet: I, place to bear in. Weill is more cautious in the explanation. He sees "in the θησαυροὺς σκοτεινούς, ἀποκρύους, ἀοράτους a somewhat mysterious allusion to baptism." But he hesitantly makes this statement. He thinks that if one wants to find out any reasonable meaning in the context, there is nothing else left, and points out that "we have to meet our demands for a really striking interpretation of the OT Proverbs have to cut down a little" (p. 29)."

[177] Cf. 7:9

[178] Cf. 8:2 εἶτα οὐκέτι ἁμαρτωλῶν ἡ δόξα.

evil.[179] In the other place Isaias now announces: "You will dwell in a high cave in a strong rock. And their water is reliable. You will see the King with glory, and your soul will meditate on the fear of the Lord."

This prophecy, too, stands in contrast to the one prophesied after 11:2 and 3, i.e., In contrast to the gloomy picture of history, it reveals the end–historical eternal glory. The power of Jesus is compared to the strong rock in whose protection man will dwell. As Christ was called a rock not desolate in 11:3, so he is now called a strong rock. If the water is described as reliable, it should be said that it never dries up, that it brings lasting happiness. In the mouth of Barnabas is the meaning of these prophetic words: the water that had to flow, since the Lord succumbed to the hostility of an evil power on the cross, nevertheless brings strength and victory against the enemy. When water is described as reliable, what is meant is that it never runs dry and that it brings constant happiness.

In the mouth of Barnabas is the meaning of these prophetic words: the water that had to flow when the Lord succumbed to the hostility of an evil power on the cross nevertheless brings strength and victory against the enemy. The glory of the Lord and the awe of Him that Isaias speaks of is in contrast to the selfish, high–handed behavior of the Lord's enemies, of which it was prophesied according to Barnabas 11:1–3.[180]

11:6–8. — Barnabas presents the words Ps. 1:3–6 for instruction. The righteous man is compared there to a tree planted by streams of water, which bears [181]fruit in its season, and whose leaves do not fall off. The sinner, on the other hand, is like the dust. "Therefore, the wicked will not stand in judgment, and sinners will not stand in the counsel of the righteous; for the Lord knows the way of the righteous, and the way of the wicked will be lost." If we compare the content of these words of Psalms with what was taught in Barnabas 11:4 and 5, it follows: like the Lord himself, the righteous are not constantly subject to the power of sinners, a time of glory is coming for them, as for the Lord.

---

[179] Many people think of Soph. 3:19: θήσομαι αὐτοὺς εἰς καύχημα καὶ ὀνομαστοὺς ἐν πάσῃ τῇ γῇ

[180] Under γή τὸν Ἰσραώβ, or, τῦ σκεῦος τοῦ πνεύματος αὐτοῦ some understand the flesh of Christ (on the cross) e.g. B. Müller p. 268, Harnack p. 52, Funk p. 74 or the mystical body of the Lord, "the baptized humanity, which is the body of Christ, in which his spirit lives and works" (Völter p. 441), " "Christ revealing himself in human hearts that are reconciled to God through his death on the cross and water baptism and transforming them into temples of God" (Veil in Hdb. z. d. N.T. Apkr. p. 222).

[181] Shouldn't this be a reminder of Jesus' right side wound?

This teaching in this form again only follows from a comparison of the Bible passages used by Barnabas. The author does not express them in this particular way after the words of the Psalm; it seems to him to be superfluous. However, following the quotation from Psalm 1, he emphasizes that the cross and salvation belong together. He writes: "Pray, take care that he has mentioned the water and the cross at the same time!" And he adds in an explanatory way: "Blessed are those who have placed their hope on the cross and have descended into the water." Barnabas also gives the further teaching in 11:8 that as the tree bears fruit "in its season", so the righteous will only receive his reward later, and that, as the tree already now bears its leaves, which it does not lose, so also every word that comes out of the mouth of the righteous in faith and love already serves for the conversion and hope of many.

11:9–11. — After it has been shown that the work of evil was foreseen by God himself, but also that his final defeat was also predicted by him, there is a call for moral conduct in the Spirit of the Lord. Just as in chapter 6 the commandment to enter the promised land flowing with milk and honey was the reason for the author to encourage moral renewal, so the probably apocryphal words also serve him for moral instruction: "And it was the land of Jacob that was praised more than all countries."– Barnabas himself thus explains this quote: "He (the Prophet) praises the vessel of his Spirit." Understanding of this explanation is given by the introduction of the missive. The same speaks of the spirit (πνεύματος) of the readers and of what is still necessary for this. Their spirit is praised, is pleasing; but for full joy and full glory, the perfection of gnosis, a more abundant exercise of love, is still lacking. Also because of joyful acts of love, the author would like to be able to praise His own loved ones. Since he now praises "the vessel of the Spirit" of Jacob with the intention of setting an example for the readers to imitate, he praises in "the vessel" that about Jacob which he wishes His own people to add to their "spirit".

Thus, "vessel of the Spirit" is the activity and manifestation of the Spirit.[182] 11:10 Barnabas quotes Ezech. 47:1 –12: "And there was a river that was going to the right,– and lovely trees came out of it; and whoever eats of them will live forever."[183] According to the clarification given by Barnabas himself, these words teach that even if we descend into the water full of the filth of sin, we still leave it "with

---

[182] ος αν, φησίν, ἀκοναη τούτων λαλουμένων καί πιστῖυση, ζηοεταί τον ἴίώνα. Veil: "Whoever hears this proclamation and believes in it...."

[183] Perhaps Barnabas already had the idea that Christ's side wound was the source of sacramental grace through the water flowing from it. It was already widespread in the 4th and 5th centuries (Ambrose, Augustine, Chrysostom and others). We encountered a similar idea as early as the 2nd century with Apollinaris of Hierapolis. In one of the surviving fragments he writes of Jo. 19:34: ἁ ὁνο πάλιν καθάρσια, ἰχίωρ καί αἱμα, λόγον και πνεύμα (v. Otto, Corpus apolog. Christian. Vol. IX, p. 487). ,

fruits in our hearts and fear and hope in Jesus in the spirit," and that everyone who hears about these fruits and then becomes a believer attains eternal life.[184] Apparently, this declaration contains an invitation to bear fruit in the heart, i.e.,to do good works.

When explaining chapter 11, I started from the premise that ὕδωρ in 11:1 means the water of Jesus' side wound. The premise had been based on the connection of ὕδωρ with σταυρούς as well as on the train of thought in the previous chapters. However, the correctness of the same is also confirmed by the fact that initially 11:2–5 becomes fully understandable only under that condition. If — as it usually happens — baptism is understood by ὕδωρ, then neither the words of the prophets in 11:3, nor the statements against the hostile powers in 11:4 fit properly into chapter 11.

In verses 8 and 11, however, there is talk of descending into the water, that is, a rather clear reference to the baptismal bath. But this does not contradict my view of ὕδωρ in verses 1–5. For while this first section of the chapter speaks of the contempt, suffering and glory of Jesus, the second part of the chapter teaches about the lot of sinners and the righteous and about the way of active love, which . . . leads the righteous to eternal glory. But the fact that baptism is mentioned in a teaching on the subjective appropriation of the glory achieved by the objective facts of salvation is understandable and very obvious, since it had already been written about water before. The purifying water of the Lord's side wound had to be reminiscent of the cleansing water of baptism[185] for the purpose that Barnabas pursued in 11:6– 11.[186] It follows from 11:7 and 9 that even 11:6–11 does not merely aim to teach

---

[184] In Zeitschrift für wiss. Theol. 1871, p. 341 H Holtzmann holds the thought of the water of the side wound of Christ in chapter 11 was completely excluded: "Before that, a longer discussion περὶ τοῦ ὕδατος καὶ περὶ τοῦ σταυροῦ; had been opened, without the author having somehow felt the temptation, by virtue of such an obvious combination to the Johannine slogan, ὕδωρ καί αἷμα (Jo. 19:34). But it is clear that Barnabas did not even know the sting through the side from which water and blood flowed; otherwise it would not have been able to please him, from Ps. 22, 21 (Chap. 5)' to prove that there is no stabbing weapon (ῥομφαία is LXX 2. Sam; 23:8) may touch on Christ." But Barnabas only wants to explain 5:15 that Christ did not fall by the sword, i.e.,that he died on the cross. But only white has become quite aware of the difficulties arising from the assumption that baptism is to be taught from the OT in chapter RL. However, this consciousness again gives him the desired reason to let the interpolator appear, which only depends on finding all the details of the NT history in the OT in advance.

[185] 4 Esdras 4:33: Et respondi et dixi: quomodo et 'quando haec? — 5:5: et de ligno sanguis stillabit. — Perhaps Barnabas was also referring to Job 14:7: ἔστιν γὰρ δένδρῳ ἐλπίς ἐὰν γὰρ ἐκκοπῇ ἔτι ἐπανθήσει καὶ ὁ ῥάδαμνος αὐτοῦ οὐ μὴ ἐκλίπῃ

[186] Compare 11:8b and my comment on it.

about baptism or to give prophecies about it, citing the same results from 11:7 and 9 it follows that both verses have absolutely nothing to do with baptism.[187]

e) The Cross (Chap. 12).

Barnabas starts from the cross (of Christ) in chapter 12. If this chapter is considered on its own, the content and meaning of it is again not clear enough. But let us take into account what has emerged as the basic idea of chapter 5:1–13, the introduction to the entire section of the epistle about Jesus' suffering! It is the same, as it turned out: "The suffering of Jesus warns against sin and teaches that the struggle against the power of evil is not fruitless, that with perseverance, despite various, seemingly insurmountable obstacles, it must eventually lead to victory, since the highest development of the evil power could only humiliate the Savior for a certain time and to a certain degree." These same thoughts recur here as in the previous chapter. But instead of pronouncing them clearly, the author by and large just strings together some OT Biblical passages and only partially states their meaning in a few short remarks.

12:1. — The cross and the fate of the crucified one are already foretold in the Old Covenant. Barnabas quotes from 4. Esdras. 4:33 and 5:5 the following passage: "And when will this be completed? This is what the Lord says: when the wood will be cut down and raised up, and when blood will drip from the wood."[188]

12:2 & 3. — Taking into account the aforementioned, previously known intentions of the writer, the OT narrative, which is used in 12:2 and 3, to prove the purpose that the cross is actually a means of helping the good to victory. Barnabas reports that in the midst of the dangers of war, Moses, on God's instructions, in order to depict the cross and the crucified one, went to an elevated position formed

---

[187] πυγμή (H S) = πυγμαχία, the fist fight (Güdemann, Relig. Stud. P. 124; Hilgenfeld p. 110; Harnack p. 54; Funk p. 75; Völter p. 445; Veil in NT Apkr. p. 160). Hefele p. 97 reads instead of πυγμή: πήγη = πάγη, the hill; "Moses now placed shield on shield in the middle of a hill." Riggenbach p. 17: "Now Moses puts one piece of weapons around the other in the middle of the pile." — Müller p. 275 objects to Hilgenfeld: "Although in the classics πυγμή should be said of fistfighting, fistfighting is never generally said for fighting, μάχη . . . The simplest way is to take πηγμή in the meaning πήγμα, scaffolding, which fits best into the context; the shields placed on top of each other (ἐν ἐφ ὁπλού) formed a scaffolding. However, the form πηγμή may not be proven further. . ." Not only this last sentence alone speaks against this view. It should also be noted that the author deliberately speaks of a hand–to–hand fight, not of a fight in general. And further, it is not clear what the assertion should mean: on a scaffold already formed by shields, shield is still placed on shield.

[188] πάλιν Μωϋσῆς ποιεῖ τύον τοῦ Ἰησοῦ, ὅτι δεῖ αὐτὸν παθεῖν, καὶ αὐτὸς ζωοποιήσει (12:5)

by shields placed one on top of the other, stretched out his hands and thereby helped His followers to victory (Ex. 17:8 et seq.).[189]

At that time, Barnabas notes, the people of Israel were reminded that they had been handed over to death and the hardships of war because of their sins, but that the hope of the cross and the crucified One permanently delivered them from the hardships of war. Those who do not put their trust in the cross have to fear the loss of their life. Barnabas writes in 12:2b: τίθησιν οὖν Μωϋσῆς ἓν ἐφ᾽ ὅπλον ἐν μέσῳ τῆς πυγμῆς. The last expression, not used in the Bible, has a special meaning for the author. He wants to say: even if we are in the midst of the struggle of sufferings and afflictions, in the evil days of the present, and the power of the enemy, "the perfect stumbling block (4:3)" presses in on us and afflicts us like the enemy in a close fist fight,[190] we don't need to despair as long as we only put our hope in the cross.

12:4–11, — While 12:2 and 3 was about the fate of the believers, here the fate of Jesus is discussed. On the cross, Christ surrenders himself to an evil power only in order to conquer it. This power is prophesied in Is. 65:2: "All day long I stretched out my hands against a disobedient people who opposed my righteous way." The story of the bronze serpent prophesies about the victory of Christ (Numbers 21:6 et seq.). The reason this narrative is cited is explicitly stated. It is to be taught that Jesus, represented in the bronze serpent, must be subject to the power

---

[189] Müller p. 277 does not refer to Jesus, "ον stands collectively, τοῦτον ον, ἕκαστον ον" ἀπολωλεκέναι has intransitive meaning and "does not refer to the death of Christ, but to those who were lost without him and the serpent". Only ἀπολώλεκα has transitive meaning, or is therefore the accusative object, and as such this relative can only refer to Jesus. Ζωοποιῆσαι remains without an acc.–obj., but this need not cause concern since the same verb is used absolutely in 12.7h. Riggenbach p. 18 follows Müller when he translates: "Once again Moses sets an example for Jesus that he must suffer and that he himself will bring to life the one whom they thought had perished." Through Muller's opinion and Riggenbach, the double opposition expressed in 12:5a is completely blurred. Barnabas emphasizes that Jesus suffers but also gives life, and that Jesus appears to perish, but the Jewish people actually perish. Harnack S, 55, Hilgenfeld p. 112, Völter p. 443 connect πίπτοντος τ. Ἰ. with Μωϋσῆς ποιεῖ τύον. But it is not reasonable to assume that a participle, separated from the associated thought by a longer interposed sentence and thus isolated without reason. Veil connects both the participle expression like ἐν σημείψ with Μ. ποιεῖ: "Another reference to Jesus, namely that that . . . gives Moses by a symbol on the occasion of the death of the Israelites."

[190] These words are not found in the Bible.

of suffering, and yet it is he who brings life,[191] and that Jesus will be believed to perish, while Israel is that which must be subject to him.[192]

The first teaching is expressed in 12:7. This view is not only reflected in this last sentence. It should also be noted that the author deliberately speaks the words of Moses to his people: "He (the serpent), although he himself is dead, can make him alive,"[193] to which Barnabas remarks in explanation: "Here again you will find the glory of Jesus;[194] for everything (lives) in him and for him." The purpose for which the narrative of the brazen serpent is mentioned, therefore, is to preach the victory and glory of the crucified One.

In 12:8–11, three more Bible passages are given to prove Christ's former final rule over the evil forces. The cross is no longer referred to in them. First, Barnabas quotes an order from Moses to Joshua, whose name already betrays God's intention to point out the coming Savior in everything. The words of Moses, according to Barnabas, are: "Take a book in your hands and write what the Lord says, namely, that the Son of God will exterminate the whole house of Amalek with the root in the last days."[195] The time determination for the extermination is missing in the traditional Bible texts. It is attached by Barnabas with special intention.

The significance of Amalek at this point arises "from the view of the Jews of that time, according to which Amalek, the first and constant enemy of Israel, was considered the root of the ancient serpent . . . It is called the evil enemy of Sammael, the shell of Amalek, or also the power of Amalek. Amalek is the head of the evil spirits and means Sammael himself."[196] The meaning of the quotation is thus: evil still has power at present, but at the end of days it will be broken, and the Son of God himself will emerge victorious in the battle and thereby reveal himself in his superhuman strength as the Son of God. "Behold, again, Jesus, not the Son of man, but the Son of God" (12:10).

The superhuman, divine power of Jesus, which provides a sure guarantee for the eventual subjection of the evil forces, is still proven against the objection that Christ is only the Son of David, with reference to that Psalm passage in which David refers to Christ as his Lord and announces the subjugation of his enemies under

---

[191] The δόξα, which Barnabas likes to talk about (8:2; n, 5; 12:7; n, 9), is not mentioned by Müller, Harnack, Funk in the indes vocabulorum.
[192] Cf. Ex. 17:14.
[193] Müller p. 28
[194] Hefele p. 101
[195] Hilgenfeld p. 114; Heydecke p. 35.
[196] LXX reads in accordance with the Hebrew texts: τῷ χριστῷ μου Κύριο. But even ancient Church fathers read κυρίῳ instead of Κύρῳ (Hieronymui in Isai. 45:1; Tertullian adv. Jud. 7, adv. Praxeam 11:28; C'prianus, ad Quir. 1, 21; Novatianus, de trin. 21).

the footstool of his feet (Ps. 109:1). It cannot be proved that Barnabas, with the quotation from Psalm 109, wants to turn against the Ebionites or against Judaizers in general. His intention is only to instruct those who take offense at the power of evil and despair of the victory of good. Because of the understanding of the teaching contained in the quotes from Psalms, Barnabas gives the Psalmist the predicate: συνίων τὴν πλάνην τῶν ἁμαρτωλῶν.

This is to say: David knows that the sinner goes astray and that his actions and doings lead to destruction, but that the one who takes Christ's side is certain of victory. The Psalmist's teaching is confirmed in 12:11 by Is. 45:1: "The Lord said to Christ my Lord,[197] whose right hand I have taken: Let the peoples obey him, and I will break the power of kings." After this quotation confirming the word of the Psalm, Barnabas explains: "See that David[198] calls him his Lord and not his Son."[199]

---

[197] Hefele p. 102, note 26: "We should add 'and Isaias', which may have remained in Barnabas's pen; or one must assume with Clericus that the words are καί πάλιν λέγει οὕτως Κυρίῳ? — διαρρήξω a later interpolation and Barnabas merely quoted the Psalm passage. The old Latin interpreter who set prophetae for Δαυείδ tried to help himself in a different way." White p. 37 considers the words Is. 45:1 to be an insertion by the interpolator, who, however, failed to "the conclusion of u must be corrected accordingly, in which now, almost comically, there is only talk of a saying from David." Völter, p. 446, also sees the Is. quote as a later, supplementary ingredient. The Isaias section alone has only the purpose , to explain the words of the psalm, for which reason in the end only David, not Isaias too, can be mentioned! Compare the strange way of quoting Mark 1:2, where the evangelist puts together a quotation from two abbreviated prophecies (from Mal. 3:1 and Is. 40:3), but only attributes the quote to Isaias as the older and greater prophet, whose saying was repeated and explained by the later Malachias.

[198] Müller p. 9 recognizes the basic idea of 12:8–11 as the teaching that Christ is Lord despite the cross, to bring appropriate relationship. With almost all of the explanations in 12:1–7 he finds merely a list of prophecies about the cross of Christ. Harnack denies any internal connection between 12:1–7 and 12:8–11 (p. LIX, note 7). — After deleting the "pure typologies," Weiss believes he can express the original idea of chapter 12 as "that according to the saying of God, the Jews in times of war and other hardships were referred to God and his salvation, but especially to hope in his messenger at the end of days, Jesus" (p. 33). The image in chapters, the life of the believers, is given a counter– image in chapter 12 in the description of the reasons for the downfall of the Israelite people (p. 34).

[199] Müller recognizes the basic idea of 12, 8-11 as the teaching that Christ is Lord despite the cross, p to bring appropriate relationship. With almost all of the explanations in 12:1-7 he finds merely a list of prophecies about the cross of Christ. Harnack denies any internal connection between 12, 1-7 and 12, 8-11 (p. LIX, note 7). — After deleting the "pure typologies," Weiss believes he can express the original idea of chapter 12 as "that according to the saying of God, the Jews in times of war and other hardships were referred to God and his salvation , but especially to hope in his messenger at the end of days, Jesus" (p. 33). The

Barnabas saw himself prompted to his writing by the fear of the power of evil (2:1). This was a great danger for the Christians to whom he addressed himself. The writer had to fear that, frightened and led astray by this, they would lose faith in the power and the victory of good, slacken in patience, perseverance and renunciation (2:2) and no longer gladly devote themselves to the works of love (1:6). He reaches into the treasure of the OT revelations, in order to give the believers a more perfect gnosis, to strengthen them in the moral struggle for good. He certainly served his purpose best by pointing out the τέλειον τῶν ἁμαρτιῶν (5:11), the time when even the Son of God became a victim of sinners, of that hostile power, through his suffering and cross, and by showing that Christ sacrificed himself only to become effective Lord over the "effective one" himself (2:1).

CHAPTER 4

THE COVENANT FOUNDATION, THE SABBATH CELEBRATION AND THE TEMPLE (CHAP. 13–16)

a) The Covenant Foundation (Chapters 13 and 14).

After Barnabas in Chap. 5–12, following the suffering of Jesus, taught the power of evil in this world and at the same time the final, eternal victory of good, he points to Chap. 13–16 on the OT Covenant Foundation, on the Sabbath celebration and the Temple of the OT Jews, in order to then teach about the true meaning of evil and to admonish for moral activity.

Just as the ancient sacrificial and fasting regulations educate people to be virtuous, the history of God's covenant also directly encourages good will and a moral lifestyle. Cape. 13 shows that God does not make his favor dependent on

picture in chapters, the life of the believers, is given a counter-picture in chapter 12 in the description of the reasons for the downfall of the Israelite people (p. 34).

external circumstances and does not make his covenant with the one who is physi-cally older. Chap. 14 teaches that fellowship with God is achieved through suffering and purity from sin.

13:1–7. — For the purposes mentioned, are described in Chap. 13 he brought three proofs of scripture. First of all, Gen. 25:21–23 is quoted, according to which Rebekah, after she had conceived, was taught by God that of the two sons she would give birth to, the elder must serve the younger. The same idea recurs in Genesis 48. Joseph brings his two sons Ephraim and Manasseh before his father Jacob and expects him to bless Manasseh as the firstborn; but Jacob blesses Ephraim because the older must serve the younger. Finally, in 13:7 the author re-minds us of the Word of God to Abraham: Behold, Abraham, I have made you the Father of the nations who believe in God in their foreskin" (Gen. 17:4 and 5). Through this declaration to Abraham, full knowledge was given.

14:1–9. — While in Chap. 13 it is shown only that old age and external circumcision have no meaning before God, the main idea follows in Chap. 14. This is introduced after S by the form ναι, ἀλλὰ ἴδωμεν.[200] ναί confirms the previous teaching of Chap. 13, ἀλλά points out to this counterpart a new, more important thought, which should now follow.[201] Chapter 14 teaches what prevents the cove-nant with God, and what conveys it. 14:1a: "Let us be clear about this, but let us see whether he has (really) given the covenant of which he swore to the fathers that he would give it to the people." From these words, some conclude that the purpose of the chapter is to reject the objection that God has not kept his promise to con-clude the covenant with Israel."[202] But it will become clear that the author is not primarily concerned with the fact of the covenant being concluded, but to prove how the covenant comes into being or is destroyed.

That is why Barnabas continues in 14:1 thus: "He gave it; but they were not worthy to receive it because of their sins." In 14:2 &3 he explains that although Moses had fasted for 40 days and nights and had received the tablets of the law, the people were not worthy of them because they had sinned and committed idolatry.[203] In 14:4 he again emphasizes why the people did not receive the covenant, in order to immediately conclude the question from it: "But in what way did we receive it?" The author himself replies that they received the covenant through the Lord him-self, namely, by the fact that he went into suffering for their sake. So the reason for

---

[200] ναι not found in H.

[201] As a rule, however, the teachings of the two chapters are not subordinated to one another as being equally important and having the same meaning.

[202] Ex. 24:18; 34:28; 31:18; 32:7–19; German 9:12–17. On the same narrative is Barn. 4:6–8 for other purposes. On the other hand, see Heydecke pp. 16 and 22–24; Völter S; 353 f.

[203] So Kayser p. 15; Heydecke p. 22; Harnack p. LIX.

acquiring the divine covenant lies in the suffering of the Lord. His suffering[204] acquires that which was denied to sinners.

In addition to the suffering of the Lord, the means by which the covenant is acquired is also the moral renewal made possible by the incarnation of the Lord. The covenant does not belong to those who fill up the measure of sins. This is the meaning of the words: the Lord "revealed himself, that they might fill up the measure of sins, and that we might receive the covenant through the Lord Jesus, who inherited it". Only after the Lord has redeemed our souls from darkness, already doomed to death and given over to the lawlessness of error, will he establish the covenant[205] in us through the Word and prepare for himself a holy people.

The three scriptures cited in the 14:7–9 teach that the one who is in possession of the covenant must be free from this. "Know therefore from what we have been redeemed!" calls Barnabas to his followers according to the first passage of Scripture Is. 42:6f. where it is said of the Redeemer that he is the light of the Gentiles, will open the eyes of the blind, free the bound from their bonds and those sitting in darkness from their prison. According to Is. 49:6f. will the Lord deliver us from darkness, according to Is. 61:1 f., etc., to free us from blindness and captivity. Blindness, captivity, darkness are to be regarded as designations of the sinful state, which makes everyone, like the Jewish people, unworthy of the covenant.[206]

b) The Sabbath Celebration (Chap. 15).

The teachings of Chap. 15 take place according to the commandment of the Sabbath celebration. The basic idea in this chapter is: just as God will celebrate his Sabbath and be able to observe a true day of rest when he has destroyed the world of evil at the end of time and handed over the wicked to punishment, so the Christian should also celebrate the Sabbath in the future once he has withdrawn from evil and made himself worthy of the divine promise by holiness and righteousness. The Sabbath rest consists in the cheerful possession of the good; it occurs when all the sufferings and hardships are overcome simultaneously with this temporality.

---

[204] ὑπομένειν.

[205] διάθηται ἐν ἡμῖν διαθήκην λόγῳ, λόγος cannot be explained as the personal Logos, as Weiss claims on p. 41. Jesus is already the subject of the sentence, λόγος is a means that the Lord uses to enter into a covenant with the individual. Is this perhaps intended to be a sacramental form? See p. 72, Anna. 1 quoted a word from Apollinaris of Hierapolis, according to which λόγος and πνεῦμα (= water and blood from Jesus' side wound) were considered means of cleansing. But perhaps τῆς πίστεως should be added to λόγῳ (cf. 16:9: ὁ λόγος αὐτοῦ τῆς πίστεως), so that the meaning would be: God makes a covenant with man when he professes faith in him.

[206] Cf. Jer. 17:24 and Ex. 31:13–17.

15:1–5. — First of all, the commandment to celebrate the Sabbath is emphasized by two scriptures. The first of these: "And purify the Sabbath of the Lord with clean hands and a pure heart," recalls Ex. 20:8 and Deut. 5:12. The second is: "If my sons keep the Sabbath, then I will show my mercy to them."[207] The commandment to keep the Sabbath holy is followed from 15:3 by an instruction about the meaning of the Sabbath based on Gen. 2:2:

"And in six days God made the works of his hands, and on the seventh day he finished them, and he rested thereon and sanctified it."[208] The six days are the six thousand years after which the Lord brings about the end of the universe (15:4). The rest on the seventh day refers to the happy time after the destruction of the power left to evil (15:5). At the conclusion of 15:5 it says: "Then on the seventh day he will rest in honor (καλῶς)." By καλῶς it is emphatically referred back to the preceding words: "If ... he has put away the time of the unlawful and judged the wicked"; it is emphasized once again by the adverb that the rest of the Lord is preceded by a reign of terror of evil, but that the former rest of God consists in the happy, complete victory over this tyrant and thus the suffering presence that goes to the heart of Barnabas and his readers (2:1; 4:3), one day it will be completely over.

When the author not only speaks of the cessation of the power of the unlawful and of the judgment of the wicked, but also writes that the Son of God will come to rest when he will have transformed the sun, moon and stars, he means to say that in the present time determined by the course of the present stars, no rest for God can yet be expected. The purpose of the quote Gen. 2:2, according to what has been said, the teaching is: a certain and limited rule (6000 years) is given to all evil and hostile things, which lasts as long as there is a time at all, but with the cessation of time it has passed.

15:6–9. — The application of this quote and its teaching to Christians follows in 15:6 and 7.[209] Just as Christ the Lord will only be able to keep his Sabbath in the future, the true Sabbath celebration and Sabbath rest will also come for Christians. Although holiness and justice are a necessary prerequisite for this celebration, a pure heart alone does not yet give the possibility of keeping the Sabbath rest. In fact, says the author, we are entirely in error if we believe that "someone can now sanctify the day which God has sanctified because he is pure in heart": εἰ οὖν ἦν ὁ θεὸς ἡμέραν ἡγίασεν νῦν τις δύναται ἁγίασαι καθαρὸς ὢν τῇ καρδίᾳ, ἐν πᾶσιν

---

[207] Barnabas: ἐν τῇ ἡμέρᾳ τῇ ἑβδόμῃ; LXX: ἐν τῇ ἡμέρᾳ τῇ ἕκτῃ. The Masoretic text, the Targum Onkelos, the Arabic Pentateuch of R. Saadia and the Vugata have the former reading. The Samaritan Pentateuch and the Peshitto agree with the LXX. See G. Hoberg „Die Genesis nach dem Literalsinn erklärt." ("Genesis explained according to the literal sense.") 2nd edition, Freiburg 1908.

[208] πέρας γέ τοι transfers the thought of Christ to Christians.

[209] καλῶς καταπαυόμενοι 15:7; cf. 15:5.

πεπλανήμεθα. Barnabas wants to say that we can only expect the Sabbath and full rest in honor[210] once the 6000 years, that is the period granted to evil, has expired,[211] just as according to Gen. 2:2 the Lord also only keeps the Sabbath after six days = 6000 years. His teaching is therefore: Anyone who wants peace and joy in this world does not know the entire world order (ἐν πᾶσιν πεπλανήμεθα).

In 15:7 a holy and pure life is now also demanded as a precondition for the beatitude of the eternal Sabbath: "Only then, when we ourselves are first sanctified, will we also be able to sanctify (the Sabbath). The sentence preceding these words summarizes both preconditions for the acquisition of Sabbath rest: "We will be able to sanctify (the Sabbath) in full rest when we will be able to do so, because we ourselves are justified, have received the promise, evil no longer exists (that is, the time of the reign of the evil one has expired), but everything is renewed by the Lord."[212] So that readers do not already expect the quiet and happy life of a true Sabbath celebration and do not take offense at the tribulations of the present, Barnabas also reminds us in 15:8 and Is. 1:13: "I don't like your new moons and Sabbaths."

The new moons and sabbaths or the "current Sabbaths" must only be over when the true Sabbath is to come for man, just as after 15:5 the sun, moon and stars must first be transformed when God is to enjoy his full rest. Hefele claims that the passage from Isaias is intended to "make the reader completely convinced" that Judaism, in contrast to Christianity, could not have the true Sabbath at all. However, it could not have the true Sabbath according to Is. 1:13, but the Christian Church

---

[210] Cr. 6:13: Ἰδού, ποιῶ τὰ ἔσχατα ὡς τὰ πρῶτα.

[211] Müller also claims that according to Barnabas the Jewish Sabbath celebration does not contradict the divine will and should have the meaning of a type (S, 302). Hevdecke p. 50: "Scriptor capitis XV. versuum 1–7 institutionem sabbati ratam agnoscit, spiritualem vero sabbati celebrations; postulate.

[212] The view is often held that Barnabas teaches in 15:9 that the Lord also ascended into heaven on the same Sunday on which he rose from the dead (e.g. Harnack p. 67 f.). But Barnabas only wants to say that the resurrection of Jesus was on a Sunday and the ascension was also on any Sunday. "But the opinion that the Ascension fell on a Sunday can also be found in later times, where conscious or unconscious ignoring of the canonical representations is out of the question, in connection with Church custom, the festival of Pentecost, which was always celebrated on a Sunday, was also celebrated as the Feast of the Ascension. Accordingly, that passage from Barnabas could at most give rise to the archaeological question as to whether a Christian Pentecost, which was also related to the Ascension, had already been celebrated back then" (Zahn, History of the N.T. Canon I. 2, p. 925). That the Ascension fell on a Sunday, or The Syrian "Doctrine of the Apostles" also teaches that it was celebrated at the same time as Pentecost. 2 and 9, as well as Eusebius, Vita Constant. IV, 64.

does not observe it either, since the true Sabbath only occurs after the Last Judgment.

Although Barnabas points to the true Sabbath with the words τὰ σάββατα οὐκ ἀνέχομαι, which is the eternal Sabbath celebration and promises and demands such a celebration for the future, it does not contradict the divine will expressed in the prophet's words if a Sabbath celebration corresponding to this temporality and imperfection is already observed on earth, and if Sabbath regulations are already issued for the present and such typical references to the hereafter are made. — If God, as 15:5 teaches, only enjoys his full and true rest after the last judgment, if therefore he now demands this rest and therefore he must also say of the whole history of the world, as long as it has not yet come to an end: οὐκ ἀνέχομαι, then no one will want to conclude from this that everything that man does here on earth is sin and violates the divine will. — What follows from this is that man's actions during his life on earth are imperfect and only in the afterlife is everything completely subject to the Divine will. ουκ ανέχομαι would therefore not be understood as a complete rejection and disregard of human history, but with regard to what the Lord has to expect after the resurrection of the dead, from a lower respect.

In the same way, the words τὰ σάββατα οὐκ ἀνέχομαι do not pronounce a Sabbath prohibition or a complete disregard for the Jewish Sabbath celebration, but that the Jewish Sabbaths are described as something inferior in comparison with the eternal Sabbath. The words "it is not the present Sabbaths that are pleasant to me, but the one that I have made, on which I will bring all things to rest, etc." (15:8b) are to be taken in the same sense as, for example, the words: it is not the present time that is pleasant to me, but the day that I have made . . . As a sign that the end of affliction and undisturbed happiness has only been granted in another world, the Christian celebrates after 15:81b and 9 only on the eighth day, because this means (as the beginning of a new week) marks the beginning of a new world.

This eighth day is a day of joy precisely because of the thought of the eternal happiness of the other world. "Therefore, we also celebrate the eighth day in joy." Since only the prospect of the future gives joy, it also has its good significance after 15:9, when Jesus rose from the dead on the eighth day and ascended to heaven on the eighth day. According to Hefele, the celebration of Sunday, of which 15:8 and 9 are mentioned, is also intended to prove that God does not want the Sabbath celebration. Just like the Sabbath, Sunday is only mentioned here as an example of a better, happier future. However, each of the two days exemplarily marks a different side of the coming, eternal happiness.

The Sabbath foreshadows rest and liberation from the hardships and sufferings of earthly life; Sunday, which opens a new week, foreshadows transformation and renewal in the afterlife. Since Barnabas speaks of the Christian Sunday celebration for this purpose, no tendency against the Jewish Sabbath celebration can be seen in 15:8 and 9. Rather, it is precisely through these verses that the Sabbath celebration even comes completely to its own right. For it is admitted that although the Sunday celebration is exemplary for the future and Sunday can never be celebrated on earth with full, true joy, nevertheless, after 15:8 and 9, the Sunday celebration should still be in order.

Why should Barnabas, despite the fact that the Sabbath rest can never be completely carried out on earth and the writer ultimately does not want to speak of the creation Sabbath and not of the Jewish Sabbath, but of the world Sabbath at the end of history, not also — the Jewish Sabbath rest want to tolerate regardless of their imperfection? Veil writes:[213] "The Jewish Sabbath celebration is also based on a misunderstanding of the Divine will, namely on the error that the Sabbath rest appointed by God refers to the seventh day of the week, while it refers to the seventh world day, i.e., the seventh millennium." If this explanation were correct, one would also have to be able to say: the Christian celebration of Sunday and the joy of Sunday are based on a misunderstanding of the Divine will, namely on the error that the joy promised by God to people is related to joys in this life and this time. Without wishing to criticize Jewish customs, Barnabas writes about the Sabbath celebration that marks the end of the world, the condemnation of evil, the eternal rest of the divine Lord and the justified.[214]

Whether the World Sabbath spoken of in chapter 15 is to be understood as the last thousand years of world history, as is almost universally assumed,[215] or whether the world Sabbath is already to be explained as the happy, eternal life,[216] is

---

[213] p. 112 Anm.

[214] N.T. Apkr. p. 146.

[215] Criticism of Judaism and its Sabbath celebrations can be found in Chap. 15 also: Kayser p. 16 f.; Hilgenfeld p. XXXII, Ap. V. p. 27; Weizsäcker p. 44; Riggenbach p. 25 and 27; Harnack p. 64; Funk p. XXVII f. Heydecke pp. 49–51, on the other hand, claims that only 15:8–9 is directed against the Jewish Sabbath celebration (cf. Theol. Literaturztg. 1876, col. 212). Völter p. 557 finds the Jewish Sabbath rejected, as long as he does not consider the chapter to be interpolated. According to Weiss p. 44, only 15:1–7 teaches a complete rejection of a Sabbath celebration on earth. Heydecke, Weiß and Völter deny Urbarnabas 15:8 and 9. White p. 44 finds a contradiction between 15:1–7 and 15:8–9, because there the rest of God took place in the 7th millennium, here in the 8th. But there is no mention of a 7th or 8th millennium, but only of the 7th and 8th days, to designate a different moment of eternal life.

[216] So from Hilgenfeld, Ap. V. p. 28, note 36; Thalhofer in Theol. Literaturblatt 1869, col. 542; Müller pp. 502, 306, 315; Heydecke p. 49 and 51; Harnack pp. 65 and 67; Sprinzl p. 222, note 5; Funk p. 84; Army p. LXXIII. Tooth, business d. N.T. Canons I. 2, p. 955: "However deeply rooted in older Jewish views and traditions the doctrine of a thousand–year reign of Christ at the end of days may be, it is difficult to imagine that Barnabas would

not clear in more detail. The author does not take a definite position either on one side or on the other. He does not care how to imagine the happy life of the future in more detail. He has only one interest in showing that the perfect life must necessarily be preceded by the sufferings and tribulations of this world and the purification and justification. Does not kick — as Weizsäcker claims (p. 48 f.) — that a chiliastic idea emerges very weakly because the great weight that the millennium empire is said to have had in the apocalypse until recently, would now have to have been broken by the destruction of Jerusalem and by the complete renunciation of the view of its holiness, the enlivening image for the thoughts would be missing and the expectation would therefore be directed all the more strongly only towards the ἄλλος κόσμος.

A chiliastic interpretation of the chapter also encounters some difficulties. "If the author really accepted a thousand–year kingdom of Christ on earth, why has he never explicitly spoken of it anywhere in the whole epistle, while he pronounces the six–thousand–year duration of the present world so clearly and bluntly and repeatedly? Why did he let a teaching slip through between the lines in such a way, which had to seem very comforting to him after all?"[217]

c) The Temple (chap. 16).

In chapter 16 Barnabas teaches: The human heart should become a temple pleasing to God. Chapter 15 had been initiated in the following form: Ἔτι οὖν καὶ περὶ τοῦ σαββάτου γέγραπται. Accordingly, chapter 16 begins: Ἔτι δὲ καὶ περὶ τοῦ ναοῦ ἐρῶ ὑμῖν. The previous chapter is closely followed by chapter 16 by two thoughts. The designation of the heavenly temple of God as τόπος τῆς καταπαύσεώς (16:2) is reminiscent of 15:5: τότε καλῶς καταπαύσεται. According to 15:8 and 9, the Sunday celebrated by Christians as the first day of a new week indicated the new creation after the end of world history; according to 16:6 et seq., the prophecy that the temple of God will be built after the end of a week indicates that the heart of man should be renewed and through the renewal made into the temple of God.

The first part of the chapter (16:1–5) teaches mainly about the Jewish temple, the second part (16:6–10) about the human heart as a temple.

16:1–5. — Barnabas speaks of the Jerusalem temple and its significance. He begins with the words: "But I will also talk to you about temple (and indeed I

---

have given this doctrine as casually as he did He should have treated it here as a self–evident prerequisite for Christians if he did not recognize Johannine prophecy among his readers."
[217] Cf. Kayser, p. 129.

will tell you)[218], how the unfortunate ones put their hope in the building by mistake[219], as if it were the dwelling of God, and not in their God, who had created them." It must not be concluded from this that "God has expressly rejected the construction of the temple"[220], or he does not want "any temple service".[221]

Barnabas does not deny the divine order of the construction of the temple. As little as in the previous chapters, he takes a principled stand against Judaism and its religious institutions in general. He only reproaches historical Judaism for not having recognized the true meaning of the construction of the Temple, for having attached too much value to it out of insufficient understanding of the divine essence.

Just as in the earlier chapters, he does not take a principled stance against Judaism and its religious institutions in general. He only reproaches historical Judaism for not recognizing the true meaning of the building of the temple and for attaching too much value to it due to an insufficient understanding of the divine essence.

He wants to rebuke a false, almost pagan conception of the nature of God, which was connected with an incorrect conception of the meaning and value of the temple. This follows from 16:2a: "For almost like the Gentiles, they assigned him his sanctuary in the temple."[222] This means that God, who calls the universe his own, is robbed of his infinity through Jewish delusion and in a delimited sanctuary was restricted and narrowed down, as if he were only a gift of consecration, that certain Jews approached pagan ideas of God, insofar as they dragged the infinite down to the finite.

---

[218] Criticism of Judaism and its Sabbath celebration take place in Chap. 15 also: Kayser p. 16 f.; Hilgenfeld p. XXXII, Ap. V. p. 27; Weizsäcker p. 44; Riggenbach p. 25 and 27; Harnack p. 64; Funk p. XXVII f. Heydecke p. 49–51, on the other hand, claims that only 15:8–9 are directed against the Jewish Sabbath celebration (cf. Theol. Literaturztg. 1876, Sp. 212). Völter, p. 557, finds the Jewish Sabbath rejected, unless he considers the chapter to be interpolated. According to White p. 44 if only 15:1–7 a complete glorification of Christ at the end of days may be justified, it is difficult to think that Barnabas should have treated this teaching as casually as he does here, as a prerequisite for Christians, if he did not know that the Johannine prophecy was recognized among his readers."

[219] Braunsberger p. 219 f. But despite these concerns, he finds an allusion to chiliasm in chapter 15 (p. 218).

[220] In his succinct way, Barnabas writes: ἔτι ds καί περί τον nnv ἐρῶ ιμίν, πῶς . . . Compare 9:1a.

[221] Hilgenfeld, Ap. V. p. 28.

[222] Riggenbach p. 25. Most expositors believe that there is a need to combat Judaism or Judaizing sects.

In order to prepare the main idea of the chapter, that the human heart should be a dwelling of God "in glory", the quoted words teach the only relative importance of the Jewish temple.[223] That no absolute value can be assigned to the construction of the temple, Barnabas also proves 16:2 by Is. 40:12 and 66:1, according to which God dwells in a temple that is not measured by human measures, but includes heaven and earth. To this proof from the words of the prophets, he adds a reference to the story that is known to the readers. He writes at the end of 16:2: "You have realized (ἐγνώκατε) that their hope is vain."

With this the writer wants to say to the readers: What the Prophet teaches, that the temple in Jerusalem cannot be the true, only dwelling of God, that therefore the hope of certain Jews was vain, you already know enough anyway. The perfect ἐγνώκατε says: Your knowledge of the matter is not only based on the present instruction of the author and the reference to the prophecy, the knowledge had already become your own in a different way before. The addressees had acquired their knowledge as eyewitnesses to the catastrophe in Jerusalem or as victims of the hard–fought inhabitants of the Jewish capital.

The true meaning of the Jewish temple is known to you, because you already know the end of its history.[224] In 16:3, the writer returns to the OT prophecies with the opening words πέρας γέ τοι πάλιν λέγει. By using them this time to teach that the Temple must be destroyed, he wants to give further proof of the importance to be attached to the Jewish Temple. Is. 49:17 and a quote from Enoch serve this purpose. The passage, which is reminiscent of Enoch 89:56 and 66, reads: "And in the last days it will come to pass that the Lord will condemn the flock of his pasture, and its fold, and its tower, to destruction."[225] In these apocryphal words, Barnabas 16:5 foretells the downfall of "the city, and the temple, and the people of Israel".

The other prophetic passage says according to Barnabas: "Behold, those who destroyed this temple will also build it up."[226] Here not only the end of the

---

[223] ἀφιέρωσαν αὐτὸν ἐν τῷ ναῷ. Many people only take ἀφιεροίν in the meaning of ἱερούν. But the compound means more; according to Henricus Stephanus, Passow and others. = to expiate, cleanse or consecrate (= ἀναιδέναί). Müller S, 323: "The verb seems to have been deliberately chosen here in order to represent God in the temple as a consecration gift, as a figurant, so to speak." Cf. the translation by Veil.

[224] Sprinzl p. 186, note 2: "The polemic is not directed . . . against the external worship of God as such, but against a purely external worship without an internal holy disposition.

[225] L does not quite understand Barnabas' intention when he translates: unde cognoscitis, quia vana spes est illorum (V reads γνῶτε). Veil's translation does not give the meaning of the passage either: "There you see that their hope is vain."

[226] Enoch, chap. 89:56 reads according to G. Beer's translation (Kautzsch, Apokr. u. Pseudep. d. A. T. II. P. 294): "I saw that he (the Lord of the sheep) left that house and their

temple is predicted, but also the reconstruction has already been pointed out.[227] The writer associates with the quotation a peculiar remark in 16:4: "Namely, because they were at war, (the temple) was destroyed by the enemies. But now they themselves, having submitted to the enemies, will again rebuild it." Barnabas wants to emphasize the reasons for the fate of the temple: the waging of war by the Jews brought the destruction of the temple, while, on the contrary, it is precisely their submission to the enemies that ensures its existence.

What, then, is Barnabas's purpose in this strange juxtaposition? How does it fit into the thought process of the Scripture and especially of the chapter? Is it the writer's only concern to establish with greater emphasis the fact of the destruction of the temple and its reconstruction by referring to secondary historical circumstances? This would be possible if the readers doubted the facts themselves. But the destruction is fully certain to them and to those who hold the authority of the Scriptures of the Old Testament, as the whole epistle shows, to keep the Old Testament Scripture so firmly, a reconstruction on the basis of quotation 16:3 will undoubtedly be. It is not for the author to do it in order to emphatically emphasize two facts and their historical statement. He has an interest other than historical.

In waging war and in submission to the enemies, the teacher of the γνῶσίς sees: more, a deeper thought. But he leaves it to the readers to guess his intentions and thoughts. But he has already offered them the opportunity to do so. Already he has in 16:2 distracted their gaze from the historical temple building erected by human hands, from a spatially delimited dwelling of God. Therefore, in 16:3 and 4, since he writes about reconstruction, their thoughts must necessarily be directed to a spiritual temple.[228] And when it says: "As subjects of the enemies they will build

---

tower and all of them 89, 66: "The lions and tigers ate and devoured the greater part of those sheep, and the wild boars ate with them; and they set fire to that tower and destroyed that house." Veil writes in Hdb. d. NT. Apocr. P. 227 on 16:5: "If with πάλιν ὡς ημελλεν etc. only a second point of evidence should be given that the Herodian Temple and the city of Jerusalem were actually destroyed according to divine prophecy, then § 5 ... It is very surprising that the author, who is otherwise familiar with the Gospel of Matthew, did not cite the Lord's Word, Matthew 24:2, instead of the apocryphal prophecy, probably taken from Enoch." But it contradicts the entire tendency of the epistle, in the main ideas N.T. to use places as evidence.

[227] Is. 49:17: καὶ ταχὺ οἰκοδομηθήσῃ ὑφ' ὧν καθηρέθης καὶ οἱ ἐρημώσαντές σε ἐκ σοῦ ἐξελεύσονται.

[228] Weiss p. 45: The quote 16:3 is contrasted with the quotes in 16:2, so that the problem that the author raises there is: "How does the Lord's promise agree with this condemnation of the temple?, according to which the destroyers will rebuild the Jerusalem temple?" Since the solution to this problem only occurs in 16:6 f., Weiss must see 16:5 (the Enoch quote) as an insertion of the interpolator, "the "I didn't understand the basics of the problem." —

the temple", the readers certainly found the moral teaching here: it is not by political greatness, not by external power that God is honored and that what certain Jews sought to achieve in vain is achieved, but by patiently enduring suffering.

16:4 could and had to remind us of the admonition repeatedly uttered earlier: the power of enemies or of evil must not give annoyance and fright to the good, he must not lose perseverance and patience because of them. After Barnabas had so emphatically and repeatedly demonstrated to the readers from the life of Je-sus that the Lord had entered into glory precisely through his suffering, the humil-iation among his enemies, it had to be obvious to them that he now wanted to explain that it will be precisely humiliation and suffering that will still make the promised temple construction possible.[229]

6–10. — In the first section of chapter 16, the writer had taught that the temple at Jerusalem could not be the true dwelling place of God, he had also said that the Jews will once again erect a true temple to God.[230] Now it is unnecessary to

---

According to Heydecke pp. 64–67 and Völter p. 358, 16:3 and 4 come from a revision of the letter.

[229] Several expositors believe that the Temple, which is to be built anew, must be understood as an external building and can therefore use 16:4 to determine the time of writing of the missive. Some find in the Temple to be rebuilt a mocking reference to the soon–to–be–built Jupiter temple in Aelia Capitolina, according to Lipsius in Schenkel's Bible Lexicon 1, 371 and in Jena Literarurztg. 1877 p. 21; Harnack, business d. old Christian Lit. II. 1. p. 423 ff.; Ladeuze p. 17 f.; Schürer, Gesch. of the Jewish People in the Age of J. Chr. 13 and 4 1901, p. 672 f. (but not in the first edition). Volkmar in Theol. Yearbook 1856 pp. 351 — 361, Journal for Science!. Theology 1861 p. 16 and otherwise claims that Barnabas thought of a new temple that the Jews hoped for, but which the Gentiles used for their own purposes. Still others are of the opinion that the writer had in mind a prospective temple intended for the Jews. This view is represented by Schürer, Lehrb. d. retest. Contemporary 1874, p. 355; Harnack, p. LXXII; A. Schlatter, Zur Topographie u. Geschichte Palästinas, 1893, p. 148 f.; the same, Die Tage Trajans und Hadrians, 1897, p. 61 ff.; Veil in Hdb. d. N.T. Apocr. P. 223 ff. Veil claims that this explanation of the passage in question offers the long–sought key to the entire Epistle of Barnabas. The entire tendency of the 16th chapter alone suggests that the writer wants to talk about the establishment of the spiritual temple in 16:4. In this sense, among others, are also expressed: Hefele p. 115 f. and 141; Hilgenfeld, Ap. V. p. 28 f.; Zeitschr. für wiss. Theol., 1858 p. 285, 1870 p. 116 f. and 1879 p. 140, B. ep.2 p. 119 fr.; Wieseler in Jahrbuch für deutsche Theol. 1870 p. 612 f.; Riggenbach p. 41 ff.; Krueger, Gesch. d. altchristl. Lit., p. 14; Funk in Theol. Qu. Sehr. 1897 pp. 623–633 and treatise, and investigation. II, p. 87 ff.; Bardenhewer, Geschichte d. alt– kirchl. Lit. I, p. 95.

[230] S writes 16:4: νυν καί αυτοί, καί οι... He is followed by Weizsäcker S 22; Müller p. 525; Harnack p. LXXII and 69 (but no longer in History of Old Christian Lit. II. 1. p. 424); Veil in Handb. to the N.T. Apkr. P. 224. The latter writes: The omission of the καί in the second

show him that and how the Christians to whom he is addressing are preparing a pleasing dwelling for God. The new section is introduced with request: "Let us examine whether there is a temple of God!" The prophetic word serves as proof of the existence of a true temple of God: "And after the completion of the week (i.e., after the dawn of a new time), a temple of God will be built in glory in the name of the Lord." A dwelling pleasing to God should be the heart of man. At first it was not a true temple of the Lord. "Before we became believers," it was "a temple actually built by hands," i.e., it was no better than the previously mentioned temple in Jerusalem, was not a temple in which God was worthily worshiped. The heart was a "transient and decaying dwelling", "full of idolatry and a habitation of demons".

It is often claimed that Barnabas could not turn to Jewish Christians at this point, but only to those who once did not believe in the one God and worshiped idolatry in the sense of polytheism.[231] Unbelief and idolatry alone are to be understood to mean living in sin, εἰδωλολατρεία is, as the author himself adds in an explanatory way, an action against God's commandments at all. The purpose of the expression is to teach that without a moral life there is no difference between a pagan and a Christian or a Jew.

The unbelief explained by idolatry is the lack of godly works.[232] A demon is to be understood as the "unclean spirit", of whom it is said in the Gospel that on

---

place was apparently intended to "replace a historical situation incomprehensible to the glossator with one known to him, namely that of the construction of Hadrian's Temple of Jupiter." However, S disturbs the in the first part of 16:4 thoughts started. The author wants to communicate the reason for the destruction of the temple and therefore also states the reason for its reconstruction in the second part of 16:4. The καί in S can be explained by the fact that the writer of S believed that Barnabas wanted to allude to a historical temple building and that he now intended to explain this historical event in more detail. By ὑπηρέται some understand the work of Jeute in the construction of the temple; see Veil in Hdb. d. N.T. Apkr. P. 224. According to Harnack, Gesch. d. old Christian Lit. Likewise, Ladeuze. P. 19. Schlatter ("The Days of Trajan and Hadrian" p. 64) points the ὑπηρίται to the Roman governor in Judea and his officials. Hilgenfeld thinks of the pagan provincials insofar as they provided auxiliary troops to the Romans (Zeitschr. f. wiss. Theol. 1870, p. 177). Funk p. 87; Bardenhewer, Gesch. d. old church. Lit. I. p. 93 and others. Under ὑπηρίται the Christians are understood to be subjects of the Roman Empire. Mayer, Ap. V. p. 109 Note 2 writes about ὑπηρίται: "Especially the lower classes in the pagan Roman Empire are already — and even more so in the future — entering the true Temple, the Church of God."

[231] Cf. on the former conversion of Israel, Rom. 10 and 11, according to which the Jews at first do not have zeal for God according to knowledge, but one day, when the Gentiles have accepted the gospel, they will also profess it.

[232] This quote is probably taken from Enoch 91:13, which was first pointed out by Völter p. 379. The passage reads: "At the end of this week they will purchase houses for their righteousness, and the house of the great King will be built in glory forever." Tobias 14:5 also

his return to the dwelling of the human heart he takes with him seven others who are worse than he. The human heart becomes a true temple after 16:8 by cleansing from sins and trusting in the Lord. Because as a result, "we have become new, once again freshly created".

16:9 deals with the question of the extent to which God takes up residence in us. The answer to the question is briefly summarized in the following words: ὁ λόγος αὐτοῦ τῆς πίστεως, ἡ κλῆσις αὐτοῦ τῆς ἐπαγγελίας, ἡ σοφία τῶν δικαιωμάτων, αἱ ἐντολαὶ τῆς διδαχῆς. After that, God dwells in man, if he confesses faith in him, allows himself to be called by his promise, possesses the wisdom of the statutes and the requirements of the doctrine. In the next sentence, the author thus continues: "(God) himself, who dwells in us[233], leads us, who had fallen to death, into the imperishable temple (= heaven[234]) by opening the door of the temple for us, i.e., opens the mouth, and gives change of mind." These words explain what God works in the person in whom he has taken up residence.[235]

16:10: "For whoever has the desire to be saved does not pay attention to the outer man,[236] but to the (divine Spirit) that is inherent in him and speaks in him." Apparently, there is a close relationship between these words and the introductory thought of the chapter. Just as the Jew who only looked at the construction of the temple and not rather at God, for whom it was built, was mistaken, so the Christian would also deviate from the path to salvation if he looked at his Christian brother, who has become the temple of God, only at the external appearance and not rather at the God living and working in him. As the contrast teaches, the "man" from whom the gaze is to be averted is to be understood as the external appearance of the Christian. But how this is to be understood in more detail is likely to emerge from earlier admonitions of Barnabas.

Since he repeatedly insists on perseverance and patience because of the "bad days", and so often refers to the suffering of Jesus for the consolation of the reader, the "man" will be the Christian who is outwardly exposed to all the evil influences of the bad days, subjected to the sufferings and tribulations of various

---

deserves consideration: καὶ πάλιν ἐλεήσει αὐτοὺς ὁ θεὸς καὶ ἐπιστρέψει αὐτοὺς εἰς τὴν γῆν καὶ οἰκοδομήσουσιν τὸν οἶκον οὐχ οἷος ὁ πρότερος ἕως πληρωθῶσιν καιροὶ τοῦ αἰῶνος καὶ μετὰ ταῦτα ἐπιστρέψουσιν ἐκ τῶν αἰχμαλωσιῶν καὶ οἰκοδομήσουσιν ιερουσαλημ ἐντίμως καὶ ὁ οἶκος τοῦ θεοῦ ἐν αὐτῇ οἰκοδομηθήσεται εἰς πάσας τὰς γενεὰς τοῦ αἰῶνος οἰκοδομῇ ἐνδόξῳ.
[233] So Hilgenfeld p. XXXII f. u. 123 f.; Kayser p. 49 f.; Müller p. 329 Braunsberger p. 182 f. and 206 f.; Riggenbach p. 29; Harnack p. 70 f.
[234] το ποιειν οσα ἡν εναντία τῶ &εῶ. Lipsius also explains the word in the above sense in Schenkels Bibellexikon I. p. 363; Weizsäcker p. 8; Funk p. 88 and in Theol. Quartalschr. 1878, p. 158. The expression is also used in a broader sense Col. 3:5.
[235] Cf. Hefele p. 117, Anm. 12; Heydecke p. 30.
[236] Matt. 12:43–45; cf. Luke 4:33.

kinds, condemned to patience and perseverance. This view is also suggested by the following 16:10 words. According to this, there must be no other horror for the one who is looking for salvation and does not want to look at the "man" other than that "that he has never heard the words of the Speaker (= God) from his mouth and, moreover, has never asked to hear him".

The warning about such horrors suggests very strongly the assumption that the readers wanted to show a false fright, i.e., that they were easily frightened by the "man", namely his sufferings and tribulations, and took offense at it. As the introductory reference to the destruction of the temple, which is well known to the readers, suggests, Barnabas also alludes[237] to the horrors associated with the destruction of Jerusalem and its temple with the quoted words. The Christian should not know such worries of a purely external nature. Anyone who knows where true salvation is to be found alone is not frightened by the destruction of the Jerusalem temple and the associated sufferings, but is astonished with horror only at the fact that the one to whom this temple was built has not yet revealed himself to him, has never really come to his awareness.[238]

---

[237] The manuscripts with the exception of H, the Latin translation and pretty much all editors and explainers of the scripture read the words αυτός εν ἡμῖν προφητεύων before αντός ἴν ἡμῖν κατοίκων. Despite the numerous counterwitnesses, preference should be given to H alone here. Because the participial expression in question has no meaning at all at this point. It cannot be counted among the following participles as a closer definition of the subject of εισάγει; because in the combination of ἐν ἡμῖν προφητεύων and ἀνοίγων there would be a tautology, and the order προφητεύων — κατοίκων — ἀνοίγων — ὁιδούς would be meaningless and planless. The participial expression in question does not fit as a fifth member next to the nouns ὁ λόγος — ἡ κλῆσις — ἡ σοφία — αἱ ἐντολαί. The quote from Clement of Alexandria also speaks against προφητεύων in this compilation. Strom. II. 20. 117 (Stählin II, p. 176), where the answer to the question of how God lives in us is also concluded with the fourth term αι ἐντολαί τῆς ὁιδαχῆς.

[238] Hetele interprets the words εισάγει εις τον ἀφ&αρτον ναόν as follows: he "made ourselves such an imperishable temple" (p. 118, note 18). Likewise Mayer p. 110 note 3. Müller claims that the author went a bit out of the picture with the words mentioned: "The heart is the temple. But now God leads us, our hearts, into the indestructible temple" (p. 353). L has already translated: fecit de nobis domum incorruptam. However, even if only the temple of the human heart was spoken of in 16:6–9, it can still be assumed that the author now leaves this image and speaks of the heavenly temple, eternal bliss, since he also immediately at the beginning of the following sentence seems to point to eternal salvation (ο γάρ πο&ών σω&ῖναι), and since the wording does not justify any other assumption. After the meaning of the words εισάγει εις . . . is no longer in doubt, is the one represented by many (e.g. Müller p. 47; Riggenbach p. 22; Hilgenfeld p. 41 f.; Weiß p. 47 and 141; Funk p. 88; Heer p. 88). To drop the claim that the entire paragraph 16:9 should be understood as an answer to the question of how God dwells in people. εισάγει, εις . . . cannot be used as an answer to that

The chapter closes according to the content with the words: "But this (i.e. what the Enoch quote 16:6 speaks of) is a spiritual temple that is being built for the Lord."[239]

---

question. The answer to the πώς; at the beginning of 16:9 is already completed before αυτός εν ημΐν κατοικών. Already this participle can no longer belong to the answer and can be counted as the fifth member of the previous ones (ο λόγος ..., η κλήσις ..., η σοφία . . αϊ έντολαι . . .), since initially it is precisely the fact that God lives in us is already presupposed as certain in the question (ο Ιλεός κατοικεί εν η/τιν 16:8), and there also Clem. Alexandr. 1. c., where the question and answer in question are quoted from Barnabas, breaks off with the fourth term.

[239] Cf. 4:11 (γενώμεθα ναὸς τέλειος τῷ θεῷ.) und 6:15 (ναὸς γὰρ ἅγιος, ἀδελφοί μου, τῷ κυρίῳ).

FIRST CONCLUSION OF THE LETTER (CHAP. 17:1 AND 2A)

All the individual treatises of chapters 2-16 had been written by Barnabas at. According to his remark in 1:7. Now, in conclusion, he explains once again in 17:2 that it had been his special intention to always use the past as a starting point in his teachings: ἐὰν γὰρ περὶ τῶν ἐνεστώτων ἢ μελλόντων γράφω ὑμῖν, οὐ μὴ νοήσητε διὰ τὸ ἐν παραβολαῖς κεῖσθαι. The meaning of these words is: for if I am writing to you about the present or the future without taking the past into account,[240] then you do not want to understand after all, because you are completely attached to the parables, i.e., the institutions and regulations of the Old Covenant (which contain a spiritual, deeper content).[241]

Because of the contrast in which the παραβολαῖ are related to the ἐνεστώτων and μελλόντων, they can only be understood in this sense. The same have special authority among the readers, as Barnabas already indicates in the previous sentence in the words: Ἐφ᾽ ὅσον ἦν ἐν δυνατῷ καὶ ἁπλότητι δηλῶσαι ὑμῖν, ἐλπίζει μου ἡ ψυχὴ τῇ ἐπιθυμίᾳ μου μὴ παραλελοιπέναι τι τῶν ἀνηκόντων εἰς σωτηρίαν.

---

[240] It is usually explained that Barnabas claims that he did not want to write about the present or the future at all. However, the entire content of the letter contradicts such a claim. The embarrassment to which this explanation must necessarily lead can only be partially avoided if Veil describes it as "things that are only just in sight" or Müller p. 341 as "the eschatological conditions" (cf. Harnack p. 72, Hilgenfeld p. 124, Weiß p. 66), or if Hefele p. 118, Heydecke p. 12, Völter p. 360 against S, H, L follow the reading type V, which deletes ενεστώτα in 17:2 and in 17:1 in a place that seems more convenient.

[241] According to the usual view, the present and future are still wrapped in the form of παραβολαί and are therefore incomprehensible. But Barnabas liked to present parables, types and allegories so that the readers could gain understanding (cf. Müller p. 342).

Especially the Old Covenant with its statutes is called δυνατῷ here, it is what pleases the addressees of a special reputation: "As far as it was possible to enlighten you in what has validity and influence (with you), and in the simple (i.e., in what is indicated by the institutions and ordinances of the Old Covenant, in their moral teachings)[242], I hope that nothing useful for your salvation has escaped my efforts." δυνατῷ is what the writer must build on if his teachings about the present and the future are to be successful.[243] He gave the instructions "as far as it was possible", i.e.,as far as the shortness of time and the external circumstances pushing for rapid writing allowed it. [244]

---

[242] Regarding ἁπλότης cf. 8:2 (νοεῖτε, πῶς ἐν ἁπλότητι λέγει ὑμῖν), where the interpretation of a prophetic passage, the teaching contained in it as ἁπλότης is denoted. In Hermas' "Shepherd" ἁπλότης is often combined with ακακία and εγκράτεια: Vis. I. 2:4; II. 3:2; III. 1:9th Vis. III. 8:7: ἐκ τῆς Εγκράτειας Ἁπλότης (γεννᾶται), ἐκ τῆς Ἁπλότητας Ακακία. Mand. 2:7: "να ἡ μετάνοια . . . ἐν ἁπλότητι εἱρεϑῇ. The word is found in the connection ἐν ἁπλότητι (τῆς) καρδίας Chron. 29:17; Sap. 1:1; Col. 3:22; Eph 6:5. St. Paul uses it in the meaning of benevolence and charity in 2 Cor. 8:2; 9:11-13 (ἁπλίτ. τῆς κοινωνίας).

[243] As a rule, ἤν and ἐν δυνατῷ are combined into one concept (= it was possible) and this expression is then thought repeatedly in order to make the infinitive ἁπλότητι δηλῶσαι dependent on it. Funk: Quantum potuit et sine obscuritate potuit vobis monstrari. See Müller p. 340 f. But this does violence to the text, δυνατόν is related to ἁπλότης, the external, exemplary facts are related to their spiritual meaning in the form ἐν δυνατῷ καὶ ἁπλότητι.

[244] Compare 1:5 and 4:9.

AN APPENDIX ATTACHED BY BARNABAS TO THE EPISTLE (CHAP. 17:2B–20 INCL.)

Through the words ταῦτα μὲν οὕτως 17:2b the main theme of the Scripture is declared closed and at the same time—since the μὲν must be followed by a δὲ —something new is announced. This is introduced in 18:1: Μεταβῶμεν δὲ καὶ ἐπὶ ἑτέραν γνῶσιν καὶ διδαχήν. Accordingly, γνῶσιν should also be taught in what follows. The same, in turn, is an understanding of moral life; because chapter 19 contains numerous calls to a virtuous life and this is followed in chapter 20 to warn against the path of darkness, a detailed catalog of sins. But if the γνῶσιν in this appendix is to be understood as an understanding of moral life, as before, and is nonetheless referred to in 18:1 as ἑτέραν γνῶσιν, then this ἑτέραν γνῶσιν is to be explained as an understanding that is gained in a new way, so it is not more after the "prophets" (1:7).

Barnabas now teaches in the γνῶσιν using a different script. He refers to them with the expression διδαχήν. The meaning of the words Μεταβῶμεν δὲ καὶ ἐπὶ ἑτέραν γνῶσιν καὶ διδαχήν is: But let us, in order to further instruct ourselves in the γνῶσιν, turn from the prophetic writings to pass over to the διδαχήν. Not only Chap. 2:17, but specifically also Chap. 19 and 20's concluding words 21:1: "It is good, then, to get to know all the written statutes of the Lord and to walk in them."[245] In 19 and 20 the admonitions of the διδαχήν are listed, in Chap. 18 and

---

[245] The "Jewish two ways" may be remembered. See also Harnack, "The Apostles' Doctrine" Lpz. 1896; Funk, "Church History." Treatise and investigation." II. pp. 108-141 and III. 1907, pp. 218-229; A. Seeberg, "Der Katechismus der Urchristenheit" ("The Catechism of Early Christianity" Lpz. 1903; ibid., "Die Didache des Judentums und der Urchristenheit" ("The Didache of Judaism and Early Christianity)" Lpz. 1908.

19, with a few brief comments. A way of light and a way of darkness are distinguished, further angels of God and angels of Satan, the lord of eternity and the prince of the present godless time.[246]

---

[246] The authenticity of chapters 18-21 has been disputed several times. S, H, V and also L speak for the same, who did not translate these four chapters himself, but indicates them at the end of chapter 17 with the words "Haec autem sic sunt" (= ταῦτα μεν οὕτως). Origen also quotes the passage in question as part of the Letter of Barnabas (de princip. III. 2:4, 7). Müller p. 347 and H. Holtzmann in yearbooks f. protest. Theol. 1885, pp. 160 f. assume a different edition of the letter by Barnabas himself. For the authenticity of the last four chapters, among other things, a: Krüger, Gesch. der altchristl. Lit. p. 14; Bardenhewer, Gesch. der altkirchl. Lit. I. p. 89; Veil in Hdb. z. d. N.T. Apokr. p. 235 ff.

CHAPTER 5

CONCLUSIONS — CHAPTER 21

As a final chapter, Chapter 21 contains multiple relationships to the introduction of the missive. In the introduction, the numerous orders (1:2 δικαιωμάτων) of God were mentioned and were invited to research in them (2:1). That is why they are mentioned again in 21:1 and 5 and it is noted that it is good to know them and to walk in them. In 1:6, the hope of eternal life was called the first teaching of the Lord and made the basis of moral activity. 21:1 and 3 is remembered for the glory in the kingdom of God and the resurrection and the reward in the hereafter, on the other hand also for the downfall of sinners along with their works.

In 1:5 Barnabas had written that it would earn him a reward if he shared with others a part of what he himself had received. What he had said about himself in the introduction, now that he has made his noble generosity known through the letter, he wants to be able to say about his believers as well. Therefore, in 21:2 the exhortation: "I would like to ask those in possession, if you accept a well-intentioned advice: you have those among you in whom you should do good, do not refrain from it!" Also, the expression μέρος in 1:5 returns again in 21:3. In 1:8 Barnabas suggests to his addressees that he does not want to approach them as a teacher. In 21:4 he writes to them quite accordingly, that they themselves should be their own good legislators and their own reliable advisers.[247]

The term γνῶσις, to which special emphasis is placed from the very beginning, must also be mentioned at the conclusion. In the same compilation with σοφία, σύνεσις, ἐπιστήμη such as 2:3[248] we find the same in 21:5. If ὑπομονή is also

---

[247] With regard to 21:2 (ἐρωτῶ . . . εἴ τινά μου γνώμης ἀγαθῆς λαμβάνετε συμβουλίαν) they are admonished to give advice (σύμβουλοι).

[248] Cf. 5:3; 6:9 and 10.

added at the last place, this is easily explained with regard to 2:2.[249] The request on independence in 21:4, insofar as one should be a teacher and advisor to oneself, results in the warning against being unattached in 21:5 and 6. Christian independence includes dependence on God, attachment to the Lord. He must give knowledge (21:5), he must teach.[250]

Barnabas does not want to be called a teacher, but God himself should influence the readers. But nevertheless, the author in 21:7 thinks: If some of his people should remember and want to believe that they have received something good from him, let this presumption cause them to strive, that his striving and his vigilance lead to something good. I am begging you for mercy". The words ἐρωτῶ ὑμᾶς, χάριν αἰτούμενος are translated by Veil: "I ask you this as a service of friend-

---

[249] M.Bacher in his work "Die Agada der babylonischen Amoräer" (Strasbourg 1878), p. 18 f., thought he had discovered the twelve-letter name of God in the Hebrew words for wisdom, insight, knowledge, and the dodecagrammaton that would later replace the Tetragrammaton JHVH. In his work "Die Stammbäume Jesu nach Matthäus und Lukas" (Bibl. Stud. XV, 1 and 2, 1910), p. 115 ff. M is correct. Heer agrees with Bacher's claim and explains that he can cite very old evidence for this from the Epistle of Barnabas, "namely from the section chapters 18-21 about the 'Two Ways', which comes from a source text that was certainly of Jewish origin." The three words σοφία, σύνεσ, ἐπιστήμη in 21:5 are said to be the translation of the three Hebrew words that form the dodecagrammaton. But Chapter 21 no longer belongs to the teaching of the "Two Ways", and synonyms of wisdom are often found compiled in the OT literature without them suggesting that name of God. Cf. Deut. 4, 6: φυλάξεσθε καὶ ποιήσετε ὅτι αὕτη ἡ σοφία ὑμῶν καὶ ἡ σύνεσις ἐναντίον πάντων τῶν ἐθνῶν ὅσοι ἐὰν ἀκούσωσιν πάντα τὰ δικαιώματα ταῦτα καὶ ἐροῦσιν ἰδοὺ λαὸς σοφὸς καὶ ἐπιστήμων τὸ ἔθνος τὸ μέγα τοῦτο. According to Heer, γνῶσις, the fourth synonym in 21:5, was already in the Jewish source as an addition to the three words that make up the twelve letter name of God. The expression γνῶσιν denotes the understanding of a secret that only the "enlightened" is aware of; it is explained by the report that the 42-letter name of God could only be pronounced by the high priest and by him only on the Day of Atonement in the Holy of Holies. In this sense, the expression γνῶσις has its good place in chapter 21, which is known to be eschatological, but it does not fit in 2:3, in which place the addition γνῶσις by Barnabas without understanding from the original, along with the words σοφία, σύνεσις, ἐπιστήμ η been taken over. "In addition to the evidence of the originality of the letter in the entirety of the Greek textual witnesses, what seems to me to be the most infallible, because hidden criterion, is now added this ratio of 2:3 and 21:5." Only γνῶσις is explained in 2:3 as in 21:5 as in the many other places of Scripture from its stated purpose in 1:5: ἵνα μετὰ τῆς πίστεως ὑμῶν τελείαν ἔχητε τὴν γνῶσιν.

[250] 21:6. V: γίνεσθε δὲ θεοδίδακτοι, ἐκζητοῦντες. The connection with δέ is missing according to H and rightly so, since 21:6 and 21:5 are equivalent in meaning.

ship." This does not convey the meaning. The χάρις is to be understood as the reward that accrues to the teacher from sharing what is his with others (1:5), and his own salvation (1:3).

The introduction had granted the addressee a certain possession of γνῶσις, it was only necessary to perfect them, they only had to increase their active love. 21:8 Barnabas praises her "beautiful vessel", which is not to be understood as her body[251], but, as already mentioned in 11:9, the external activity of the good disposition, the "spirit" (πνεῦμα). To this praise he adds the last admonition for more active moral activity: "Do not follow any of you, but research incessantly (in the orders of God) and fulfill every commandment!" In a hurry, the writer put together the epistle. He had explained this in 1:5 and emphasized it again to 21:9. What the readers have to expect as a reward for willing hearing is joy: 1:8 and 21:9. The words εἰς τὸ εὐφρᾶναι ὑμᾶς in 21:9 should claim authenticity despite H because of their kinship relationship to 1:8.[252]

---

[251] So Veil in N.T. Apokr. p. 166.

[252] The numerous relationships between the final chapter and the introduction are telling evidence of the authenticity of Chap. 21.

CONCLUSION

CHAPTER 1

FINAL REMARKS

1. Time of origin, purpose and literary character of the Epistle of Barnabas.

In view of the anonymity and the relatively late attestation of the Epistle of Barnabas[253], the detailed consideration and penetrating explanation of its contents obviously means the only way in which the questions about its time of origin, its purpose and its literary character, which have already been dealt with many times, can be brought closer to their definitive solution.

1. The time conditions from which the letter grew out of can be seen with considerable certainty from the letter itself. According to what Barnabas writes openly and clearly, it was "dreadful days" (2:1) in which it came into being. The rule is in the hands of the "evil prince" (4:13). He rules over the present ungodly time (18:2). There is a danger that the "black" will creep in everywhere (4:9; cf. 2:10; 20:1). However, a more detailed investigation provides a more precise picture.

On the one hand, temptations to sin, to weakening in active love, and on the other hand, horrors of a political nature have given rise to the epistle. The congregation or congregations to which Barnabas writes are in fear and terror because of the dangers and suffering that threaten from outside, but Barnabas tries to divert attention and concern away from the inner spiritual dangers. The time and the external political situation can be seen from 5:8; 9:4 and 16:2. 10:5:8 shows, as we have seen above, that the Apostles have already died and have proven their love for the Lord through their death.

As already mentioned, the remark in 9:4 that the circumcision has been abolished means that the circumcision has been abolished — referring to the Emperor Hadrian's ban on circumcision before the Bar-Kochba War. When 16:2 et seq. speak of a destruction of the Jewish temple and, as follows from 16:10, the author must warn of the horrors associated with this destruction of the temple, then one has to think of the destruction of the Jewish temple by Hadrian in the

---

[253] Cf. Harnack, Gesch. der altchr. Lit. I, 1 p. 58 ff.

year 133 or 134[254] and of the tribulations associated with the aforementioned wars. Perhaps there are also allusions in chapter 4 to the turmoil and suffering of these sad political conditions in Palestine.

In fact, Barnabas writes in 4:1 that it is necessary to look for what one can save. Those to whom the author turns, probably sought salvation from the Roman armies in vain. At this point Barnabas admonishes: "Let us flee completely from all the works of lawlessness![255] and immediately after that: "Let us not give rest to our soul ...!" Those who have spoken too softly may have intended to flee for fear of the external enemy and to seek peace and security from him. The words in 4:10: "Do not separate yourselves for yourselves alone, as if you were already justified!" may have had their first reason in the shy hiding from external enemies.

Probably this external behavior has reminded the moral preacher of an undue seclusion from the world of those who are not yet justified. In 4:11 there is the admonition: "Let us become a perfect temple for God; if (God) dwells in us, let us strive for the fear of God and fight for observance of His commandments!" Shouldn't there be an allusion here to the fate of the imperfect temple, to the fear of people, to political struggles? Even the introduction of the letter reminds of a warlike time. 2:2 f. is spoken in images taken from the life of war. Fear and endurance are called 2:2 allies, fortitude and renunciation are called comrades-in-arms. In 2:3, we are talking about the case when these allies and comrades-in-arms "hold out impeccably in the cause of the Lord".

In 2:1 the author says that he wants to distract from external circumstances; for he wants people to "take care of themselves" and not of the one who causes the evil days. In section 5:13-17,[256] it is noticeable that a reminder for spiritual renewal is precisely the word: "Enter into the Promised Land!" is taken as a basis. It is understandable that Barnabas is using this very Biblical quotation, when worries about the conquest and devastation of Palestine have prompted the Scripture. The same political occasion also explains it by the fact that the words are inserted in the treatise on water 11:9: "And it was the land of Jacob that was praised more than any land."

Chapter 9, which deals with circumcision, has, as has been shown, interrupted the train of thought. But the chapter has its good reason when it is taken

---

254 Ed. This was the Third Temple, the Temple of Bar-Kochba the so-called "Messias" recognized by Rabbi Akiba and official Jewry.

255 Schlatter's "Die Tage Trajans und Hadrians" ("The Days of Trajan and Hadrian") pp. 45-49 has proven in detail and thoroughly that Hadrian destroyed a Temple in Jerusalem.

256 Cf. 4:10.

into account that the imperial ban on circumcision prepared the war of annihilation against the Jewish people.

What is strangely touching at the end of the chapter is the heartfelt outpouring that no one has received a teaching that would have come more from the writer's heart. But it can be understood if the chapter reminds us of the confusion that the readers are currently exposed to. If we consider that Hadrian, in his fight against Judaism, issued an edict[257] not only against circumcision but also against the Sabbath celebration, then it is natural that he also devoted a special discussion to the Sabbath commandment (Chapter 15). The repeated emphasis on having to write in a hurry[258] is also understandable given the political unrest. It may be noticeable, however, that Barnabas' external unfortunate circumstances are not discussed in more detail. But it wasn't necessary. Readers knew him. They only needed instruction about what they could forget in the great external tribulations and what could help them to overcome them comfortingly.[259]

2. The addressees, although devout Christians, since they were tribal relatives of the Jewish people, took an active part in the fate of the same, they themselves had to watch and experience the horrors of the Bar-Kochba war. The horror of these historical circumstances and a lack of concern for spiritual and moral development and perfection in relation to the many political worries they caused prompted the epistle. This twofold occasion corresponds to a twofold task of the writer: he wants to invigorate them morally and provide religious consolation.

a) Barnabas urgently reminds the readers that they are temples of God. "Let us become spiritual men, a perfect temple for God (4:11)!" A holy temple, my brothers, is the dwelling place of our hearts in the Lord."[260] Faith must manifest itself in the joyful activity of charity (1:6). Let the fellow man hear of the good works, so that he too may believe (11:11). Whoever does not avoid evil and does not pursue good, there is no covenant with God for him (4:6 f.; 14). The Lord has asked for a circumcision of the heart (Chap. 9) and the like.[261]

b) The introductory greeting 1:1: "Rejoice, sons and daughters, in the name of the Lord (Jesus Christ)" and the following words are explained by the in-

---

[257] Schlatter p. 5 f.

[258] 1:5; 4:9; 21:9.

[259] Schlatter himself places the writing of the letter in the year 130-131, before the beginning of the Bar-Kochba War (132-135). Loc. cit. p. 1.

[260] 6:15; cf. 16:6 ff.

[261] See especially Chap. 10 and 19-21.

tention to distract from the sad earthly conditions and to comfort them in the introduction: "I want to show you some things that will make you happy in the present circumstances (1:8)."

Barnabas opens readers' eyes to the better future, since Christ "will come into his inheritance" (4:3). The Christian must first have passed through this world of afflictions if he wants to celebrate true Sabbath rest, just as the Lord God keeps Sabbath rest only after he has dismissed the time of the wicked and judged the wicked (15:5 ff.). Barnabas repeatedly emphasizes that it was precisely through suffering and tribulation that Christ acquired eternal glory, in order to show that the same path leads Christians to eternal happiness (chap. 5–12).

In 7:11 we find the precious word that Barnabas puts into the mouth of the Lord: "Those who want to see me and gain my kingdom must necessarily endure tribulations and sufferings before they gain me." In chapter 8 we read the admonition, which is valuable for all time, that there will indeed be bad and terrible days in the kingdom of God, but that we will find salvation precisely in them. The one basic idea of the Letter can be reflected in the words of the Savior in the Gospel: "And when lawlessness increases, love will grow cold in many; but he who endures to the end will be saved" (Mt. 24:12 f.), or in the other words of the Lord: "Verily, verily, I say to you: 'You will weep and weep, but the world will rejoice; you will be sad, but your sadness will become joy"[262] (Jn. 16:20). With such thoughts, something is also touched by the saying attributed to Barnabas, which is found elsewhere: "In bad competitions, the winner is the one who is the lesser; because he comes out (as a winner) because he is richer in mistakes."[263]

The point may be that those who are the first in this ungodly time should not be admired as the best, because in it the first cannot be the best at all. The tendency of the writer, which dominates the whole letter, to be a consolation to the faithful in the dreary times, perhaps prompted his identification with the apostle Barnabas, whose earliest witness, as is known, is Clement of Alexandria. The name Barnabas is indeed interpreted in the history of the Apostles as "the Son of Consolation".[264]

---

[262] ἐν ἀμίλλαις πονηραίς ἀθλιώτερος ὁ νικήσας, διότι ἀπέρχεται πλέον ἔχων τής ἁμαρτίας (Grabe, Spicilegium ss. patrum ut et haereticorum saec. I. II. III. 2. Aufl. Oxon. 1700 vol. I. p. 302 f.).

[263] ἰν ἀμίλλαις πονηραῖς ἀθλιώτερος ὁ νικήσας, διότι ἀπέρχεται πλέον εχων τής αμαρτίας (Grabe, Spicilegium ss. patrum ut et haereticorum saec. I. II. III. 2nd ed. Oxon. 1700 vol. I. p. 302 f.).

[264] υἱὸς παρακλήσεωςActs 4:36. Etymologically, Barnabas' is often explained as בן הנבואה = "son of prophecy". In "Acts of the Apostles" (Freibg. 1892), following A. Klostermann, Felten derives the name from the Aramaic בר נחמה = "Son of Consolation". About υἱὸς τοῦ θεοῦ

Anyone who follows the moral admonitions and teachings of the epistle and knows how to console himself despite suffering and persecution is credited with full possession of Gnosis. Gnosis is therefore not only an understanding of the circumstances of this life and a knowledge of the duties of life, but is also living according to this knowledge. Through this conception of Gnosis, the author shows himself to be dependent on that spiritual movement which, with the intention of effectively countering the Hellenistic religions and rejecting the accusation of spiritual inferiority and shoddiness,[265] described not only the confession of the one God, but also life according to his commandments as wisdom, knowledge, understanding, philosophy.[266] The epistle of Barnabas, by that conception, ranks with the Psalms, Job, Proverbs, Wisdom, Sirach, in which books religious moral life is understood as wisdom and knowledge and sin is described as folly.

3. What has been said about the occasion of the epistle shows that the writing must be regarded as a real epistle. The form of the letter, which is shown in the greeting of the readers in the first chapter, in the wishes of the final chapter, in the comments there about the readers' memory of the author and about the writer's intention, as well as in the comments that recur several times in the repeated addressing of the readers as ἀδελφοί or τέκνα, in the repeated direct address προσέχειν, μάθετε and the like, is not just disguise and fiction.

As such, it has already been considered by Ewald.[267] Hennecke asserts in the NT Apocrypha: "The few passages according to which it might seem as if the author was really familiar with the circumstances of his reading audience (1:3) and as if he were writing a letter at all, . . . they are an affixed ornament that is intended

---

= "Son of (God) Nebo" see Deißmann, "Bibelstudien" 1895, p 175; "Neue Bibelstudien" 1897, p. 15.

[265] On this accusation see Josephus c. Apion. II. 12:14, 20; I Cor. 1:22: Ἕλληνες σοφίαν ζητοῦσιν."

[266] This term is particularly found among Jewish writers of the Diaspora. Philo proudly calls the Jews philosophers (de mutatione nominum). He explains that Jewish teachers everywhere proclaim their "wisdom" and that they "philosophize" publicly on every Sabbath (de vita Mosis 111. 27). Moses is the greatest philosopher (Philo, de mundi opificio 2; cf. Josephus c. Ap. 1:22; II. 36:39, 41). The author of Aristeas' letter particularly seeks to characterize the Jewish religion as a philosophy. See Paul Krüger, "Philo und Josephus als Apologeten des Judentums" Leipzig 1906, p. 7 f. and p. 18 ff. — On the significance of Gnosis in Hermetic literature see R. Reitzenstein, "Die helle¬nistischen Mysterienreligionen" (Leipzig 1910). According to this, Gnosis is "a kind of new life, the highest perfection of the soul, liberation from the body, the way to heaven, the means of salvation, the true worship of God and piety, just as ἀγνωσία θεον is always love of the body and of sin" (p. 38).

[267] Geschichte des Volkes Israel VII (Göttingen 1859) p. 138

to make the literary deception complete.[268] According to this view, Hennecke does not classify the Epistle of Barnabas under the "epistles", but under the "teaching letters and sermons". W. Wrede[269] firmly declares the epistolary cladding of the writing to be a fiction (pp. 87 et seq.). H. Jordan asserts in S. "Geschichte der altchristlichen Literatur" ("History of Early Christian Literature"[270]) p. 139: "The Letter of Barnabas now stands completely on the border of what could at best still be described as an "epistle"; it is a doctrinal and admonishing treatise in purely external letter form", and he therefore does not count it among the letters of the Apostolic Fathers Clement, Ignatius and Polycarp, but places it as an "epistle" next to the Letter to the Hebrews. However, we are missing a written conclusion and more precise information about the personal circumstances of the sender and the addressee. But according to the comments about the reason for the letter, it reveals very special, concrete circumstances.

Wrede is not familiar with the writer's thrice made remark that he is forced to write quickly, i.e., he translates the words γράφειν (γράψαι, πέμπει)to ἐπούδαοα with "I tried hard to write." But wrongly, as the supplement κατὰ μικρὸν in 1:5 and the contrast to πολλὰ δὲ θέλων γράφειν in 4:9 shows. Wrede explains that Barnabas had taken special pains to give the writing an epistolary form for the purpose of fiction. "All in all, even the written remarks occupy a not inconsiderable space."[271] But if Barnabas has time to take special care of the letter form in order to fake, why does he so often miss any form so much in the treatises of the letter that are important to him that it is sometimes difficult to clearly understand what he wants? The epistolary form is not a fiction, it necessarily arises effortlessly, without further ado, from the circumstances.

O. Pfleiderer[272] explains the missive as a "homily written in letter form". Although one could be reminded of homilies, but nevertheless the writing is not to be called a homily. However, it may be assumed that the writing, which is actually a letter, repeatedly wants to draw on teachings that had already been presented in homilies. Some of the overly brief forms and many unclear phrases suggest that the readers had previously been informed so precisely on some points that they were now able to understand the writer despite the poor phrasing.

---

[268] p. 83; Cf. p. 141.

[269] „Das literarische Rätsel des Hebräerbriefes. "The literary riddle of the letter to the Hebrews. With an appendix on the literary character of the Epistle of Barnabas.", Göttingen 1906. (Forschungen zur Rei. u. Lit. des A. u. N. Test. 8. Heft.)

[270] Leipzig 1911.

[271] Wrede, p. 93.

[272] "Das Urchristentum, seine Schriften und Lehren in geschieht. Zusammenhang." (Berlin 1902) p. 553.

Perhaps it is precisely in what is written in chapters 6-12 about Jesus' sufferings and about his relationship to the sufferings of the Christian that one can find a homily that was given earlier. But what is said in this passage about the Promised Land (6:8-19; 11:9), about circumcision (chap. 9), about the dietary commandments (chap. 10), should be regarded as an inclusion in the homily, because these parts have their special reason in the circumstances of the time prompting the letter. A use of what is already available can be assumed if only because Barnabas also borrowed something older in chapters 19 and 20.

Since the epistle of Barnabas is to be regarded as a real letter and not as an "homily", it must be attributed in terms of its literary character to the letters of the Apostolic Fathers Clement, Ignatius and Polycarp.

II. The Doctrinal Content Of The Letter And Its Position To The NT And The Letters Of The Apostolic Fathers

Decisive for the position of the Letter of Barnabas to the NT and the letters of the Apostolic Fathers, given the lack of self-testimony of its author, is the specific nature of his doctrinal content. A brief presentation of the Christian teachings contained in the epistle[273] is all the more relevant here, since our investigation has revealed a number of new conceptions of its intellectual content. The question of which thoughts and teachings enabled the writer to comfort and morally revive in the aforementioned times of great need is best answered from the point of view of the history of salvation.

1. Very much of the Old Covenant is taken into account by Barnabas. The revelations of the OT, it's writings are almost the only religious textbook for him and his circles. NT Writings seem hardly to be considered for religious instruction as yet. In any case, Barnabas never uses the books of the NT to prove and confirm his main theses. NT Quotes one might guess in 4:4 "Many are called, but few are chosen (Mt. 22:14)" and in 5:9 "He came not to call the righteous, but sinners (Mt. 9:13)." Of those words it is expressly said that they are written in the OT. The quotation 13:7 "Behold, Abraham, I have made you the Father of the nations who believe in the Lord in the foreskin," reminds of Rom. 4:11. Some other words and thoughts are found in a similar way in the writings of NT But it cannot be asserted with certainty that they are used. With regard to the quotation in 4:14, since some unknown writings are sometimes used, one can think of a no longer preserved book of the Old Covenant.

---

[273] Cf. the statements by Hefele and Sprinzl. See also V. Schweitzer, „Über Glaube und Werke im Barnabasbrief", Der Katholik 1904, Vol. 29, p. 273 ff.

With regard to the other passages, it may be assumed that Barnabas drew from the oral tradition. A special preference for the writings of the Old Covenant arises from the purpose of the Scriptures to perfect gnosis on the basis of the OT (1:5-7), and from the prestige that the writings of the OT in particular enjoyed among the addressees because of their exemplary character (17:1 f.). Above all, the author likes to use the five books of Moses, the prophets Isaiah and Jeremiah and the Psalms. The Deuterocanonical books are not used, if not for example in 6:7 an allusion to wisdom. 2:12 should be found.

As in the NT, the letters of Barnabas are not quoted either., Judges, Ruth, Ecclesiates, Song of Solomon, Esdras, Nehemiah, Esther, Obadiah, Nahum, Sophronias. In 4:3 and 16:5 and 6, reference is made to Enoch; in 16:5 with the formula: λέγει γὰρ ἡ γραφή (12:1 is reminiscent of 4 Esd. 4:33; 5:5. Only rarely are the authors of the cited books mentioned by name. Moses is mentioned in 6:8; 10:1-11; 12:6; David in 10:10; 12:10; Isaias in 12:11; Daniel in 4:5. In 10:2 there is explicit mention of Deuteronomy, in 15:1 of the Decalogue. Unknown quotes are 2:10; 6:13; 7:4-8; 11:9. As a rule, the quoted writer is called a prophet. Also Moses (6:8-13; 14:2), the Psalmist (5:13; 6:4-6; 11:6), the author of 2 Kings (9:1), 4 Esd. (12:1) and the unknown writings in 7:4 and 11:9 explicitly bear the name Prophet.

In 1:7, all the writers of the Old Covenant, through whom God revealed himself, are called prophets. The one who speaks through the biblical writers is God (5:12), is the Father (2:9), the Lord,[274] the Spirit of the Lord (9:2). Christ revealed himself in the prophets; from him they have the grace of prophecy.[275] — Mostly the quotes are reproduced freely. What is remarkable is the peculiar mixing of two scriptures in 9:8, where it is stated as the word of the scripture. "And Abraham circumcised 318 men out of his house." The fact of circumcision is taken from Gen. 17:23 et seq., but the number alone is borrowed from Gen. 14:14.

According to the Epistle of Barnabas, the Old Covenant has an absolute meaning that is valid for all times in the written revelations as well as in the various ceremonies. He is a teacher and educator for both the Jew and the Christian. The Christian teacher and preacher Barnabas draws from him for his Christian teaching, for the presentation of the suffering and glory of Jesus, for the sentence that for the sake of Jesus the Christian must not only practice justice, but also suffer in order to find glory.

Of the ceremonies and customs which are used by the preacher of the Gospel as a means of teaching and education, the ceremony concerning the two

---

[274] E.g. 6:3, 12; 9:1 (λέγει κύριος ἐν τῷ προφήτῃ).

[275] 5:6. In several places the "Lord" who revealed himself in the Old Testament is understood to mean Christ (cf. 6:3, 14; 7:3).

goats on the Feast of Atonement (chap. 7), regarding the red heifer (chap. 8), circumcision (chap. 9), the dietary laws (chap. 10) and the Sabbath celebration (chap. 15). The two goats, one of which is destined for the sacrificial altar, the other is cursed and then crowned with scarlet-red wool, together indicate the one Lord Jesus Christ and teach that Jesus, although he has been condemned to the shameful sacrifice of the cross, will nevertheless be crowned with glory. By placing the red wool on a thorn bush, man is reminded to patiently accept suffering (which is symbolized in the thorn bush) in order to thus attain the glory of the kingdom of Jesus (which is represented by the red wool).

The fact that at the sacrifice of the red heifer, sinful men should first slaughter and burn the cow, but then innocent boys should collect the ashes, suggests that the glory of sinners is only temporary, and after sinners the good ones will gain lasting prestige. Furthermore, if those boys are to lay scarlet wool and hyssop at the same time when the people are sprinkled on a wood, then it is indicated that in the kingdom of Jesus (which is referred to by the wood) bad and bitter days (which are represented by the hyssop) lead to eternal glory.

The meaning of the law of circumcision is circumcision of the heart. By circumcising 318 men, Abraham pointed to Jesus and his cross through this very number (= $\iota\eta + \tau$). By prohibiting the eating of certain animals, as well as by allowing the eating of certain other animals, God wants to warn against certain sins and encourage a certain way of life. The Sabbath celebration reminds us that, just as God only rested after the six days of creation work, only after the sufferings and tribulations of human history does eternal, blissful rest, no longer disturbed by the reign of evil, come about.

Also, some facts from the history of the Jewish people are still valuable for the Christian preacher and the Christian people. When God let the people of Israel move into a new, promised land, God's plan is thus made known to transform man once — in Christ — into glory, to transform him into a child of God (6:8 ff.). Since the covenant tablets had been destroyed by Moses because of the idolatry of the Israelite people, Barnabas draws the lesson from this that even the Christian of the covenant with God is only safe as long as he practices works of righteousness (4:6, 8:14).

From the fact that Moses stretched out his hands in the middle of the battle against the Amalekites and in this way helped his people to victory, it follows that the cross and the crucified one are able to deliver from the tribulations (12:2 f.). From the story of the bronze serpent it can be seen that Jesus, who is represented in it, is subject to the power of suffering and yet it is he who brings life (12:5-7). The right to a typological explanation of the bronze serpent is expressly established. The same is required because this action willed by God contradicts a divine commandment. The erection of the bronze serpent is in contrast to the commandment:

"You shall have neither a cast nor a carved image of God." From this contrast it follows that the purpose of the bronze serpent is to be a role model.

2.   The question now arises whether, according to the Epistle of Barnabas, the Old Covenant in its history, its writings, its customs and institutions only had the same meaning for the Jew as for the Christian, whether he only wanted to point out Christ and only to educate for a life of patience and humility and in the hope of eternal participation in the glory of the Messiah, or whether the Jew was also specifically obliged to observe the Jewish ceremonies and institutions, in order to be a member of a specially chosen people of God in pre-Christian times through this observation.

It is not possible to find a sufficiently clear answer to this question from the letter. Regarding Israel as the chosen divine people, it can be concluded from the remark that the Lord has prepared the new people for himself (5:7); the new people of the Lord presupposes an old one. But that the belonging to the ancient people of God, the participation in the OT order of salvation of his time, which was mediated by observing the Jewish commandments of sacrifice and fasting, the law of circumcision, the laws of food, by participating in the temple cult, has not been noticed anywhere, but cannot be denied either.

According to the missive, these Jewish, divinely ordained institutions and ceremonies are so much a means of preparation for the NT and have such an important educational significance that by those who do not want to understand this meaning, even the sharp expression is used, they are bewitched by an evil angel (9:4). In the portrayal of Barnabas, the Old Covenant seems to be almost completely absorbed into the New, so that there seems to be little left even for the relative independence of an OT salvific sanatorium. This may be related to his view of historical Judaism.

This view may have prevented him from particularly pointing out an independent meaning of the Old Covenant. Barnabas finds little divine wisdom and divine spirit in Judaism as a whole, which has become a historical phenomenon; hence the claim of seduction by an evil angel. He still has a lot to criticize about this people. He emphasizes that God himself complains about Israel's sacrifices and fasting in Isaiah 1 and 58. Barnabas seems to deny the spirit of humility and love in which sacrifices and fasting should be carried out to the people of Israel and only assigns it to the new people of God (chapters 2 and 3).

Twice he feels he has to mention that the Jews, during their stay at Sinai, made themselves unworthy of the covenant with God through idolatry (4:7; 14:1 ff.). When mentioning their temple, he criticizes the fact that these "poor ones" did not recognize its significance and in a certain respect have become like the pagans. They themselves are to blame for the downfall of the temple due to their rebellious, restless nature (16:1-4). He denies them knowledge and understanding of the divine ordinances (8:7; 10:12).

When Barnabas speaks of the Old Covenant, he does not use the designation "the Lord's people," "the people of God," etc., and never at all the designation "the Law." He probably once wrote about the "first people", but in order to immediately assign this honorable title to the NT people (13:1 ff.). Also, he speaks 3:6 of the "laws of those", but τῷ ἐκείνων νόμῳ means the context according to ἀνομία. On the other hand, Barnabas mentions NT Relations "the new law of our Lord Jesus Christ (2:6)" and "the new people", which was prepared by the Lord Jesus Christ and for Him.[276] So who is Jesus and who is the new people with the new law?

3. Jesus Christ is the Son of God,[277] — "the Lord of the whole world, to whom God said at the creation of the world: Let us make man according to our image and likenesses (5:5)!" He is the beloved of the Father (3:6; 4:3-8). Unlike the father, who is called δεσπότης, he is called κύριος.[278] In 6:17 he is perhaps to be understood by τῷ λόγῳ. The Son of God became man. If he had not appeared in the flesh, then the human eye would not have been able to see him; that not even the sun, which is only the work of his hands, is able to see (5:10). Jesus appeared as the teacher of Israel (5:8), he came to call sinners (5:9), performed signs and miracles (5:8), established a kingdom,[279] the Church (7:11).

His teaching is briefly summarized in three points: "The hope of life is the beginning and the end of our faith; and righteousness is the beginning and the end of judgment; Love, which manifests itself in joyful, happy activity, is a testimony to righteousness (1:6)." Jesus chose for himself twelve apostles, who were to proclaim his gospel (5:9), and who also actually preached "the remission of sins and the sanctification of the heart" (8:3) and responded with love to the love of their Master (5:8). Christ sacrificed "the vessel of the Spirit (7:3)". He was insulted, beaten, spit on, crucified (7:9). Taking the suffering upon himself, he declared that he was the Son of God (7:9). When he was crucified, he was soaked with vinegar and gall (7:3). Barnabas probably also points out that water flowed from the side wound of Jesus (chap. 11). Christ rose from death to life by his own power.[280]

He abolished death and showed the resurrection from the dead (5:6). The resurrection took place on a Sunday (15:9). The Lord also ascended into heaven on a Sunday (ibid.). He will receive full glory in heaven. "One day they will see him, clothed in a long purple robe (7:9)." But even after his ascension, Jesus continues

---

[276] 5:7; 7:5; cf. 3:6.

[277] 5:9. 11:7, 2:9; 12:10.

[278] 1:6, 7; cf. 4:3.

[279] 4:13; 7:11; 8:5-6.

[280] 5:7 (τὴν ἀνάστασιν αὐτὸς ποιήσας).

to work on earth in the community of his believers. He lives in them. It is he who opens the Christian's mouth when he confesses his faith. He introduces him to heaven (16:9). His rule and glory is finally shown in his judgeship. "The Son of God is Lord and will judge the living and the dead."[281] "The Son of God will end the time of the wicked, judge the wicked, and transform the sun, moon, and stars, and then rest in honor on the seventh day (15:5)."

The purpose of the freely willed incarnation and the freely willed suffering[282] of Jesus is remission of sins and sanctification[283]; he has come to put away death (5:6) and to give life (7:2; 12:5). The purpose of Jesus' suffering and Jesus' power and glory is to teach that even the children of God (4:9), the good ones, can only be delivered to the evil power for a certain period of time.[284]

4. How does Barnabas elaborate on the "new people" that Jesus Christ has prepared for himself? This people receives from Jesus the covenant which he inherited (14:5). The covenant is concluded with the member of the new people, the Kingdom of the Lord, the Church in his soul. The Lord "makes the covenant in us by the Word".[285] "The seal of the covenant of the beloved Jesus is pressed into our hearts in the hope of faith in Him (4:8)". The conclusion of the covenant in the soul of man consists in the fact that the Lord "redeems from darkness the souls already fallen to death and abandoned to the wickedness of error (14:5)" and sanctifies his people.[286]

Remission of sins and sanctification of the heart are also called the content of the gospel, the preaching of the apostles (8:3). According to the above quotation, the means of becoming part of the covenant of Jesus is the "Word" (λόγος). If πίστεως is added to λόγος, which could be justified by 16:9, then the confession of faith in Jesus is considered as a basis for obtaining the covenant with God. According to the above quotation, "the hope of faith in him" is also mentioned as a prerequisite of the covenant. According to these words, both faith in Jesus and hope[287] rooted in faith are required of those who want to belong to the new kingdom. External sacramental means of sanctification are recalled only in chapter 11:8:

---

[281] 7:2; cf. 5:7.

[282] Cf. 5:6-11 et al. places.

[283] 5:1; 6:11 ff.; 14:5 ff.

[284] Cf. Chap. 5-8 as well as 11 and 12.

[285] 14:5. Only H reads διάθηται ἡμῖν (st. ἐν ἡμῖν) διαθήκην ἐν ἡμῖν but is justified because of the same meaning in 4:8.

[286] 14:6, cf. 5:1

[287] Cf. 11:8; 12:3; 16:8.

"Blessed are those who have descended into the water in the hope of the cross." Perhaps, among the above-mentioned λόγος in 14:5, it is worth remembering a sacramental form for acquiring the covenant with Christ.[288]

The means of preserving the covenant and obtaining eternal life are summarized in 16:9 in the answer to the question of how God dwells in us. The answer shows that the Christian of the Covenant can rejoice as long as he "confesses faith in God, allows himself to be called by his promise, possesses the wisdom of the statutes and the requirements of the doctrine". The citizen of the divine Kingdom has the social duty to influence others through faith and love and also to win others for faith and the hope of eternal life (11:8).

The very introduction emphasizes that the joy of good works should bear witness to the righteousness that exists in the divine judgment (1:6). The Christian must ensure that "the black man does not receive shelter (4:10)", that "the evil one does not provide a shelter for error in us and throw us out of our lives (2:10)". He must keep away from "the ruler of the present ungodly age (18:2)", from the "dark way" in which "the angels of Satan command (18:1)". He walks under the rule of the One who is "the Lord from eternity to eternity", on the "path of light", "over which the light-bearing angels of God are placed (18:1 f.)".

"On the one hand, the righteous man walks in this world, on the other hand, he expects holy eternity (10:11)". But faith and hope, justice and holiness alone are not enough. Anyone who believes that the happiness of the eternal divine kingdom must be granted to him simply because he lives a holy life is completely in error (15:6). Whoever wants to belong to the kingdom of God also needs suffering. Anyone who wants to see the Lord and come to His kingdom may only find him after tribulations and sufferings.[289] The name Christian is not found for the one who is only allied with Christ.

On the other hand, he is described as a "child of God (4:9)", as a "spiritual man (4:11)", as "a spiritual temple built for the Lord (16, 10)", a "perfect temple for God (4:11)", "a holy temple for the Lord (6:15)". Man is renewed in Christianity to such an extent that it is necessary to speak of a "new form", of a new creation (6:11). Barnabas considers only the kingdom of God in man; there is no mention of an external organization of the Church. The gloomy, passionate times in which he writes compel him to divert attention from all external circumstances at all. He does not look "at man, but at the one who dwells and speaks in him (16:10)". The contrast between the kingdom founded by Christ and the people of Israel is particularly evident in three sentences.

---

[288] See the Apollinarius passage p. 72.
[289] 7:11; cf. 8:6.

Christ fulfills the promise to the fathers (5:7). The new people believe "in integrity (3:6)", i.e., he knows that it is required by the divine commandments of fasting to avoid all injustice and to practice works of mercy. "The new law of our Lord Jesus Christ, which is not required by the yoke of external compulsion, has a sacrifice that is not offered by the external man (2:6)"; i.e.,the new law is written in the heart of the believer and is observed freely not as a result of penal provisions, but as a result of correct knowledge and correct disposition, and the sacrifice of the New Covenant is humility and sacrificial love. To denote the opposite of the OT and NT Covenant Barnabas does not use as does St. Apostle Paul the juxtaposition of law and faith, or such a sharp contrast as "ministry of death", "ministry of damnation" and "ministry of the Spirit", "ministry of righteousness".[290]

5. The expression "Kingdom of the Lord" also refers to eternal life in the Epistle of Barnabas. While the "kingdom of the Lord" in 4:13 and 8:6 means the new people of God on earth, "the kingdom of the Lord" means "The kingdom of God" in 7:11 and 21:1 a different, better, future life. The same, like the Christian's earthly life (2:10; 4:9), is only referred to as "life".[291] The same designations indicate an essential correspondence of the two realms of life, which, however, is not explained in more detail. In any case, the kingdom of the beyond is regarded only as a perfection of the worldly. Barnabas writes that the believer already has a foretaste of the future life here (1:7). But the difference between the two kingdoms is precisely determined.

One day the believer will rise again (21:1) and live forever.[292] He will be allowed to see Jesus (7:9, 11). He will be the lord of the earth and will rule over the animals of the field, the fish and the birds of the sky (6:17 f.). The evil forces will no longer be able to harm him (15:7), he will be glorified (21:1). But such happiness can only be granted to him when "everything has been renewed by the Lord (15:7)", when the Lord "has taken away the time of the wicked, judged the wicked and transformed the sun, moon and stars (15:5)."

A special court is not distinguished from the general court. Eternal life is considered a world Sabbath, and its glory is called a Sabbath rest, while this time is related to the six days preceding the creation Sabbath (15:3 ff.). Barnabas does not attempt to give a specific time for the onset of the Last Judgment; There are no chiliastic ideas to be found in his letter. Eternal life is also called the imperishable temple, into which God introduces the believer by dwelling in him, speaking through him and giving him a change of mind (16:9). The eternal life of the good is opposed to the destruction of the evil along with their works. The sinner "will

---

[290] 2 Cor. 3:7-9.
[291] 1:4, 6; cf. 6:17.
[292] 8:5; cf. 11:10-11.

perish together with his works (21:1)". This destruction is "eternal death with punishment (20:1)". While virtue confers resurrection, sin brings "retribution (21:1)."

6. Numerous teachings that have already been handed down in the writings of the New Testament recur in the Epistle of Barnabas, but often in a strange, new form because they were written from strange, external circumstances. Because the letter, like all the books of the New Testament, arose from the need of the moment and the violence of the circumstances, it again stands alongside these. Just as little as it aims at an only reasonably comprehensive presentation of the content of faith. Just like the NT in the narrower sense, he wants the writings to be a textbook or teaching book for the faith. Neither this nor the other intend to convert to the Christian faith. In the same way, they address those who have already been won over to the gospel through preaching and only want to support oral instruction through the written word.

The Epistle of Barnabas can be brought into special relation to the Epistle to the Hebrews, since, like it, it is addressed to Christians from Judaism and often takes into account ancient institutions and orders. But in contrast to the Epistle to Barnabas, the Epistle to the Hebrews mostly pursues dogmatic and apologetic purposes. While this refers to the Old Covenant in order to demonstrate the sublimity of the New, the Old Covenant for the Epistle of Barnabas only has the purpose of providing material for admonitions and consoling words from a Christian moral preacher. To this end, he also exercises harsh criticism of the Jewish people here and there.

But this criticism does not give it a place next to the Pauline Epistles. For Barnabas only blames the conduct of the Jewish people, while, according to his epistle, the institutions and orders of the Old Covenant are still of the utmost importance for the Christian, as long as they are understood correctly. Paul fights for the gospel and its doctrine of freedom mainly against the law of the Jewish people, Barnabas fights for the gospel and its admonition to love, patience and perseverance against the moral behavior of the Jewish people. Barnabas judges sharply, Paul judges more sharply. If the content of the letter to Barnabas cannot now be placed alongside the Pauline letters, even if the Jewish law is held in higher esteem by Barnabas than by Paul, then on the other hand it cannot be asserted that the Jewish Christian Barnabas still wants to save some Jewish institutions and customs in their original and closest meaning for his Jewish–Christian readership — as far as possible.

A peculiarity of the missive compared to the NT Books lie in the means they use for instruction. While they provide dogmatic and moral instruction on the basis of the teachings of the Old Covenant, Jesus' preaching and the various facts from his life, Barnabas relies on introductory and transitional remarks and on chapters 19 and 20, the "Didache apart from the writings and customs of the Old Testament and does not recall the suffering of Jesus directly as an established fact, but only with the help of prophetic words and ancient types.

Since he presents Jesus in a complicated way with the help of the OT, his letter does not have as invigorating and powerful an effect on the reader as the Gospels, and his teaching style is unlikely to make the same powerful impression as the preaching style of Saint Paul, who sought to bring Jesus the crucified one alive and vividly "before his eyes" (cf. Gal. 3:1), and who, as a man crucified with Christ in his sufferings and persecutions, advocated for his suffering Savior.

7. What separates the Epistle of Barnabas from the dogmatic attempts and the apologetic-polemical works of the oldest Christian literature is its purpose to comfort and morally invigorate. Although it is a textbook of Gnosis, it has no place in the Gnostic or Antignostic literature. Gnosis, about which its author writes so often, has nothing to do with the Gnostic Christological errors. When he speaks of Jesus, his divinity and humanity, his life, suffering and death, his resurrection and ascension, he only wants to create the necessary prerequisites to be able to act as a moral preacher and comforter, but he has no intention of to establish and defend the doctrine of Jesus' divinity and humanity.

The letter differs from apologetic-polemic literature particularly in the way it uses the Old Testament, its writings and institutions. The abundant use of the Old Covenant is not done to prove to Jews that Jesus is the Messiah and that Christianity is the true kingdom of God, nor to demonstrate to Gentiles the divinity of the religion of Christ based on the fulfillment of old prophecies. In the epistle, prophecies are the means of teaching that the Christian's sufferings are based on the divine plan for the world. Closer connections exist between the Epistle of Barnabas and the letters of the Apostolic Fathers Clement[293], Ignatius and Polycarp. Not only can they be put together according to their literary character, as has already been proven above, but their content also shows several points of contact.

The exhortation to Christian life in love, humility and patience for the sake of the Savior and eternal glory is in the same way the main content of the writings of these fathers. The teaching about Jesus boils down to the idea: Jesus Christ is the ideal exemplar of the Christian. Instead of a learned explanation about Jesus' person, it is repeatedly stated: the believer must humble himself in order to reach God, since Jesus, the God, has humbled himself to human suffering. The reference to the facts of salvation and a more or less clear indication that Jesus was God and man at the same time is sufficient for those fathers. The story of Jesus and the Christological mystery is mentioned, but little is proven. The letters mentioned are addressed to religious personalities or congregations. Since these writings likewise

---

[293] Only I Clem will be taken into account as the remaining Clementines are fraudulent.

speak of the intention of consolidating the young Church through moral revival and strengthening and thus ensuring it externally, they make the moral life of the faithful an apologia to the external enemy, a wisdom before the world.

Despite many similarities, each of the above-mentioned fathers also has something peculiar about the Epistle of Barnabas. The closest thing to it is the letter of St. Clement, because he also makes extensive use of the writings of the OT for moral instruction, and because quotations from the Pentateuch, the Psalms and the prophets are constantly repeated here and there. But Clement does not use the OT typologically.[294] He addresses the community at Corinth with direct and clearly stated moral demands (cf. chap. 22); he questions the history of OT according to examples of virtuous life[295] and also according to deterrent examples of sin;[296] with the words of the prophet Isaiah, he presents Jesus as an example of humility (16).

Furthermore, the Epistle of Clement aims at something more than the Epistle of Barnabas and is not limited to the same teaching and educational resources as it. In addition to the admonitions on moral life, he also includes regulations of a legal nature. Prompted by the disruption of the legal order in the Christian community in Corinth, Clement admonishes obedience to the legally appointed superiors and demands that "sacrifice and service of God"[297] be celebrated at legally appointed times and hours (40 ff.). Occasionally he inserts an apologetic treatise on the resurrection from the dead (24-26).

In addition to the examples from the history of Israel, current Church history (5 f.) and profane history (55) serve him for moral revival and encouragement. He even makes nature a moral and religious teacher (20 and 24 f.). With regard to the use of teaching and educational resources, Clement stands higher than Barnabas. Since he lives for Gentile and Jewish Christians, he shows a wider view than the latter, who only looks into the former Holy Land to instruct Christians who come from Judaism. Since Clement, in contrast to Barnabas, gratefully utilizes everything that nature and history offers him, it is striking that he draws as little as the latter from the precious moral sayings, especially the Lord's Sermon on the Mount.[298] The life and suffering of Jesus may have been regarded by both writers as the most powerful sermon of the Son of God.

The differences between the Barnabas Epistle and the Ignatius Epistles are greater. Although the Bishop of Antioch, like Barnabas, is fortunate enough to be able to rejoice in the firm faith of the addressees in his letters, he nevertheless takes

---

[294] The typological explanation in 12:7 is to be seen as a side note.

[295] Cf. Chap. 9-12; 17; 18; 31; 53.

[296] Cf. Chap. 4; 45; 51:5.

[297] προσφοράς καί λειτουργίας (40:2).

[298] Only 46:8 is a word of Jesus quoted.

some occasion to remind the faithful of the dangers that threaten the faithful from the outside through Judaizers and Gnostics.[299] In order to encourage and strengthen people to live in Christ and to teach the suffering Jesus, he does not need the Old Testament. He only occasionally reminds us of the same thing in individual, short phrases. Even if he points out the dangers of the false teachers mentioned, he does not need OT revelations.[300] The writings of the Old Testament are not the authority with which he supports the Christian exhortations and teachings; His authority is the Christian bishop with his priests and deacons. Through unity with the Christian dignitaries and joint participation in the service of the Church they celebrate, he wants to educate for Christ and strengthen him in Christ.[301]

Unlike Clement, he emphasizes this unity because it is endangered; He demands subordination to bishop and priest because it is a means of Christian education for him, just as the Old Testament commands Barnabas to view the bishop as the Lord himself (Eph. 6:1) and to honor (Epistle of Ignatius to the Trallians 3:1), himself to submit to the bishop like Jesus (Trallians 2:1), and explains that what the bishop finds good is pleasing to God (Smyrnians 8:2). He emphasizes the authority of the bishop so much because he wants to influence his addressees not through reference to the written word, but through life. He values personal life so highly that, instead of allowing the prophets to speak, he declares that the prophets lived according to Christ[302], who is their teacher.[303]

Since Ignatius values a truly Christian, living example so highly, it is also his lively desire to be an example himself and to teach and work by his own example.[304] He who is already fortunate enough to walk the path of suffering for his Divine Lord and has the strength to rejoice that he has the chains, "the spiritual pearls" (Eph. 11:2), and may soon be mauled by wild beasts in Rome,[305] is in fact a bishop to all to whom he addresses in his letters, in whom the suffering and patient Christ seems to reveal himself, so that truly OT or NT Citations[306] can be dispensed with.

Since this Holy Power of a great personality speaks from the Ignatian letters, it gives them so much life and strength that the Epistle of Barnabas seems dry

---

[299] Cf. Magn. 8:1; 10:3. Sm. 2.

[300] Eph. 15:1; Magn. 12; 13:1; Trall. 8:2.

[301] Cf. Eph. 2:2; 4; 5; 13. Magn. 7. Trall. 7. Ph. 4.

[302] Magn. 8:2; 9:2; regarding the value of personality cf. Trail. 3:2.

[303] Magn. 9:2; Cf. Barn 5:6.

[304] Cf. Trall. 10; 12:2; Sm. 4:2

[305] Cf. Ro. 2; 4; 5.

[306] Jesus' words are only found in Sm. 3:2 and perhaps Ro. 6:1 and Eph. 14:2; Pauline and Johannine phrases are common.

and lifeless, and that at first glance one would like to be inclined to deny the literary character of a real letter to the Epistle of Barnabas, whose author does not want to gain form and life in the mind of the reader, compared to those whose author does not want to gain form and life in the spirit of the reader.

The Polycarp letter also shows its peculiarity compared to our missive. He does not rely on the writings of OT in a similar way to this, nor does he, like Clement and Ignatius, urge submission to the ecclesiastical authorities. Like these two writers, he seeks to give examples from the latest Christian history and, in the difference between Barnabas, Clement and Ignatius, he particularly likes to refer to sayings of Jesus and words from the NT.[307]

Barnabas thus educates for Christ and for Christian life through the Old Covenant with its history, its writings, institutions and customs, Clement above all through the exemplary historical figures of the OT, Ignatius through submission to the bishop as the vicar and the example of Christ and through his own example, Polycarp through writings of the N.T.

---

[307] Cf. 2:3; 6:2; 7:2; 12:3; especially 12:1, where Polycarp expresses confidence that the Philippians will trust in holy Writings are practiced, which, according to the following sentence and the entire contents of the letter, must above all be writings from the N.T. Polycarp writes: "I am convinced that you are well trained in the holy things. Scriptures and none of them are unknown to you. But it is not my place (to give you any further training). Only (I want to warn you) with the words of the scriptures (= Ps. 4:5 and Eph. 4:26): 'Be angry and do not sin, and do not let the sun go down on your anger'!"

SAINT BARNABAS THE APOSTLE

Barnabas (originally Joseph), styled an Apostle in Holy Scripture, and, like St. Paul, ranked by the Church with the Twelve, though not one of them; b. of Jewish parents in the Island of Cyprus about the beginning of the Christian Era. A Levite, he naturally spent much time in Jerusalem, probably even before the Crucifixion of Our Lord, and appears also to have settled there (where his relatives, the family of Mark the Evangelist, likewise had their homes — Acts 12:12) and to have owned land in its vicinity (4:36-37). A rather late tradition recorded by Clement of Alexandria (Stromata II.20) and Eusebius (Church History II.1) says that he was one of the seventy Disciples; but Acts (4:36-37) favours the opinion that he was converted to Christianity shortly after Pentecost (about A.D. 29 or 30) and immediately sold his property and devoted the proceeds to the Church. The Apostles, probably because of his success as a preacher, for he is later placed first among the prophets and doctors of Antioch (xiii, 1), surnamed him Barnabas, a name then interpreted as meaning "son of exhortation" or "consolation". (The real etymology, however, is disputed. See Encyl. Bibli., I, col. 484.) Though nothing is recorded of Barnabas for some years, he evidently acquired during this period a high position in the Church.

When Saul the persecutor, later Paul the Apostle, made his first visit (dated variously from A.D. 33 to 38) to Jerusalem after his conversion, the Church there, remembering his former fierce spirit, was slow to believe in the reality of his conversion. Barnabas stood sponsor for him and had him received by the Apostles, as the Acts relate (9:27), though he saw only Peter and James, the brother of the Lord, according to Paul himself (Galatians 1:18-19). Saul went to his house at Tarsus to live in obscurity for some years, while Barnabas appears to have remained at Jerusalem. The event that brought them together again and opened to both the door to their lifework was an indirect result of Saul's own persecution. In the dispersion that followed Stephen's death, some Disciples from Cyprus and Cyrene, obscure men, inaugurated the real mission of the Christian Church by preaching to the Gentiles. They met with great success among the Greeks at Antioch in Syria, reports of which coming to the ears of the Apostles, Barnabas was sent thither by them to investigate the work of his countrymen. He saw in the conversions effected the fruit of God's grace and, though a Jew, heartily welcomed these first Gentile converts. His mind was opened at once to the possibility of this immense field. It is a proof how deeply impressed Barnabas had been by Paul that he thought of him immediately for this work, set out without delay for distant Tarsus, and persuaded

Paul to go to Antioch and begin the work of preaching. This incident, shedding light on the character of each, shows it was no mere accident that led them to the Gentile field. Together they laboured at Antioch for a whole year and "taught a great multitude". Then, on the coming of famine, by which Jerusalem was much afflicted, the offerings of the Disciples at Antioch were carried (about A.D. 45) to the mother-church by Barnabas and Saul (Acts 11). Their mission ended, they returned to Antioch, bringing with them the cousin, or nephew of Barnabas (Colossians 4:10), John Mark, the future Evangelist (Acts 12:25).

The time was now ripe, it was believed, for more systematic labours, and the Church of Antioch felt inspired by the Holy Ghost to send out missionaries to the Gentile world and to designate for the work Barnabas and Paul. They accordingly departed, after the imposition of hands, with John Mark as helper. Cyprus, the native land of Barnabas, was first evangelized, and then they crossed over to Asia Minor. Here, at Perge in Pamphylia, the first stopping place, John Mark left them, for what reason his friend St. Luke does not state, though Paul looked on the act as desertion. The two Apostles, however, pushing into the interior of a rather wild country, preached at Antioch of Pisidia, Iconium, Lystra, at Derbe, and other cities. At every step they met with opposition and even violent persecution from the Jews, who also incited the Gentiles against them. The most striking incident of the journey was at Lystra, where the superstitious populace took Paul, who had just cured a lame man, for Hermes (Mercury) "because he was the chief speaker", and Barnabas for Jupiter, and were about to sacrifice a bull to them when prevented by the Apostles. Mob-like, they were soon persuaded by the Jews to turn and attack the Apostles and wounded St. Paul almost fatally. Despite opposition and persecution, Paul and Barnabas made many converts on this journey and returned by the same route to Perge, organizing churches, ordaining presbyters and placing them over the faithful, so that they felt, on again reaching Antioch in Syria, that God had "opened a door of faith to the Gentiles" (Acts 13:13-14:27; see article SAINT PAUL).

Barnabas and Paul had been "for no small time" at Antioch, when they were threatened with the undoing of their work and the stopping of its further progress. Preachers came from Jerusalem with the gospel that circumcision was necessary for salvation, even for the Gentiles. The Apostles of the Gentiles, perceiving at once that this doctrine would be fatal to their work, went up to Jerusalem to combat it; the older Apostles received them kindly and at what is called the Council of Jerusalem (dated variously from A.D. 47 to 51) granted a decision in their favour as well as a hearty commendation of their work (Acts 14:27-15:30; see articles COUNCIL OF JERUSALEM; SAINT PETER). On their return to Antioch, they resumed their preaching for a short time. St. Peter came down and associated freely there with the Gentiles, eating with them. This displeased some disciples of James; in their opinion, Peter's act was unlawful, as against the Mosaic law. Upon their remonstrances, Peter yielded apparently through fear of displeasing them, and refused to eat any longer with the Gentiles. Barnabas followed his example. Paul considered that they "walked not uprightly according to the truth of the gospel" and upbraided them before the whole church (Galatians 2:11-15). Paul seems to have carried his point. Shortly afterwards, he and Barnabas decided to revisit their missions. Barnabas wished to take John Mark along once more, but on account of the previous defection Paul objected. A sharp contention ensuing, the Apostles agreed to separate. Paul was probably somewhat influenced by the attitude recently taken by Barnabas, which might prove a prejudice to their work. Barnabas sailed with John Mark to Cyprus, while Paul took Silas an revisited the churches of Asia Minor. It is believed by some that the church of Antioch, by its God-speed to Paul, showed its approval of his attitude; this inference, however, is not certain (Acts 15:35-41).

Little is known of the subsequent career of Barnabas. He was still living and labouring as an Apostle in 56 or 57, when Paul wrote First Corinthians (9:5-6). from which we learn that he, too, like Paul, earned his own living, though on an equality with other Apostles. The reference indicates also that the friendship between the two was unimpaired. When Paul was a prisoner in Rome (61-63), John Mark was attached to him as a disciple, which is regarded as an indication that Barnabas was no longer living (Colossians 4:10). This seems probable.

Various traditions represent him as the first Bishop of Milan, as preaching at Alexandria and at Rome, whose fourth (?) bishop, St. Clement, he is said to have converted, and as having suffered martyrdom in Cyprus. The traditions are all late and untrustworthy.

With the exception of St. Paul and certain of the Twelve, Barnabas appears to have been the most esteemed man of the first Christian generation. St. Luke, breaking his habit of reserve, speaks of him with affection, "for he was a good man, full of the Holy Ghost and of Faith". His title to glory comes not only from his kindliness of heart, his personal sanctity, and his missionary labours, but also from his readiness to lay aside his Jewish prejudices, in this anticipating certain of the Twelve; from his large-hearted welcome of the Gentiles, and from his early perception of Paul's worth, to which the Christian Church is indebted, in large part at least, for its great Apostle. His tenderness towards John Mark seems to have had its reward in the valuable services later rendered by him to the Church.

The feast of St. Barnabas is celebrated on 11 June. He is credited by Tertullian (probably falsely) with the authorship of the Epistle to the Hebrews, and the so-called Epistle of Barnabas is ascribed to him by many Fathers.

—The Catholic Encyclopedia, 1912

THE EPISTLE OF BARNABAS

I

[1]All hail in peace, you sons and daughters, in the name of our Lord Jesus Christ, who loved us.

[2]Seeing that the divine fruits of righteousness abound among you, I rejoice exceedingly and above measure in your happy and honoured spirits, because you have with such effect received the grace of the spiritual gift. [3]Wherefore also I inwardly rejoice the more, hoping to be saved, because I truly perceive in you the Spirit poured forth from the rich Lord of love. So greatly did the much-desired sight of you astonish me respecting you.. [4]I am therefore persuaded of this, and fully convinced in my own mind, that since I began to speak among you I understand many things, because the Lord has accompanied me in the way of righteousness. I am also on this account bound by the strictest obligation to love you above my own soul, because great are the faith and love dwelling in you, while you hope for the life which He has promised. [5]Considering this, therefore, that if I should take the trouble to communicate to you some portion of what I have myself received, it will prove to me a sufficient reward that I minister to such spirits, I have hastened briefly to write unto you, in order that, along with your faith, you might have perfect knowledge. [6]Well then, there are three ordinances of the Lord; the hope of life, which is the beginning and end of our faith; and righteousness, which is the beginning and end of judgment; love shown in gladness and exultation, the testimony of works of righteousness. [7]For the Lord has made known to us by His prophets both the things which are past and present, giving us also the first-fruits of the knowledge of things to come, which things as we see accomplished, one by one, we ought with the greater richness of faith and elevation of spirit to draw near to Him with reverence. I then, not as your teacher, but as one of yourselves, will set forth a few things by which in present circumstances you may be rendered the more joyful.

II

[1]Since, therefore, the days are evil, and Satan possesses the power of this world, we ought to give heed to ourselves, and diligently inquire into the ordinances of the Lord. [2]Fear and patience, then, are helpers of our faith; and long-suffering and continence are things which fight on our side. [3]While these remain pure in what respects the Lord, Wisdom, Understanding, Science, and Knowledge rejoice

along with them. ⁴For He has revealed to us by all the prophets that He needs neither sacrifices, nor burnt-offerings, nor oblations, saying thus; ⁵*What is the multitude of your sacrifices unto Me, says the Lord? I am full of burnt-offerings, and desire not the fat of lambs, and the blood of bulls and goats, not when you come to appear before Me: for who has required these things at your hands? Tread no more My courts, not though you bring with you fine flour. Incense is a vain abomination unto Me, and your new moons and sabbaths I cannot endure.* ⁶He has therefore abolished these things, that the new law of our Lord Jesus Christ, which is without the yoke of necessity, might have a human oblation. ⁷And again He says to them, *Did I command your fathers, when they went out from the land of Egypt, to offer unto Me burnt-offerings and sacrifices? But this rather I commanded them, Let no one of you cherish any evil in his heart against his neighbour, and love not an oath of falsehood.*¹ ⁹We ought therefore, being possessed of understanding, to perceive the gracious intention of our Father; for He speaks to us, desirous that we, not going astray like them, should ask how we may approach Him. ¹⁰To us, then, He declares, *A sacrifice to God is a broken spirit; a smell of sweet savor to the Lord is a heart that glorifies Him that made it. We ought therefore, brethren, carefully to inquire concerning our salvation, lest the wicked one, having made his entrance by deceit, should hurl us forth from our [true] life.*

III

¹He says then to them again concerning these things, *Why do you fast to Me as on this day, says the Lord, that your voice should be heard with a cry? I have not chosen this fast, says the Lord, that a man should humble his soul.* ²*Nor, though you bend your neck like a ring, and put upon you sackcloth and ashes, will you call it an acceptable fast.*² ³To us He says, *Behold, this is the fast that I have chosen, says the Lord, not that a man should humble his soul, but that he should loose every band of iniquity, untie the fastenings of harsh agreements, restore to liberty them that are bruised, tear in pieces every unjust engagement, feed the hungry with your bread, clothe the naked when you see him, bring the homeless into your house, not despise the humble if you behold him, and not [turn away] from the members of your own family (seed).* ⁴*Then shall your dawn break forth, and your healing shall quickly spring up, and righteousness shall go forth before you, and the glory of God shall encompass you;* ⁵*and then you shall call, and God shall hear you; while you are yet speaking, He shall say, Behold, I am with you; if you take away from yourself the chain [binding others], and the stretching forth of the hands [to swear falsely], and words of murmuring, and give cheerfully your bread to the hungry, and show compassion to the soul that has been*

---

¹ Jeremiah 7:22; Zechariah 8:17
² Isaiah 58:4-5

humbled.³ ⁶To this end, therefore, brethren, He is long-suffering, foreseeing how the people whom He has prepared shall with guilelessness believe in His Beloved. For He revealed all these things to us beforehand, that we should not as rush forward as novices to shipwreck ourselves as rash acceptors of their laws.

IV

¹It therefore behooves us, who inquire much concerning events at hand, to search diligently into those things which are able to save us. Let us then utterly flee from all the works of iniquity, lest these should take hold of us; and let us hate the error of the present time, that we may set our love on the world to come: ²let us not give loose reins to our soul, that it should have power to run with sinners and the wicked, lest we become like them. ³The final stumbling-block (or source of danger) approaches, concerning which it is written, as Enoch says, *For for this end the Lord has cut short the times and the days, that His Beloved may hasten; and He will come to the inheritance.* ⁴And the prophet also speaks thus: *Ten kingdoms shall reign upon the earth, and a little king shall rise up after them, who shall subdue under one three of the kings.* ⁵In like manner Daniel says concerning the same, *And I beheld the fourth beast, wicked and powerful, and more savage than all the beasts of the earth, and how from it sprang up ten horns, and out of them a little budding horn, and how it subdued under one three of the great horns.* ⁶You ought therefore to understand. And this also I further beg of you, as being one of you, and loving you both individually and collectively more than my own soul, to take heed now to yourselves, and not to be like some, adding largely to your sins, and saying, The covenant is both theirs and ours. ⁷Ours it is; but they lost it in this way for ever, after Moses had just received it. For the Scripture says, *And Moses was fasting in the mount forty days and forty nights, and received the covenant from the Lord, tables of stone written with the finger of the hand of the Lord.*⁴ ⁸But turning away to idols, they lost it. For the Lord speaks thus to Moses: *Moses go down quickly; for the people whom you have brought out of the land of Egypt have transgressed.*⁵ And Moses understood, and cast the two tables out of his hands; and their covenant was broken in pieces, in order that the covenant of the beloved Jesus might be sealed upon our heart, in the hope which flows from faith in Him. ⁹Now, being desirous to write many things to you, not as your teacher, but as becomes one who loves you, I have taken care not to fail to write to you from what I myself possess, with a view to your purification. We

---

³ Isaiah 58:6-10
⁴ Exodus 31:18, Exodus 34:28
⁵ Exodus 32:7; Deuteronomy 9:12

take earnest heed in these last days; for the whole [past] time of our faith will profit us nothing, unless now in this wicked time we also withstand coming sources of danger, as becomes the sons of God. That the Black One may find no means of entrance, [10]let us flee from every vanity, let us utterly hate the works of the way of wickedness. Do not, by retiring apart, live a solitary life, as if you were already [fully] justified; but coming together in one place, make common inquiry concerning what tends to your general welfare. [11]For the Scripture says, W*oe to them who are wise to themselves, and prudent in their own sight!*[6] Let us be spiritually-minded: let us be a perfect temple to God. As much as in us lies, let us meditate upon the fear of God, and let us keep His commandments, that we may rejoice in His ordinances. [12]The Lord will judge the world without respect of persons. Each will receive as he has done: if he is righteous, his righteousness will precede him; if he is wicked, the reward of wickedness is before him. Take heed, [13]lest resting at our ease, as those who are the called [of God], we should fall asleep in our sins, and the wicked prince, acquiring power over us, should thrust us away from the kingdom of the Lord.[14]

[3]And all the more attend to this, my brethren, when you reflect and behold, that after so great signs and wonders were wrought in Israel, they were thus [at length] abandoned. Let us beware lest we be found [fulfilling that saying], as it is written, *Many are called, but few are chosen.*[7]

V

[1]For to this end the Lord endured to deliver up His flesh to corruption, that we might be sanctified through the remission of sins, which is effected by the sprinkling of His blood. [2]For the scripture concerning Him, partly with reference to Israel, and partly to us; and says thus: *He was wounded for our transgressions, and bruised for our iniquities: with His stripes we are healed. He was brought as a sheep to the slaughter, and as a lamb which is dumb before its shearer.*[8] [3]Therefore we ought to be deeply grateful to the Lord, because He has both made known to us things that are past, and has given us wisdom concerning things present, and has not left us without understanding in regard to things which are to come. [4]Now, the Scripture says, *Not unjustly are nets spread out for birds.*[9] This means that the man perishes justly, who, having a knowledge of the way of righteousness, rushes off into

---

[6] Isaiah 5:21

[7] Matthew 22:14

[8] Isaiah 53:5, 7

[9] Proverbs 1:17

the way of darkness. [5]And further, my brethren: if the Lord endured to suffer for our soul, He being Lord of all the world, to whom God said at the foundation of the world, *Let us make man after our image, and after our likeness,*[10] understand how it was that He endured to suffer at the hand of men. [6]The prophets, having obtained grace from Him, prophesied concerning Him. And He (since it behooved Him to appear in flesh), [7]that He might abolish death, and reveal the resurrection from the dead, endured [what and as He did], in order that He might fulfil the promise made unto the fathers, and by preparing a new people for Himself, might show, while He dwelt on earth, that He, when He has raised mankind, will also judge them. [8]Moreover, teaching Israel, and doing so great miracles and signs, He preached [the truth] to him, and greatly loved him. [9]But when He chose His own apostles who were to preach His Gospel, [He did so from among those] who were sinners above all sin, that He might show *He came not to call the righteous, but sinners to repentance.* [10]Then He manifested Himself to be the Son of God. For if He had not come in the flesh, how could men have been saved by beholding Him? Since looking upon the sun which is to cease to exist, and is the work of His hands, their eyes are not able to bear his rays. [11]The Son of God therefore came in the flesh with this view, that He might bring to a head the sum of their sins who had persecuted His prophets to the death. [12]For this purpose, then, He endured. For God says, *The stroke of his flesh is from them; and when I shall smite the Shepherd, then the sheep of the flock shall be scattered.*[11] [13]But He himself willed thus to suffer, for it was necessary that He should suffer on a tree. For he that prophesied said concerning Him, *Spare my soul from the sword, fasten my flesh with nails; for the assemblies of the wicked have risen up against me.*[12] [14]And again he says, *Behold, I have given my back to scourges, and my cheeks to strokes, and I have set my countenance as a firm rock.*[13]

VI

[1]When, therefore, He has fulfilled the commandment, what says He? *Who is he that will contend with Me? Let him oppose Me: or who is he that will enter into judgment with Me? Let him draw near to the servant of the Lord.*[14] *Woe unto you, for you*

---

[10] Genesis 1:26

[11] Zechariah 13:7

[12] Psalms 22:16,17

[13] Isaiah 50:6-7

[14] Isaiah 50:8

shall all wax old, like a garment, and the moth shall eat you up.[15] And again the prophet says, Since as a mighty stone He is laid for crushing, *behold I cast down for the foundations of Zion a stone, precious, elect, a corner-stone, honourable.* [3]Next, what says He? *And he who shall trust in it shall live forever.* Is our hope, then, upon a stone? Far from it. But inasmuch as the Lord has set his flesh [as a foundation] with power; for He says, *And He placed me as a firm rock.*[16] [4]And the prophet says again, *The stone which the builders rejected, the same has become the head of the corner.* And again he says, *This is the great and wonderful day which the Lord has made.* [5]I write the more simply unto you, that you may understand. I am the off-scouring of your love. [6]What, then, again says the prophet? *The assembly of the wicked surrounded me; they encompassed me as bees do a honeycomb, and upon my garment they cast lots.* [7]Since, therefore, He was about to be manifested and to suffer in the flesh, His suffering was foreshown. For the prophet speaks against Israel, *Woe to their soul, because they have counselled an evil counsel against themselves,*[17] *saying, Let us bind the just one, because he is displeasing to us.* [8]And Moses also says to them, *Behold these things, says the Lord God: Enter into the good land which the Lord swore [to give] to Abraham, and Isaac, and Jacob, and inherit it, a land flowing with milk and honey.*[18] [9]What, then, says Knowledge? Understand you: Trust, she says, in Him who is to be manifested to you in the flesh — that is, Jesus. For man is earth in a suffering state, for the formation of Adam was from the face of the earth. [10]What, then, means this: *into the good land, a land flowing with milk and honey?* Blessed be our Lord, who has placed in us wisdom and understanding of secret things. For the prophet says, *Who shall understand the parable of the Lord, except him who is wise and prudent, and who loves his Lord?*[19] [11]Since, therefore, having renewed us by the remission of our sins, He has made us after another type, that we should possess the soul of children, inasmuch as He has created us anew by His Spirit. [12]For the Scripture says concerning us, while He speaks to the Son, *Let Us make man after Our image, and after Our likeness; and let them have dominion over the beasts of the earth, and the fowls of heaven, and the fishes of the sea.*[20] And the Lord said, on beholding the fair creature man, *Increase, and multiply, and replenish the earth.*[21] These words refer to the Son. [13]Again, I will show you how, the Lord

---

[15] Isaiah 50:9

[16] Isaiah 50:7

[17] Isaiah 3:9

[18] Exodus 33:1; Leviticus 20:24

[19] Cf. Matthew 11:25

[20] Genesis 1:26

[21] Genesis 1:28

speaks concerning us. He has accomplished a second creation in these last days. The Lord says, *Behold, I will make the last like the first.* In reference to this, then, the prophet proclaimed, *Enter into the land flowing with milk and honey, and have dominion over it.*[22] [14]Behold, therefore, we have been recreated anew, as again He says in another prophet, *Behold, says the Lord, I will take away from these, that is, from those whom the Spirit of the Lord foresaw, their stony hearts, and I will put hearts of flesh within them,*[23] because He was to be manifested in flesh, and to dwell among us. [15]For, my brethren, the habitation of our heart is a holy temple to the Lord.[24] [16]For again says the Lord, *And wherewith shall I appear before the Lord my God, and be glorified? He says, I will confess to you in the Church in the midst of my brethren; and I will praise you in the midst of the assembly of the saints.* We, then, are they whom He has led into the good land. [17]What, then, means the milk and honey? This, that as the infant is kept alive first by honey, and then by milk, so also we, being quickened and kept alive by the faith of the promise and by the word, shall live and be lords of the earth. [18]Now we have already said above; *Let them increase and multiply, and rule over the fishes.*[25] Who then is able [now] to govern the beasts, or the fishes, or the fowls of heaven? For we ought to perceive that to govern implies authority, so that one should command and rule. [19]If, therefore, this does not exist at present, yet still He has promised it to us for the hereafter. When we ourselves also have been made perfect so that we may become heirs of the covenant of the Lord.

VII

[1]Understand, then, you children of gladness, that the good Lord has foreshown all things to us, that we might know to whom we ought in all things to render thanksgiving and praise. [2]If therefore the Son of God, being Lord and future Judge of the living and the dead, suffered that His wound might give us life, let us believe that the Son of God could not suffer except for our sakes. [3]But moreover, when fixed to the cross, He had vinegar and gall given Him to drink. Hearken how the priests of the temple gave previous indications of this. Seeing that there is a commandment in scripture, *Whatsoever shall not observe the fast shall surely die*, the Lord commanded, because He was in His own person about to offer the vessel of His Spirit

---

[22] Exodus 33:3
[23] Ezekiel 11:19, Ezekiel 36:26
[24] Ephesians 2:21
[25] Genesis 1:28

as a sacrifice for our sins, that the type also which was given in Isaac who was offered upon the alter should be fulfilled. ⁴What, then, says He in the prophet? *And let them eat of the goat which is offered, with fasting, for all their sins.* Attend carefully: *And let all the priests alone eat the inwards, unwashed with vinegar.* ⁵Wherefore? Since you are to give Me, who am to offer My flesh for the sins of My new people, gall with vinegar to drink, eat you alone, while the people fasteth and waileth in sackcloth and ashes; that He might show that He must suffer at their hands. ⁶Attend ye to the commandments which He gave. *Take two goats, of goodly aspect, and similar to each other,, and offer them, and let the priest take the one for a whole burnt offering for sins.* ⁷ But the other one—what must they do with it? *Accursed*, says He, *is the one.* Mark how the type of Jesus now is revealed. ⁸*And all of you spit upon it, and pierce it, and encircle its head with scarlet wool, and thus let it be driven into the wilderness.* And when all this has been done, he that took the goat into the wilderness leads it, and takes off the wool, and puts it upon the shrub which is called Rachia, of which also we are accustomed to eat the fruits when we find them in the field. the same whereof we are wont to eat the shoots when we find them in the country. Of this briar alone is the fruit thus sweet. ⁹Why then, again, is this? Give good heed. *The one upon the altar, and the other accursed.* and why is the one that is accursed crowned? Because they shall see Him then in that day having a scarlet robe about his body down to his feet; and they shall say, Is not this He whom we once despised, and pierced, and mocked, and crucified? Truly this is He who then declared Himself to be the Son of God. ¹⁰For how like is He to the goat! With a view to this, it says *the goats to be of goodly aspect, and similar*, that, when they see Him then coming, they may be astonished by the likeness of the goat. Therefore, behold, the type of Jesus who was to suffer. ¹¹But why is it that they place the wool in the midst of thorns? It is a type of Jesus set forth for the Church, since whoever should desire to bear away the scarlet wool it behoved him to suffer many things, owing to the terrible nature of the thorn, and through affliction to win the mastery over it. Thus, He says, they that desire to see Me, and to attain unto My kingdom, must lay hold on Me through tribulation and affliction.[26]

VIII

¹Now what do you suppose means the type, that a command was given to Israel, that men of the greatest wickedness should offer a heifer, and slaughter and burn it, and, that then boys should take the ashes, and put these into vessels, and bind

---

[26] Acts 14:22

round a stick purple wool along with hyssop, and that thus the boys should sprinkle the people, one by one, in order that they might be purified from their sins? ² Understand ye how in all plainness it is spoken unto you; the calf is Jesus: the sinful men offering it are those who led Him to the slaughter. After this it is no more men (who offer); the glory is no more for sinners. ³And the boys that sprinkle are those that have proclaimed to us the remission of sins and purification of heart. To these He gave authority to preach the Gospel, being twelve in number, corresponding to the twelve tribes of Israel. ⁴But why are there three boys that sprinkle? To correspond to Abraham, and Isaac, and Jacob, because these were great before God. ⁵ And why was the wool placed upon the tree? Because by the tree Jesus holds His kingdom, so that through the cross those believing on Him shall live forever. ⁶But why was hyssop joined with the wool? Because in His kingdom there shall be evil and foul days, in which we shall be saved; for he who suffers pain in the flesh is healed through the foulness of the hyssop. ⁷And on this account the things which stand thus are clear to us, but obscure to them because they did not hear the voice of the Lord.

IX

¹He speaks moreover concerning our ears, how He has circumcised both them and our heart. The Lord says in the prophet, *In the hearing of the ear they obeyed me.* And again He says, *By hearing, those shall hear who are afar off; they shall know what I have done.*²⁷ And, *Be circumcised in your hearts, says the Lord.*²⁸ ²And again He says, *Hear, O Israel, for these things says the Lord your God.*²⁹ And once more the Spirit of the Lord proclaims, *Who is he that wishes to live for ever, let him hear the voice of my servant.* And again He says, *Hear, O heaven, and give ear, O earth, for God has spoken.* ³⁰These are in proof. And again He says, *Hear the word of the Lord, you rulers of this people.* ³¹And again He says, *Hear, you children, the voice of one crying in the wilderness.* Therefore He has circumcised our ears, that we might hear His word and believe, for the circumcision in which they trusted is abolished. ³For He declared that circumcision was not of the flesh, but they transgressed because an evil angel deluded them. ⁴He says to them, *These things says the Lord your*

---

²⁷ Isaiah 33:13
²⁸ Jeremiah 4:4
²⁹ Jeremiah 7:2
³⁰ Isaiah 1:2
³¹ Isaiah 1:10

God — (so I find a the commandment) — *Sow not among thorns, but circumcise yourselves to the Lord.* And why speaks He thus: *Circumcise the stubbornness of your heart, and harden not your neck?*[32] And again: *Behold, says the Lord, all the nations are uncircumcised in the flesh, but this people are uncircumcised in heart.*[33] [5]But you will say, Yes, in truth the people are circumcised for a seal. But so also is every Syrian and Arab, and all the priests of idols: are these then also within the bond of His covenant? Yes, the Egyptians also practise circumcision. [6]Learn then, children of love, concerning all things richly, that Abraham, the first who enjoined circumcision, looking forward in spirit to Jesus, practiced that rite, having received the mysteries of the three letters. [7]For the Scripture says, *And Abraham circumcised ten, and eight, and three hundred men of his household.* What, then, was the knowledge given to him in this? Learn the *eighteen* first, and then the *three hundred.* The ten and the eight are thus denoted — Ten by 'I', and Eight by 'H'. Here thou hast JESUS (IHSOYS). And because the cross in the 'T' was to have grace, He saith also *three hundred.* So He reveals Jesus in the two letters, and in the remaining one the cross. [8]He knows this, who has put within us the innate gift of His covenant. No one has learned from me a more genuine word of knowledge than this, but I know that you are worthy.

X

[1]Now, wherefore did Moses say, *You shall not eat the swine, nor the eagle, nor the hawk, nor the raven, nor any fish which is not possessed of scales,* he received in his understanding three ordinances. [2]Moreover, the Lord says to them in Deuteronomy, *And I will establish my ordinances among this people.*[34] So then it is not a commandment of God that they should not bite with their teeth, but Moses spake it in spirit. [3]For this reason he named the swine, as much as to say, You shall not join yourself to men who resemble swine. For when they live in pleasure, they forget their Lord; but when they come to want, they acknowledge the Lord. Just as the swine, when it eats, does not recognize the Lord; but when hungry it cries out, and on receiving food is quiet again. [4]*Neither shalt thou eat eagle nor falcon nor kite nor crow. Thou shalt not, He saith, cleave unto, or be likened to, such men who now not how to provide food for themselves by toil and sweat, but in their lawlessness seize what belongeth to others, and as if they were walking in guilelessness watch and search about*

---

[32] Deuteronomy 10:16
[33] Jeremiah 9:25-26
[34] Deuteronomy 4:1

for some one to rob in their rapacity, just as these birds alone do not provide food for themselves, but sit idle and seek how they may eat the meat that belongeth to others, being pestilent in their evil-doings. [5]*And you shall not eat, he says, the lamprey, or the polypus, or the cuttlefish.* He means, You shall not join yourself or be like to such men as are ungodly to the end, and are condemned to death. In like manner as those fishes, above accursed, float in the deep, not swimming on the surface like the rest, but make their abode in the mud which lies at the bottom of the sea. [6]*Moreover, You shall not, he says, eat the hare.* Wherefore? You shall not be a corrupter of boys, nor like such. For the hare gains one passage in the body every year; for according to the number of years it lives it has just so many orifices. [7]Moreover, *You shall not eat the hyena.* He means, You shall not be an adulterer, nor a corrupter, nor resemble them that are such. Wherefore? Because that animal annually changes its sex, and is at one time male, and at another female. [8]Moreover, he has rightly detested the weasel. For he means, You shall not be like to those whom we hear of as committing wickedness with the mouth, on account of their uncleanness; nor shall you be joined to those impure women who commit iniquity with the mouth. For this animal conceives by the mouth. [9]Moses then issued three doctrines concerning meats with a spiritual significance; but they received them according to fleshly desire, as though they referred to eating. [10]David, however, comprehends the knowledge of the three decrees, and speaks in like manner: *Blessed is the man who has not walked in the counsel of the ungodly, even as the fishes [referred to] go in darkness to the depths [of the sea]; and has not stood in the way of sinners,* even as those who profess to fear the Lord, sin like swine; *and have not sat on the seat of the destroyers*—as the birds that are seated for prey. You have now the complete lesson concerning eating. [11]But Moses says still further, *You shall eat every animal that is cloven-footed and ruminant.* What does he mean? He who, on receiving food, recognizes Him that nourishes him, and being satisfied by Him, is visibly made glad. Well spoke he, having respect to the commandment. What, then, does he mean? That we ought to join ourselves to those that fear the Lord, those who meditate in their heart on the commandment which they have received, those who both utter the judgments of the Lord and observe them, those who know that meditation is a work of gladness, and who ruminate upon the word of the Lord. But what means the cloven-footed? That the righteous man also walks in this world, yet looks forward to the holy world to come. You see how wise a lawgiver Moses was. [12]But how was it possible for them to understand or comprehend these things? We then, rightly understanding his commandments, explain them as the Lord intended. For this purpose He circumcised our ears and our hearts, that we might understand these things.

XI

¹Let us further inquire whether the Lord took any care to signify beforehand the water and the cross. Concerning the water, indeed, it is written, in reference to the Israelites, that they would not receive that baptism which leads to the remission of sins, but would procure another for themselves. ²The prophet therefore declares, *Be astonished, O heaven, and let the earth tremble at this, because this people has committed two great evils: they have forsaken Me, a living fountain, and have hewn out for themselves broken cisterns.* ³*Is my holy hill Zion a desolate rock? For you shall be as the fledglings of a bird, which fly away when the nest is removed.*³⁵ ⁴And again says the prophet, *I will go before you and make level the mountains, and will break the brazen gates, and bruise in pieces the iron bars; and I will give you the secret, hidden, invisible treasures, that they may know that I am the Lord God.*³⁶ ⁵*And He shall dwell in a lofty cave of the strong rock.* Furthermore, what says He in reference to the Son? *His water is sure; you shall see the King in His glory, and your soul shall meditate on the fear of the Lord.*³⁷ ⁶And again He says in another prophet, *The man who does these things shall be like a tree planted by the courses of waters, which shall yield its fruit in due season; and his leaf shall not fade, and all that he does shall prosper.* ⁷*Not so are the ungodly, not so, but even as chaff, which the wind sweeps away from the face of the earth. Therefore the ungodly shall not stand in judgment, nor sinners in the counsel of the just; for the Lord knows the way of the righteous, but the way of the ungodly shall perish.* ⁸You perceive how He pointed out the water and the cross at the same time. For this is the meaning; Blessed are they who, placing their trust in the cross, have gone down into the water; for, says He, they shall receive their reward at his *proper season*: then He declares, I will recompense them. But now He says, *Their leaves shall not fall off.* This means, that every word which proceeds out of your mouth in faith and love shall tend to bring conversion and hope to many. ⁹Again, another prophet says, *And the land of Jacob shall be extolled above every land.*³⁸ This means the vessel of His Spirit, which He shall glorify. ¹⁰Further, what says He? *And there was a river flowing on the right, and from it arose beautiful trees;*

---

³⁵ Isaiah 16:1-2
³⁶ Isaiah 45:2-3
³⁷ Isaiah 33:16-18
³⁸ Zephaniah 3:19

and whosoever shall eat of them shall live forever.[39] This means, that we indeed descend into the water laden with sins and defilement, but rise up from it, bearing fruit in our heart, resting our fear and hope on Jesus in the spirit. And whosoever shall eat of these shall live for ever, He means: Whosoever, He declares, shall hear these things spoken and shall believe, shall live forever.

XII

[1]In like manner He points to the cross of Christ in another prophet, who says, *And when shall these things be accomplished? And the Lord says, When a tree shall be bent down, and again arise, and when blood shall flow out of wood.* Here again you have an intimation concerning the cross, and Him who should be crucified. [2]Yet again He speaks of this in Moses, when Israel was attacked by strangers. And that He might remind them, when assailed, that it was on account of their sins they were delivered to death, the Spirit speaks to the heart of Moses, that he should make a figure of the cross, and of Him about to suffer thereon; for unless they put their trust in Him, they shall be overcome forever. Moses therefore placed one weapon above another in the midst of the hill, and standing upon it, so as to be higher than all the people, he stretched forth his hands, and thus again Israel was victorious. But when again he let down his hands, they were again slain with the sword. [3]For what reason? That they might know that they could not be saved unless they set their hope in Him. [4]And in another prophet He declares, *All day long I have stretched forth My hands to an unbelieving people, and one that gainsays My righteous way.*[40] [5]Again Moses makes a type of Jesus, how that He must suffer, and that He Himself whom they shall think to have destroyed shall make alive in an emblem when Israel was falling. For the Lord caused all manner of serpents to bite them, and they died (forasmuch as the transgression was wrought in Eve through the serpent), that He might convince them that by reason of their transgression they should be delivered over to the affliction of death.[41] [6]Moreover Moses, when he commanded, *You shall not have any graven or molten image for your God,* yet he himself did so that he might reveal a type of Jesus. Moses then makes a brazen serpent, and places it upon a beam, and by proclamation assembles the people. [7]When, therefore, they had come together, they besought Moses that he would offer sacrifice in their behalf, and pray for their recovery. And Moses spoke unto them, saying, *When any one of*

---

[39] Ezekiel 47:12

[40] Isaiah 65:2

[41] Numbers 21:6-9; John 3:14-18

you is bitten, let him come to the serpent placed on the pole; and let him hope and believe, that even though dead, it is able to give him life, and immediately he shall be restored. [42] And they did so. You have in these things also the glory of Jesus; for in Him and to Him are all things.[43] [8]What, again, says Moses to Jesus (Joshua) the son of Nun, when he gave him this name, as being a prophet, that all the people might give ear to him alone, because the Father reveals all things concerning His Son Jesus? [9]This name then being given him when Moses sent him to spy out the land, he said, *Take a book into your hands, and write what the Lord declares, that the Son of God will in the last days cut off from the roots all the house of Amalek.*[44] [10]Behold again it is Jesus, not a son of man, but the Son of God, and He was who was manifested, both by type and in the flesh.[45] Since then men will say that Christ is the son of David, David himself prophesieth being afraid and understanding the error of sinners; *The Lord said unto my Lord, Sit thou on My right hand until I set thine enemies for a footstool under Thy feet.* [11]And again, thus says Isaiah, *The Lord said to Christ, my Lord, whose right hand I have holden, that the nations should yield obedience before Him; and I will break in pieces the strength of kings.*[46] Behold how David calls Him Lord and not son.

XIII

[1]Now let us see whether this people or the first people has the inheritance, and whether the covenant had reference to us or to them. [2]Hear now what the Scripture says concerning the people. *Isaac prayed for Rebecca his wife, because she was barren; and she conceived.* [47] Furthermore also, *Rebecca went forth to inquire of the Lord; and the Lord said to her, Two nations are in your womb, and two peoples in your belly; and the one people shall surpass the other, and the elder shall serve the younger.*[48] [3]You ought to understand who Isaac is, and who Rebecca is, and in whose case He has shown that the one people is greater than the other. [4]And in another prophecy Jacob speaks more clearly to his son Joseph, saying, *Behold, the Lord has not deprived me of your presence; bring your sons to me, that I may bless*

---

[42] Numbers 21:9

[43] Colossians 1:16

[44] Exodus 17:14

[45] 1 Timothy 3:16

[46] Isaiah 45:1

[47] Genesis 25:21

[48] Genesis 25:23

them. ⁵And he brought Manasseh and Ephraim, desiring that Manasseh should be blessed, because he was the elder. With this view Joseph led him to the right hand of his father Jacob. But Jacob saw in the spirit a type of the people that should come afterwards. And what says he? *And Jacob crossed his hands, and laid his right hand upon the head of Ephraim, the second and younger, and blessed him. And Joseph said to Jacob, Transfer your right hand to the head of Manasseh, for he is my first-born son.* ⁴⁹ *And Jacob said, I know it, my son, I know it; but the elder shall serve the younger: yet he also shall be blessed.* ⁵⁰ ⁶You see on whom he laid his hands, that this people should be first, and heir of the covenant. ⁷If then, still further, the same thing was intimated through Abraham, we reach the perfection of our knowledge. What, then, says He to Abraham? Because you have believed, it is imputed to you for righteousness: *Behold, I have made you the father of those nations who believe in the Lord while in uncircumcision.*

XIV

¹Yes it is even so; but let us inquire if the Lord has really given that testament which He swore to the fathers that He would give to the people. He did give it; but they were not found worthy to receive it, on account of their sins. ²For the prophet declares, *And Moses was fasting forty days and forty nights on Mount Sinai, that he might receive the testament of the Lord for the people.* ⁵¹ *And he received from the Lord two tables, written in the spirit by the finger of the hand of the Lord.* ⁵² And Moses having received them, carried them down to give to the people. ³And the Lord said to Moses, *Moses, Moses, go down quickly; for your people has sinned, whom you brought out of the land of Egypt.* ⁵³ *And Moses understood that they had again made molten images; and he threw the tables out of his hands, and the tables of the testament of the Lord were broken.* ⁴Moses received them, but they themselves were not found worthy. But how did we receive them? Moses received them being a servant,⁵⁴ but the Lord himself, having suffered in our behalf, has given them to us, that we should be the people of His inheritance. ⁵But He was made manifest, in order that at the same time they might be perfected in their sins, and we might receive the covenant through Him who inherited it, even the Lord Jesus, who was prepared beforehand hereunto, that appearing in person He might redeem out of darkness

---

⁴⁹ Genesis 48:18

⁵⁰ Genesis 48:19

⁵¹ Exodus 24:18

⁵² Exodus 31:18

⁵³ Exodus 32:7; Deuteronomy 9:12

⁵⁴ Hebrews 3:5

our hearts which had already been paid over unto death and delivered up to the iniquity of error, and thus establish the covenant in us through His word. [6]For it is written how the Father charged Him to deliver us from darkness, and to prepare a holy people for Himself. [7]The prophet therefore declares, *I, the Lord Your God, have called You in righteousness, and will hold Your hand, and will strengthen You; and I have given You for a covenant to the people, for a light to the nations, to open the eyes of the blind, and to bring forth from fetters them that are bound, and those that sit in darkness out of the prison-house.*[55] We perceive then whence we were redeemed. [8]And again, the prophet says, *Behold, I have appointed You as a light to the nations, that You might be for salvation even to the ends of the earth, says the Lord God that redeems you.* [9]And again, the prophet says, *The Spirit of the Lord is upon me; because He has anointed me to preach the Gospel to the humble: He has sent me to heal the broken-hearted, to proclaim deliverance to the captives, and recovery of sight to the blind; to announce the acceptable year of the Lord, and the day of recompense; to comfort all that mourn.*[56]

XV

[1]Further, also, it is written concerning the Sabbath in the Decalogue which He spoke, face to face, to Moses on Mount Sinai, *And sanctify the Sabbath of the Lord with clean hands and a pure heart.*[57] [2]And He says in another place, *If my sons keep the Sabbath, then will I cause my mercy to rest upon them.*[58] [3]Of the Sabbath He speaks in the beginning of the creation: *And God made in six days the works of His hands, and made an end on the seventh day, and rested on it, and sanctified it.* [3]Give heed, my children, to the meaning of this expression, He finished in six days. [4]Give heed, children, what this means; *He ended in six days.* He means this, that in six thousand years the Lord shall bring all things to an end; for the day with Him signifyeth a thousand years; and this He himself bears me witness, saying; *Behold, the day of the Lord shall be as a thousand years.* Therefore, children, in six days, that is in six thousand years, all things shall come to an end. [5]*And He rested on the seventh day.* This means; when His Son, shall come, and shall destroy the time of the Lawless One, and shall judge the ungodly, and shall change the sun, and the moon, and the stars, then shall He truly rest on the seventh day. [6]Moreover, He says, *You shall hallow it with pure hands and a pure heart.* If, therefore, any one can now hallow the day which God has hallowed, though he is pure in heart, we are utterly astray.

---

[55] Isaiah 42:6-7
[56] Isaiah 61:1-2
[57] Exodus 20:8; Deuteronomy 5:12
[58] Jeremiah 17:24-25

[7]But if after all then and not till then shall we truly rest and hallow it, when we shall ourselves be able to do so after being justified and receiving the promise, when iniquity is no more and all things have been made new by the Lord, we shall be able to hallow it then, because we ourselves shall have been hallowed first. [8]Finally, He says to them, *Your new moons and your Sabbath I cannot endure.*[59] You perceive what His meaning is: Your present Sabbaths are not acceptable to Me, but that which I have made, namely when, giving rest to all things, I shall make the beginning of the eighth day, that is, a beginning of another world. [9]Wherefore, also, we keep the eighth day with joyfulness, the day also on which Jesus rose again from the dead. And when He had manifested Himself, He ascended into the heavens.

XVI

[1]Moreover, I will also tell you concerning the temple, how the wretched [Jews], wandering in error, trusted not in God Himself, but in the temple, as being the house of God. [2]For almost after the manner of the Gentiles they worshipped Him in the temple. But what saith the Lord abolishing the temple? Learn you. *Who has meted out heaven with a span, and the earth with his hand? Have not I saith the Lord?*[60] *Heaven is My throne, and the earth My footstool: what kind of house will you build to Me, or what is the place of My rest?*[61] You perceive that their hope is vain. [3]Moreover, He again says, *Behold, they who have cast down this temple, even they shall build it up again.* [4]It has so happened. For through their going to war, it was destroyed by their enemies; and now: they, as the servants of their enemies, shall rebuild it. [5]Again, it was revealed that the city and the temple and the people of Israel were to be given up. For the Scripture says, *And it shall come to pass in the last days, that the Lord will deliver up the sheep of His pasture, and their sheep-fold and tower, to destruction.* And it so happened as the Lord had spoken. [6]Let us inquire, then, if there still is a temple of God. There is — where He himself declared He would make and finish it. For it is written, *And it shall come to pass, when the week is completed, the temple of God shall be built in glory in the name of the Lord.*[62] [7]I find, therefore, that a temple does exist. How then, shall it be built in the name of the Lord. Understand you. Before we believed in God, the habitation of our heart was corrupt and weak, as being indeed like a temple made with hands. For it was

---

[59] Isaiah 1:13

[60] Isaiah 40:12

[61] Isaiah 66:1

[62] Daniel 9:24-27; Haggai 2:10

full of idolatry, and was a habitation of demons, because we did whatsoever was contrary to God. [8]*But it shall be built in the name of the Lord.* Give heed that the temple of the Lord may be built in glory. [9]How? Understand you. Having received the remission of our sins, and hoping in the name of the Lord, we have become new creatures, formed again from the beginning. Wherefore in our habitation God truly dwells in us. How? His word of faith; His calling of promise; the wisdom of the ordinances; the commands of the teaching; He himself dwelling in us; opening to us who were enslaved by death the doors of the temple, that is, the mouth; and by giving us repentance leads us into the incorruptible temple. [10]He then, who wishes to be saved, looks not to man, but to Him who dwells in him, and speaks in him, amazed at never having either heard him utter such words with his mouth, nor himself having ever desired to hear them. This is the spiritual temple built for the Lord.

XVII

[1]So far as it was possible with all simplicity to declare it unto you, my soul hopes that I have not omitted anything of the matters pertaining unto salvation and so failed in my desire. [2]For if I should write to you about things immediate or future, you would not understand, because such knowledge is hid in parables. So much then for this.

XVIII

[1]But let us now pass to another sort of knowledge and doctrine. There are two ways of doctrine and authority, the one of light, and the other of darkness. But there is a great difference between these two ways. For over one are stationed the light-bringing angels of God, but over the other the angels of Satan.[63] [2]And the one is the Lord from all eternity and unto all eternity, whereas the other (i.e., Satan) is prince of the season of iniquity that now is.

XIX

[1]This then is the way of light, if any one desires to travel on his way to the appointed place, he must be zealous in his works. The knowledge, therefore, which is given to

---

[63] 2 Corinthians 12:7

us for the purpose of walking in this way, is the following. [2]You shall love Him that made you, you shall fear Him that created you, you shall glorify Him that redeemed thee from death; you shall be simple in heart, and rich in spirit. You shall not join yourself to those who walk in the way of death. You shall hate doing what is unpleasing to God: you shall hate all hypocrisy. You shall not forsake the commandments of the Lord. [3]You shall not exalt yourself, but shall be of a lowly mind in all things. You shall not take glory to yourself. You shall not take evil counsel against your neighbour. You shall not allow over-boldness to enter into your soul. [4]You shall not commit fornication: *you shall not commit adultery*: you shall not be a corrupter of boys. You shall not let the word of God issue from your lips with any kind of impurity. You shall not make a difference in a person to reprove him for a transgression. You shall be meek: you shall be *quiet*. You shall be *fearing the words* which you have heard. You shall not bear a grudge against thy brother. [5]You shall not be of doubtful mind as to whether a thing shall be or not.[64] *You shall not take the name of the Lord in vain*. You shall love your neighbour more than your own soul. You shall not murder a child by abortion, nor again shall you kill it when it is born. You shall not withdraw your hand from your son or daughter, but from their infancy you shall teach them the fear of the God. [6]You shall not be found coveting your neighbor's goods, nor shall you be avaricious. You shall not be joined in soul with the haughty, but you shall be reckoned with the righteous and lowly. Receive as good things the trials which come upon you, knowing that nothing is done without God. You shall not be of double mind or of double tongue, for a double tongue is a snare of death. [7]You shall be subject to the Lord, and to thy masters as a type of God, with modesty and fear. You shall not issue orders with bitterness to your maidservant or your man-servant, who trust in the same God, lest they should cease to fear that God who is above both; for He came to call men not according to their outward appearance,[65] but according as the Spirit had prepared them.[66] [8]You shall communicate in all things with your neighbour; you shall not call things your own; for if you are partakers in common of things which are incorruptible, how much more should you be of those things which are corruptible! You shall not be hasty with your tongue, for the mouth is a snare of death. As far as possible, you shall be pure for your soul's sake. [9]*Do not be ready to stretch forth your hands to take, while you contract them to give*. You shall love, as the apple of your eye, every one *that speaks to you the word of the Lord*. [10]*You shall remember* the day of judgment night and day, and you shall seek out day by day the persons of the saints, either laboring

---

[64] James 1:8
[65] Ephesians 6:9
[66] Romans 8:29-30

by word and going to exhort them and meditating how you may save souls by your word, or you shall work with your hands for a redemption for thy sins. [11]You shall not hesitate to give, nor murmur when you give. Give to every one that asks you, and you shall know who is the good Recompenser of the reward. You shall preserve what things you have received in charge, neither adding to nor taking from them. You will utterly hate the Evil One. You will judge righteously. [12]You shall not make a schism, but you shall pacify those that contend by bringing them together. You shall confess your sins. You shall not go to prayer with an evil conscience. This is the way of light.

XX

[1]But the way of the Black One is crooked, and full of cursing; for it is the way of eternal death with punishment, in which way are the things that destroy men's souls—idolatry, over-confidence, arrogance of power, hypocrisy, double-heartedness, adultery, murder, rapine, haughtiness, transgression, treachery, malice, self-sufficiency, poisoning, magic, avarice, want of the fear of God; [2]persecutors of good men, hating the truth, loving lies, not perceiving the reward of righteousness, not cleaving to the good nor to the righteous judgment, paying no heed to the widow and the orphan, wakeful not for the fear of God but for that which is evil; men from whom gentleness and forbearance stand aloof and far off; loving vain things, pursuing a recompense, not pitying the poor man, not toiling for him that is oppressed with toil, ready to slander, not recognizing Him that made them, murderers of children, corrupters of the creatures of God, turning away from him that is in want, oppressing him that is afflicted, advocates of the wealthy, unjust judges of the poor, sinful in all things.

XXI

[1]It is good therefore to learn the ordinances of the Lord, as many as have been written above, and to walk in them. For he who does these things shall be glorified in the kingdom of God; whereas he who chooses their opposites shall be destroyed with his works. For this cause there will be a resurrection, on this account a retribution. [2]I beseech you who are superiors, if you will receive any counsel of good advice from me, keep among yourselves those to whom you may do good: do not forsake them. [3]For the day is at hand on which all things shall perish with the Evil One. *The*

Lord is near, and His reward. [4]Again, and yet again, I beseech you: be good lawgivers to one another; continue faithful counselors of one another; take away from among you all hypocrisy. [5]And may God, who rules over all the world, give to you wisdom, intelligence, understanding, knowledge of His judgments, patience. [6]And be taught of God, inquiring diligently what the Lord asks from you; and do it that you maybe safe in the day of judgment. [7]But if you have any remembrance of good, call me to mind when you practice these these things, in order that both my desire and watchfulness may lead to some good result. I beseech you, entreating this as a favor. [8]So long as the good vessel (of the body) is with you, do not fail in any one of those things, but unceasingly seek after them, and fulfill every commandment; for these things are worthy. [9]For this reason I was the more eager to write to you so far as I was able, that I might give you joy. Fare ye well, children of love and peace. The Lord of glory and of every grace be with your spirit. Amen.

ABOUT THE AUTHOR

Fr. Dr. Phillip Haeuser
23 April 1876 — 25 February 1960

Philipp Haeuser was born on April 23, 1876, in Kempten, into a family of devout Catholics. He studied philosophy and theology at the University of Munich from 1895-1899. Haeuser loved his Church. He entered the Gregorian Seminary in Munich in 1897 and was ordained a priest on July 20, 1899 by Bishop Petrus von Hötzl for the Augsburg diocese.

He served as prefect of studies at the seminary in Neuberg from 1900-1909. Parallel to his church activities, he conducted research on early Christian literature during this time, and on July 7, 1911, he received his doctorate in theology from the Albert-Ludwigs-University of Freiburg.

His dissertation was upon the Epistle of Barnabas, which you have in your hand, and he was awarded a Doctorate in Theology. He published a number of theological works and from 1928 took over the translation of the *Ecclesiastical History* of Eusebius of Caesarea, which was published in print in 1932. Haeuser's translation is still the basis of the authoritative edition today.

Before and during the period of National Socialism, Haeuser published other writings that reinterpreted Christian motifs in a masculine, non-feminine way, for example in his *Der Kämpfer Jesus* (*The Fighter Jesus*) written with the pseudonym P. Willibald, where he fought the idea of Christ as a pacifist, a wimp, and portrayed him as a heroic figure, a fighter for God.

He served as a priest in Strassburg in the diocese of Augsberg, and was politically active against Catholic liberalism, philo-judaism and other Marxist culture war philosophies crippling Catholicism even to our day.

Imprisoned after the war by the Allies, he was sentenced to 5 years in the Regensburg work camp, after they had pushed his bishop to dismiss him from his parish, and done all they could to persecute him, including banning him from teaching, preaching, being an editor, writer or radio commentator for 10 years.

Struggling on in the cause of justice he signed a letter, "Dr. Haeuser, innocent, suffering, and imprisoned priest".

Contrary to the Allies and their pressuring upon the diocese, it should be noted that Mayor Günter of Strassberg on October 10, 1945 told the Vicar General of the diocese that the previous Sunday 510 parishioners had voted positively for Father Haeuser to remain their pastor. Günter stated,

> "Our pastor here is held in the highest esteem, and the entire parish of Strassberg has owed him the utmost gratitude for thirty-four years. A dismissal would be the greatest ingratitude and would provoke bitterness. Through his conciliatory ways, our pastor has held the parish together in peace and quiet despite the greatest difficulties, even in the most troubled times. A dismissal would threaten the peace and quiet."

Released in 1948 due to health, in 1953 the Augsberg diocese named him "emeritus", which allowed him to preside at the daily liturgy. He also regularly made hospital visits to parishoners and performed other pastoral works. In November 1957, he retired to the Cistercian Sisters' monastery at Oberschoenenfeld, after serving the Strassburgers for 46 years.

Feted before his departure with a farewell celebration by the citizens of Strassburg, whom had given him honorary citizenship many years before, Fr. Hauser spoke to the huge crowd in the Reichsadler Restaurant saying:

> "Together with the citizens of Strassberg we've experienced many beautiful and joyful years, but also hard and bitter ones. We

144 • FR. PHILLIP HAEUSER

have understood each other, and we will always understand each other, and that is why we will never forget each other."

The newspaper reporter who covered the event commented:

"In the old parish church that he loved and trusted he often preached from the pulpit that life is a struggle, must be a struggle, since only thus does it lead the way to the stars."

Fr. Haeuser resided at the monastery in Oberschönenfeld until his death on February 25, 1960.

www.ingramcontent.com/pod-product-compliance
Lightning Source LLC
Chambersburg PA
CBHW031138270326
41929CB00011B/1672